A BEST PRACTICE GUIDE TO ASSESSMENT AND INTERVENTION FOR AUTISM AND ASPERGER SYNDROME IN SCHOOLS

of related interest

Your Special Student
A Book for Educators of Children Diagnosed with Asperger Syndrome
Josie Santomauro and Margaret-Anne Carter
Illustrated by Carla Marino
ISBN 978 1 84310 660 9

Hints and Tips for Helping Children with Autism Spectrum Disorders
Useful Strategies for Home, School, and the Community
Dion E. Betts and Nancy J. Patrick
ISBN 978 1 84310 896 2

Reaching and Teaching the Child with Autims Spectrum Disorder
Using Learning Preferences and Strengths
Heather MacKenzie
ISBN 978 1 84310 623 4

The Verbal Behaviour Approach
How to Teach Children with Autism and Related Disorders
Mary Lynch Barbera
With Tracy Rasmussen
ISBN 978 1 84310 852 8

Asperger Syndrome in the Inclusive Classroom
Advice and Strategies for Teachers
Stacey W. Betts, Dion E. Betts and Lisa N. Gerber-Eckard
ISBN 978 1 84310 840 5

The Complete Guide to Asperger's Syndrome
Tony Attwood
Hardback ISBN 978 1 84310 495 7
Paperback ISBN 978 1 84310 669 2

Managing Meltdowns
Using the S.C.A.R.E.D. Calming Technique with Children and Adults with Autism
Deborah Lipsky and Will Richards
ISBN 978 1 84310 908 2

A BEST PRACTICE GUIDE TO ASSESSMENT AND INTERVENTION FOR AUTISM AND ASPERGER SYNDROME IN SCHOOLS

Lee A. Wilkinson

Jessica Kingsley Publishers
London and Philadelphia

First published in 2010
by Jessica Kingsley Publishers
116 Pentonville Road
London N1 9JB, UK
and
400 Market Street, Suite 400
Philadelphia, PA 19106, USA

www.jkp.com

Library of Congress Cataloging in Publication Data
A CIP catalog record for this book is available from the Library of Congress

British Library Cataloguing in Publication Data
A CIP catalogue record for this book is available from the British Library

ISBN 978 1 84905 811 7

Printed and bound in the United States by
Thomson-Shore, 7300 Joy Road, Dexter, MI 48130

To the Memory of
Inez Patricia James
1951–2005
Friend and Colleague

ACKNOWLEDGMENTS

I would like to thank the professionals at Jessica Kingsley Publishers for their invaluable assistance in bringing this book to fruition. I am especially grateful to my wife Amy, for her love, support and unwavering patience during the preparation of this book. I would also like to extend my gratitude to the children on the spectrum, their families, and professionals, with whom I have worked over the past many years. From you I have learned so much.

CONTENTS

FOREWORD

As editor-in-chief of *Autism Spectrum Quarterly,* I have had the pleasure of previously working with Dr. Lee A. Wilkinson regarding two outstanding articles that he wrote for the Magajournal®. So, when he graciously asked me if I would write the foreword for his book, despite a busy schedule, I enthusiastically accepted, knowing that his writing skills and clarity of purpose would make the manuscript an "easy read". While that is indeed true—and will undoubtedly be great news for busy professionals—*A Best Practice Guide to Assessment and Intervention for Autism and Asperger Syndrome in Schools* is so much more than that. It is a landmark contribution destined to become a classic in the field of autism spectrum disorders (ASDs).

It was obvious from the quotation by Dr. Lorna Wing in the preface that this book would be grounded in the best of practices. It did not disappoint. Moreover, in the preface the author promises to "provide the reader with a balance of conceptual, practical, and empirical information", and that is exactly what readers will find throughout this comprehensive and well-documented treatise on assessment and intervention for children with autism spectrum conditions.

Chapter 1 introduces the reader to case vignettes of Jeremy and Sally, two children with different expressions of ASD who serve to illuminate aspects of the assessment and intervention process. While the children are referenced throughout the book, in Chapter 4 they serve as illustrative examples of how to apply best-practice techniques to the identification and assessment of children on the autism spectrum. As such, Dr. Wilkinson provides readers with a well-designed and easy-to-follow blueprint for application of procedures in the school setting.

The book is exquisitely and meticulously organized, making it an easy-to-access reference guide as well as a comprehensive text book and training manual. The author segues into assessment by way of first emphasizing the important role of screening in the early identification of children on the autism spectrum. Along the way, Dr. Wilkinson makes a strong and convincing case for adopting a *dimensional,* as opposed to a *categorical* approach to autism spectrum conditions, given that the former focuses on adaptive functioning which will serve the child well over the long haul, in contrast to the latter approach which focuses on the descriptive and more immediate elements of behavior. Leaving nothing to chance, the author lays out a Multistep Guide for Screening that provides school personnel with a "how to" for application.

The *Best Practice in Assessment* chapter again emphasizes the importance of using a comprehensive developmental approach that targets adaptive functioning and provides a context for understanding the qualitative aspects of the disability. This chapter also provides guiding principles for assessment and evaluation, as well as 10 components of best-practice assessment and evaluation. There is also a treasure trove of assessment instruments listed and later discussed. In some cases, the entire instrument is presented in either the chapter or an appendix, while in others clear-cut examples are given.

Leaving no stone unturned, Dr. Wilkinson goes beyond assessment procedures to examine some of the scientifically-based and controversial interventions in ASD. He not only stresses the importance of using an individualized approach to intervention, but also notes that treatment should be *comprehensive, intensive,* and designed to *facilitate generalization* of acquired skills. To ensure understanding, Dr. Wilkinson outlines a real-world example of an empirically-based classroom intervention for Jeremy (one of the students in his above-noted case vignettes).

The remaining chapters cover special needs education and the current status of the field, as well as directions for future research. What comes next will warm the hearts of busy professionals in all fields. There are frequently asked questions and glossaries of terms and acronyms, followed by appendices covering everything from assessment instruments (accompanied by a terrific ready-to-use, comprehensive assessment worksheet), to diagnostic criteria, sample IEP goals and objectives, resources, and so much more.

Sadly, the comprehensive assessment of children with ASD across domains (e.g. communication/language, executive function, etc.) has long been an amorphous, if not murky area with respect to determining the needs of children with ASD. Dr. Wilkinson has made an enormous contribution to the field by comprehensively and systematically illuminating not only what needs to be done, but also how to go about doing it. That "recipe" alone would be worth the read, but he goes on to supply the actual "ingredients" (in the form of both formal and informal assessment procedures and instruments) that, when properly applied, can "serve up" intervention protocols that are based upon the documented needs of children with autism spectrum conditions. This is a very important book, and it is an honor and privilege to recommend it to both seasoned professionals and those who are new to the field.

Diane Twachtman-Cullen, Ph.D., CCC-SLP
Editor-in-Chief, *Autism Spectrum Quarterly*

PREFACE

All of the features that characterize Asperger syndrome can be found in varying degrees in the normal population.

Lorna Wing (1981)

Lorna Wing's seminal paper, "Asperger's syndrome: A clinical account," introduced the terms Asperger syndrome and autistic triad to the clinical literature (Wing 1981). It was her intention to stress that the syndrome was part of a spectrum of conditions and that there were no clear boundaries separating it from other autistic disorders (Wing 2005). Today, we recognize that, in practice, it is difficult to reliably distinguish between Asperger syndrome, autism, and other disorders on the spectrum (Attwood 2006; Mayes and Calhoun 2003; Mayes, Calhoun, and Crites 2001; Witwer and Lecavalier 2008). Many clinicians and researchers are in agreement that Asperger syndrome is not a separate diagnostic entity, but rather high-functioning or a mild variant of autism (Attwood 2006; Mayes and Calhoun 2003; Macintosh and Dissanayake 2006; Ozonoff, Dawson, and McPartland 2002). My intent is not to actively engage in the ongoing debate as to whether Asperger syndrome and autism are the same or different disorders, but rather to focus on the behavioral and educational issues pertinent to the understanding of children with social-communication difficulties, regardless of the diagnostic label or classification subtype. Indeed, the question remains as to whether there is any value in defining a particular autism subtype as distinct from the rest of the continuum (Wing 1993, 2005). At present, we have no definitive answer to this question. There is no question, however, that we are witnessing an ever increasing number of more capable school-age children being diagnosed with ASD in our schools.

PURPOSE OF THIS BOOK

While there is no shortage of books describing the controversies and challenges associated with the diagnosis and treatment of ASD, there is a need for an up-to-date text that provides educators and support professionals with a best practice guide to screening, assessment, and intervention. My primary aim in preparing this book was to provide school-based professionals with a practical and scientifically based approach to the evaluation and treatment of Asperger syndrome and high-functioning autism spectrum disorders (ASD). It is written from a real-world perspective based on my experience as both an applied researcher and practitioner. The contents are intended to provide the reader with a balance of conceptual, practical, and empirical information in order to bridge the research-to-practice gap in identifying, assessing, and treating school-age children at risk for autism-related conditions. While acknowledging differing scientific views, this guide provides information and recommendations that are consistent with current scientific research and empirically based practice, rather than speculation, theory, subjective and anecdotal reports. Quick reference and "best practice" boxes are included throughout the book to alert the reader to critical topics.

This book is guided by a fundamental premise that autistic traits exist along a spectrum of severity with respect to the core symptomatology. Because mild deficits in social and communicative competence have a continuous distribution in the population of school-age children, even mild autistic-like traits can be associated with teacher-reported problems in socialization and a wide range of behavioral and academic difficulties (Skuse *et al.* 2009). Consequently, social skills deficits that fall below the threshold for a clinical diagnosis of ASD can still result in functional impairment. As a result, it is important to focus on those children whose differences in social and communication functioning might indicate a need for support and intervention services. We must assess autistic traits dimensionally and recognize the potential impact on the functioning and well-being of more capable children with autism spectrum conditions. Finally, this book contains a focused discussion and review of the current research only when necessary so as to ensure that children are not "lost" in the ongoing debate regarding classification schemes, and that the individual child remains the focus of attention.

AUDIENCE

Autism is considered a universal disorder that affects children across all socioeconomic and educational levels. This book is intended to be a resource for practitioners in educational and school psychology, child and adolescent clinical psychology, general and special education, counseling, educational administration, social work, and for graduate and pre-service students. It is designed as a guide to help school professionals (teachers, counselors, speech and language therapists, psychologists, case managers, and many others) make informed decisions regarding the assessment, identification, and treatment of autistic spectrum disorders (ASD). Importantly, it serves as a best practice reference for all professionals who have the responsibility for the screening, assessment, and education of school-age students who may have neurodevelopmental disorders such as ASD. Because the dramatic increase in the number of school-age children being identified with ASD extends well beyond the United States to Europe and other countries, this book will also find an audience among the international educational community who shares the challenges of screening, evaluating, and intervention planning to meet the unique needs of children with ASD.

ORGANIZATION OF THE TEXT

This book consists of seven chapters. Chapter 1 begins with the case vignettes of Jeremy and Sally and a discussion of the challenges facing educators. The reader is then provided with an overview of Asperger syndrome and the autism spectrum disorders (ASD). Chapter 2 focuses on the screening and identification of children in need of further assessment. Instruments are reviewed and a multi-step screening process described. Chapter 3 addresses evidence-based assessment practices, including individual instruments and a developmentally based procedure. In Chapter 4, the case examples of Jeremy and Sally are presented to illustrate best practice in the assessment of ASD. Chapter 5 focuses on intervention practices and describes current scientifically based interventions and treatments for ASD. Chapter 6 provides information on the identification of special educational needs and specialized services. Chapter 7 concludes with a discussion of the current status of the field and future directions for research.

Lee A. Wilkinson

Chapter 1

INTRODUCTION
AND OVERVIEW

If you've met one student with autism, you've met one student with autism.

JEREMY

Jeremy is a seven-year-old first grade student with a history of behavioral problems both at school and home. His educational history includes long-standing difficulties in the areas of social interaction, attention, and impulse control and aggression. Although an engaging child with a precocious vocabulary, Jeremy has a "blunt" communicative style and is insensitive to many nonverbal social cues. As a result, he frequently misreads the communication of others. Jeremy is also described as highly argumentative, resistant, immature, and not well accepted by other children. Although capable academically, he demonstrates significant difficulty in the areas of appropriateness of response, task persistence, attending and topic maintenance. Few children want to play, sit or work with Jeremy. He is considered "bossy" with other students and has significant nonacademic challenging behaviors such as interrupting, distracting others, and constantly talking about topics of special interest such as the solar system. Jeremy seems to have his own agenda and rules which he expects other students to follow. Among Jeremy's strengths are his well-developed visualization skills and memory for facts and details. He also has a strong desire for structure, rules, and order.

SALLY

Sally is a nine-year old fourth grade student who has difficulties relating and communicating with peers and adults, transitioning problems, poor task completion, and occasional oddities in behavior. Although she does not display behavioral challenges such as temper tantrums or "meltdowns," Sally often ignores her teacher's requests and refuses to participate in classroom activities. She is not interested in seeking out other girls and seems to prefer the company of adults. Although an able student, Sally has few friends in school and at home. She is considered "odd" by her peers and often seems to be in her own "world." In class, she is a quiet and reserved student who usually stays on the periphery of the group and prefers solitary activities such as creating small, imaginary worlds with blocks and figures, and playing games involving puppies or kittens for long periods of time. At home, Sally is viewed as a "sweet" and agreeable child who is compliant and well liked by her adult relatives. Yet, Sally's parents also express concern about their daughter's periods of aloofness, inattentiveness, and lack of initiative and social responsiveness.

THE CHALLENGE TO SCHOOL PROFESSIONALS

What do Jeremy and Sally have in common? How do they differ? They share the core diagnostic features often referred to as the autistic "triad" or the three key areas of atypicality: social impairment, communication deficits, and narrow interests/repetitive behavior. However, these features are manifested in very different ways. For example, Jeremy's behavioral profile is characterized by externalizing problems such as aggression, disruption/ tantrums, noncompliance, and poor self-regulation. In contrast, Sally's social problems are not as apparent because of her non-externalizing behavior profile, withdrawal, passivity, and lack of initiative and social engagement. Nevertheless, both demonstrate the core, defining feature of autism spectrum disorder (ASD); an impairment in social relatedness (Wing 2005).

While Jeremy and Sally might receive a common clinical or educational label, their unique individual needs present a challenge to the educators and other school professionals who are struggling to cope with the increasing numbers of students with ASD in the classroom. In fact, most students with social-communication disabilities receive their education in mainstream classrooms with teachers who often have limited experience and training in working with children with special needs (Myles and Simpson 2002; Wilkinson 2005). These children frequently experience problems related to their social-communication deficits such as poor regulation of attention, emotional distress, academic difficulties, and high rates of challenging behavior (Ghaziuddin 2005; Klin and Volkmar 2000; Simpson and Myles 1998; Tantam 2003). As a result, they are at risk for academic underachievement, school drop-out, peer rejection, and internalizing disorders such as anxiety and depression (Adreon and Stella 2001; Myles and Simpson 2002). Providing effective behavioral supports and interventions for children like Jeremy and Sally presents a major challenge to their families and the educational communities that serve them.

ASD in 100 Words or Less

Autism spectrum disorders (ASD) occur in 1 percent of the population, are strongly heritable, and result from atypical neurodevelopment. Autism and Asperger syndrome (AS) are characterized by an uneven developmental profile and a pattern of qualitative impairments in communication and socialization, and by a limited (and often unusual) range of activities or interests. This triad of impairments exists on a continuum that varies in severity of symptoms, age of onset, and association with other childhood disorders. Although many children are not identified until school age, ASD is a life-long condition that has implications for education, social development, and community adjustment.

Source: Adapted with permission from Simon Baron-Cohen 2008a.

OVERVIEW

Autism spectrum disorders (ASD), including autistic disorder, Asperger's disorder, and pervasive developmental disorder not otherwise specified (PDDNOS) are disorders of childhood onset characterized by impairment in social interaction and communication, as well as restricted or stereotyped patterns of behavior or interests (American Psychiatric Association 2000). Autism is considered a universal disorder. Epidemiological studies indicate a worldwide increase in the prevalence of autism spectrum disorders (ASD) over the past decade. The pervasive developmental disorder (PDD) category, also commonly referred to as ASD, represents one of the fastest growing disability categories in the world (Centers for Disease Control and Prevention 2002; Cimera and Cowan 2009). In the United States, ASD is more prevalent in the pediatric population than cancer, diabetes, spina bifida, and Down syndrome (Filipek *et al.* 1999). The increase in the number of school-age children with ASD extends beyond the United States into Europe and other countries (Fombonne *et al.* 2006; Volkmar 2005; Wing and Potter 2002). Undoubtedly, autism and autism-related disorders are no longer rare conditions and it is likely that most school professionals will meet students with ASD in their schools.

The recognition of more capable children with autistic disorder has shifted our conceptualization toward a dimensional perspective of ASD. Surveys focusing on a broader definition of ASD (or broad phenotype), of which autism is a single form, have reported progressively rising annual incidence and prevalence estimates markedly higher than in early studies (Wing and Potter 2002). For example, recent studies indicate that rates for both

ASD and autistic disorder are three to four times higher than 30 years ago (Fombonne 2003). A recent review of 37 epidemiological studies conducted in 13 different countries and regions between 1966 and 2004 concluded that the best estimate of the prevalence of all ASDs in Europe and North America combined is approximately 0.6% (60/10,000 or approximately 1 per 160) of the population (Fombonne 2005). This convergence of estimates is noteworthy, especially when coming from studies with improved methodology. Although we do not have a representative sample for the United States, the Centers for Disease Control and Prevention (CDC) *Autism and Developmental Disabilities Monitoring* (ADDM) (2002) report indicates an average prevalence estimate of 6.7 per 1000 children aged eight years (or approximately 1 in 150 children with an ASD). In the United Kingdom, the Medical Research Council's (MRC) *Review of Autism Research: Epidemiology and Causes* (2001) reported that there was good agreement that ASD affects approximately 60 per 10,000 children under eight years of age. This marked increase in the incidence of autism-related conditions is also reflected in the rates among a sample of nearly 60,000 children 9 to 10 years of age in South London indicating a prevalence of 116 per 10,000, or nearly double the estimated rate of 60 per 10,000 across countries (Baird *et al.* 2006; Fombonne 2005). At the present time, the best estimate is that autism now affects approximately 1 in 100 children aged 5 to 16 years of age in the United Kingdom, or approximately 133,500 children (Office of National Statistics 2005). Based on these statistics, we can expect that a majority of mainstream schools will have one or more children with ASD (Fombonne *et al.* 2001).

The occurrence of autism is also evident in the number of students with ASD receiving special educational services. For example, the number of students receiving assistance in the United States grew more than 900 percent from 1994 to 2006 (US Department of Education 2006). Figure 1.1 displays the cumulative growth of autism cases from 1992 to 2006 for ages 6–22 in the United States and outlying areas. Although a change in special education policy and greater availability of services seem likely to have contributed to this increase, a similar rise in rates has been reported in the United Kingdom (Office of National Statistics 2005; Wing and Potter 2002). The number of students with autism having a statement of special needs in England increased approximately 44 percent from 2004 to 2008 (Autism Education Trust 2008). Figures for the number of students with ASD receiving additional services and interventions beyond the usual curriculum showed an even greater increase of 74 percent for the same time period.

Unquestionably, the prevalence of ASD is substantially greater than previously recognized. Surveys of the prevalence of autism not only indicate an increase in the number of cases meeting standard diagnostic criteria, but a significant rise in the number of milder cases that fail to meet the full criteria for classification or diagnosis (Chakrabarti and Fombonne 2001; Skuse, Mandy, and Scourfield *et al.* 2009; Yeargin-Allsop *et al.* 2003). A number of explanations for this dramatic increase in the incidence and prevalence of ASD have been advanced. They include: changes in diagnostic criteria; improved identification; growing awareness among parents and professionals; conception of autism as a spectrum disorder; and greater availability of services (Fombonne 2005; Wing and Potter 2002). Whatever the reasons, the current prevalence figures carry clear-cut implications for school professionals across the globe who share the challenge of identifying and providing early educational intervention for an increasing number of children with some form of ASD who may comprise approximately 1 percent of the child population (Department for Education and Skills 2002; Fombonne 2005).

THE PERVASIVE DEVELOPMENTAL DISORDERS

Autism affects individuals throughout the world. There is international and cross-disciplinary agreement on the primary characteristics and validity of autism as a diagnostic category. At present, there is no other developmental disorder for which internationally accepted criteria exist (Volkmar 2005). The *Diagnostic and Statistical Manual of Mental Disorders* (4th edn, rev. text [*DSM-IV-TR*]); (American Psychiatric Association 2000) and the 10th edition of the International Classification of Diseases (*ICD-10)* (World Health Organization [WHO] 1993) list categories of pervasive developmental disorders (PDD) which include autism and four other associated disorders. Table 1.1 shows a comparison of the *DSM-IV* and *ICD-10* classifications.

Table 1.1 Comparison of *DSM-IV* and *ICD-10* diagnoses

DSM-IV	*ICD-10*
Autistic Disorder	Childhood Autism
Asperger's Disorder	Asperger's Syndrome
Childhood Disintegrative Disorder	Other Childhood Disintegrative Disorder
Rett's Disorder	Rett's Syndrome
Pervasive Developmental Disorder Not Otherwise Specified (PDDNOS)	Atypical Autism Other Pervasive Developmental Disorder Pervasive Developmental Disorder Unspecified

Source: American Psychiatric Association 2000, and World Health Organization 1993.

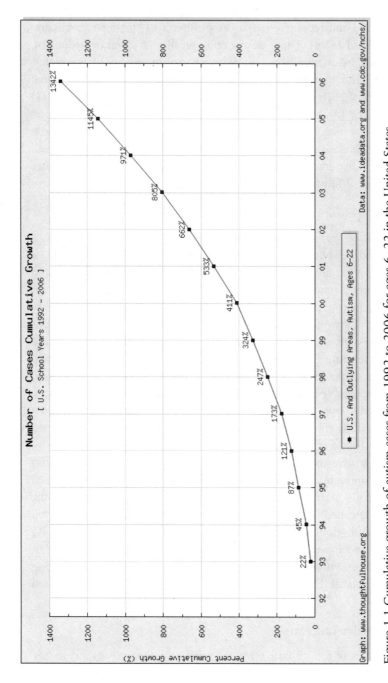

Figure 1.1 Cumulative growth of autism cases from 1992 to 2006 for ages 6–22 in the United States

Source: U.S. Department of Education, Office of Special Education Programs, Data Analysis System (DANS), OMB #1820-0043: *Children with disabilities receiving special education under Part B of the Individuals with Disabilities Act 2006.* Data updated as of July 15, 2007

The synonymous terms autistic spectrum disorder and pervasive developmental disorder refer to a wide continuum of associated neurobehavioral disorders, including but not limited to, three core-defining features: impairments in (a) reciprocal social interactions and (b) verbal and nonverbal communication, and (c) restricted and repetitive behaviors or interests (American Psychiatric Association [APA] 1994). These delays or atypicality in social development, communication, neurocognition, and behavior vary in severity of symptoms, age of onset, and association with other childhood disorders (National Research Council 2001). The five pervasive developmental disorders are: (1) austistic disorder, (2) Asperger's disorder, (3) Rett's disorder, (4) childhood disintegrative disorder, and (5) pervasive developmental disorder not otherwise specified (PDDNOS). As continuous and generally lifelong disorders, all have serious clinical implications for personal, social, educational, and other important areas of functioning.

The autistic triad

The constellation of impairments encompassing communication, social interaction, and behavior and interests has been referred to as the "triad of impairments" (Wing and Gould 1979). All children with autism and related conditions demonstrate the three aforementioned core-defining features (American Psychiatric Association 1994). There is, however, marked variability in the severity of symptomatology across children and many misconceptions about students with autism. Symptoms differ from one child to another and may change over time. Symptom expression falls along a continuum and will vary from the marked impairment of strictly defined (classic or Kanner's) autism to more capable children with higher cognitive and linguistic abilities. For example, the level of intellectual functioning can range from children with intellectual disability (InD) to those who score in the superior range on traditional IQ tests and, as in the case of Jeremy and Sally, from those who are socially intrusive to those who are social isolates; and from those who have limited communication skills to those with a precocious and advanced vocabulary. While a large percentage of children will exhibit (what in the United States is called) intellectual disability or mental retardation, or (what in the United Kingdom is termed) a learning disability, a broad range of IQ scores is observed in autism. Children who meet the criteria for autism but without intellectual disability or learning disability are described as having *high-functioning autism* (HFA). The features of each ASD/PDD are summarized below.

Autistic disorder (autism)

Autistic disorder is the clinical term for what is frequently called *autism*. First described by Leo Kanner over 60 years ago, autism is the most common and typical of the ASD/PDD subtypes. It is generally described as a developmental disorder of neurobiologic origin defined on the basis of behavioral and developmental features. Children diagnosed with autistic disorder demonstrate impairments in the three core developmental areas or triad: social skills, communication, and behaviors, activities, and interests, with delays or abnormalities in at least one of these categories present prior to three years of age. Table 1.2 shows the *DSM-IV* core domains and examples of autistic symptoms. In the social domain, symptoms include impaired use of nonverbal behaviors (e.g. eye contact, gestures), failure to develop appropriate peer relationships, and limited social-emotional reciprocity. Delays or impairment in communication include problems with reciprocity in conversation, peculiar or repetitive speech and language, and deficits in joint attention and imaginary play. Behavioral features are characterized by

Table 1.2 Core domains of autism and examples of behavioral characteristics

Core domain	Examples of behavioral characteristics
Social interaction	Inability to respond to social cues Inappropriately intrusive in social situations Problems with turn-taking Difficulty establishing and maintaining eye contact Trouble with back and forth social interactions
Communication	Delayed use of gestures Echoing what is said directly, later, or in a slightly changed way Oddities in volume, cadence, and pitch (prosody) Pronoun reversal or misuse Scripted language Problems with reciprocal conversations
Restricted/stereotyped patterns of behavior/ interests	Interest in parts of objects Preoccupation with topics or intense interest in details Stereotypic movements (e.g. rocking, flapping, twirling) Preoccupation with tasting and smelling objects Unusual response to sounds Insistence on routines, resisting change

Note. A diagnosis of Autistic Disorder requires the presence of six or more symptoms, with at least two being symptoms of impaired social interaction, at least one being a symptom of impaired communication, and at least one a symptom of restricted/stereotyped behavior/ interests.

Source. American Psychiatric Association 2000.

circumscribed interests, inflexible adherence to routines, stereotyped body movements, and preoccupation with sensory qualities of objects. According to the current *DSM-IV-TR* criteria, individuals must exhibit six symptoms falling within the three core domains. They must manifest at least two of the following four symptoms in socialization: marked impairment in use of multiple nonverbal behaviors; failure to develop peer relationships; lack of spontaneous seeking to share enjoyment, interests, or achievements; and lack of social or emotional reciprocity. They must present with at least one of the following qualitative communication impairments: delay or total lack of spoken language; impairment in the ability to initiate or sustain conversation; stereotyped or repetitive language; or lack of make-believe or imitative play. Finally, they must present with one of the following: restrictive, repetitive or stereotypic behavior, interest, or activity; an encompassing preoccupation with one or more stereotyped and restricted patterns of interest; apparent inflexible adherence to specific, nonfunctional routines or rituals; stereotyped and repetitive motor mannerisms; or persistent preoccupation with parts of an object. Delays or abnormal functioning in at least one of the three core developmental areas must be present by the age of three.

Asperger's disorder (Asperger's syndrome)

First described by Hans Asperger in 1944, also known as Asperger syndrome (AS), Asperger's disorder is a relatively new diagnostic category, having been added to the current *DSM-IV* and *ICD-10* revisions (*DSMIV-TR*; American Psychiatric Association 2000). This early social disability is pervasive and affects all areas of the child's functioning and development. Although the diagnostic criteria are still evolving, the clinical description of Asperger syndrome consists of severe and sustained impairment in social reciprocity and restricted, repetitive patterns of behavior, but no cognitive impairment or history of delayed language development as in autistic disorder. However, because it is often difficult to identify individuals with significant impairment in social and behavioral domains who do not have some degree of communication deficit, it is possible that someone who meets the *DSM-IV-TR* criteria for Asperger's disorder will also meet the criteria for autistic disorder. The two tend to be more alike than different and can be thought of as lying on the same autistic spectrum (Wing 2005; Witwer and Lecavalier 2008). Even though there may be few functional differences between children identified with Asperger syndrome and those with high-functioning autism (HFA), it is important to note that according to the *DSM-IV-TR* classification system, if the criteria for autistic disorder are met, this precludes a diagnosis of Asperger syndrome. Nevertheless, in practice there is a frequent interchangeable use of Asperger syndrome with other milder variants of typical (classic) autism, including both high-functioning autism (HFA) and PDDNOS (Mayes, Calhoun, and Crites 2001).

Childhood disintegrative disorder

Also known as Heller's syndrome, childhood disintegrative disorder is a very rare condition that has symptoms similar to autism, including both impaired social interaction and stereotyped patterns of interests and behaviors. Children with this disorder are likely to be male and demonstrate severe deficits in cognitive functioning, self-help, and other skills areas. The *DSM-IV-TR* criteria include a significant regression in skills following two years of typical development in at least two of the following areas of development: language, social skills or adaptive behavior, bowel or bladder control, play, or motor skills. Although the course of childhood disintegrative disorder is similar to that of autism, it is the distinct pattern of regression leading to profound impairment that distinquishes childhood disintegrative disorder from autistic disorder. If the loss of skills occurs before two years of age (sometimes called autistic regression), a diagnosis of autism is given rather than childhood disintegrative disorder. Childhood disintegrative disorder can be difficult to diagnose since it is often unclear whether a marked regression has actually occurred or whether the regression is associated with a neuropathological progression.

Rett's disorder

Rett's disorder is a very rare progressive neurodevelopmental disorder affecting girls exclusively. Although children with Rett's disorder experience no problems in prenatal or perinatal development and show normal motor development throughout the first five months of life, progressive deterioration of function begins in the first or second year of development. Previously acquired fine motor skills are lost and the typical hand-wringing movement of the disorder appears. Affected girls also develop a wide-based gait and gradually lose gross motor function. The concomitant loss of language skills, interest in the environment, and social interaction result in a presentation similar to autism. Rett's disorder is usually associated with severe or profound levels of cognitive impairment.

Pervasive developmental disorder not otherwise specified (PDDNOS)

This category tends to be used quite frequently and is often referred to as a diagnosis of exclusion. Children diagnosed with pervasive developmental disorder not otherwise specified (sometimes called atypical autism) experience difficulty in at least two of the three symptom categories of autistic disorder, but do not meet the complete diagnostic criteria for any other ASD. Although children with this diagnostic classification typically have milder symptoms, PDDNOS is often used when there is a severe and pervasive impairment in the development of reciprocal social interaction along with impairment in either verbal or nonverbal communication skills or with the presence of stereotyped behaviors, interests, and activities. Clinicians and researchers tend to use this category when case history information is unavailable or inadequate; when impairment in one of the core areas (social, communication, restricted interests) is very mild or absent; when onset is over three years of age; and for conditions other than autism where there is a significant impairment in social skills (Towbin 2005).

AUTISM SPECTRUM DISORDERS IN THE SCHOOL

Rett's disorder and childhood disintegrative disorder are rare conditions and often refered to as nonautistic ASD/PDDs in terms of course and outcome. While both share some features with ASD at earlier points in development, their relationship with other autism spectrum disorders is not clear (Johnson, Myers and Council on Children with Disabilities 2007; Volkmar and Klin 2005). Moreover, both Rett's disorder and childhood disintegrative disorder are characterized by a limited response to intervention and poor prognostic outcome compared to children with ASD. Throughout this book, the term autism spectrum disorder refers to a broad definition of autism, including the "classic" (or Kanner's autism) form of the disorder, as well as milder variants such as Asperger's disorder, high-functioning autism, and pervasive developmental disorder not otherwise specified. ASD is the clinical term that most closely captures the relationships among these disorders and commonality among the core characteristics. They are the subtypes observed and identified most frequently in school-age children and thus have the greatest relevance for the school professional. The ASD subtypes are usually ranked as more to less severe as one travels along the continuum from autistic disorder to high-functioning autism and Asperger's disorder to PDDNOS. A note of caution: use of the term autism spectrum disorder or ASD is meant to be descriptive and is not a formal diagnostic classification. Table 1.3 summarizes the characteristics and features of each ASD subtype.

Wing (2005) has described three groups of children with ASD that are useful when considering identification, educational planning, and provision of services in schools. The "aloof group" corresponds most closely to Kanner's or classic autism. It comprises children who are socially indifferent to others and who are most likely to have moderate levels of intellectual disability. Children in the aloof group are typically identified in early childhood and prior to school entrance. The "passive group" tends to have a higher level

Table 1.3 Characteristics of autism spectrum disorders

Characteristic	Autistic disorder*	Asperger's disorder	PDDNOS
Social skills	Very poor	Poor	Variable
Language and communication	Usually poor	Fair	Fair to good (a)
Repetitive interests and activities	Variable	Marked	Variable (a)
Intellectual ability	Severe InD to normal	Mild InD to normal	Mild InD to normal
Age of onset	0 to 36 months	Usually > 36 months	Variable
Sex ratio	M > F	M > F	M > F
Overall degree of impairment	Variable	Mild	Mild

Note. * Includes high-functioning autism (HFA)

(a) At least one of these two features must be present

Source: American Psychiatric Association 2000.

of cognitive functioning than the aloof group, with intellectual ability often average to above. The major characteristics of students in this group include a lack of spontaneous social approaches to others, poor communication skills, stereotyped movements, and odd responses to sensory stimuli. Children in the passive group may not be identified until school age and are likely to meet the *DSM-IV* criteria for Asperger's disorder or PDDNOS. The "active-but-odd" group is probably the group most often observed in school settings. It consists of students who make spontaneous approaches to others, but who do not engage in reciprocal social interaction. Characteristics include average to superior cognitive ability, but marked impairment in the pragmatic aspects of communication and the presence of behavior problems and coexisting childhood disorders. The diagnosis and identification of children in the active-but-odd group can be challenging because many autistic features may be overlooked or attributed to other conditions. This group is apt to meet the criteria for HFA, Asperger syndrome, or PDDNOS. Of course, these subgroups are not clinically validated categories and overlap with respect to their features. However, they provide us with a framework in which to conceptualize the continuum of ASD in the schools.

Clinical and educational classification

The specific criteria for autism are not the same among the different diagnostic and classification systems. Although a variety of systems exist, the *Individuals with Disabilities Education Act of 2004* (IDEA) in the United States, the *SEN Code of Practice* in the United Kingdom, and the *Diagnostic and Statistical Manual of Mental Disorders*, 4th edn, Text Rev. (*DSM-IV-TR*) have made the greatest impact on the assessment and classification of school-aged children with autism (Kamphaus, Reynolds, and Imperato-McCammon 1999).

In psychiatry and psychology, the most widely used diagnostic system is the *DSM-IV-TR*, which was first developed by the American Psychiatric Association in 1952 and is now in a revised fourth edition. The current *DSM* classification system, which includes autistic disorder, Asperger's disorder, and PDDNOS, has stimulated a considerable amount of research over the past 15 years (Volkmar *et al.* 2004). Nonetheless, there continue to be questions regarding the utility of distinguishing between the ASD subtypes. As noted earlier, there is a consensus on the validity of autistic disorder as a diagnostic category and agreement on its clinical features. However, many clinicians and researchers question whether there are true differences between individuals diagnosed with AS and those with autistic disorder without intellectual disability or HFA (Macintosh and Dissanayake 2004; Volkmar and Klin 2005). Indeed, research suggests that there are few differences between primary school-aged children with Asperger syndrome and HFA and that they are likely variants of the same underlying syndrome (Macintosh and Dissanayake 2004, 2006).

Neither the *IDEA* nor the *SEN* were intended as diagnostic or classification systems for childhood disorders. Rather, they are government legislation designed to serve children with special educational needs in public schools (Kamphaus *et al.* 1999). Unlike the *DSM*, which is a diagnostic and classification system based primarily on empirical research, the *IDEA* legislation specifies categories of "disabilities" to determine eligibility for special educational services. The definitions of these categories, including autism, are the most widely used classification system in the United States. Although the *SEN Code of Practice* in the United Kingdom does not define categories of special educational need, the English system enables help to be provided to students on the basis of assessments of their individual "special educational needs." We will discuss both the educational and clinical systems of identifying ASD further in Chapter 5.

Gender differences

Autism spectrum disorders are much more common in males than females in the general population. In fact, boys are three to four times more likely than girls to be identified with ASD. Likewise, referrals for evaluation of boys are ten times higher than for girls (Attwood 2006). Although few studies have examined gender differences in the expression of autism, we do have several tentative explanations for this disparity. Since females are socialized differently, ASD may not be manifested in the same way as typical male behavioral symptoms (Wilkinson 2008a). For example, girls might not come to the attention of parents and teachers because of better coping mechanisms and the ability to "disappear" in large groups (Attwood 2006). Girls on the higher end of the spectrum also tend to have fewer special interests, better superficial social skills, better language and communication skills, and less hyperactivity and aggression than boys. As in Sally's case description, social impairment and pragmatic deficits may not be readily apparent because of a non-externalizing behavioral profile, passivity, and lack of initiative. Girls who have difficulty making sustained eye contact and appear socially withdrawn may also be perceived as "shy," "naive," or "sweet" rather than having the social impairment associated with ASD (Wagner 2006). As a result, parents, teachers, and clinicians may not observe the obvious characteristics associated with the male prototype of autism spectrum conditions such as Asperger syndrome and HFA. This lessens the probability of a girl being identified as having the core symptoms of ASD. Over reliance on the male model with regard to diagnostic criteria might also contribute to a gender "bias" (Wilkinson 2008a). Clinical instruments tend to exclude symptoms and behaviors that may be more typical of females with ASD.

Research suggests that higher-functioning girls on the spectrum tend to show less severe forms of ASD compared to higher-functioning boys (Klinger, Dawson, and Renner 2003). This has led some researchers to suggest that males have more autistic traits than females and that these traits may be related to a sex-linked biological factor (Baron-Cohen 2008b). Although a comprehensive review of this subject is beyond the scope of this chapter, we should recognize that there may be sex differences in the expression of the broader autism phenotype and that a qualitative difference in social connectedness and reciprocity may well differentiate the genders (Attwood 2006; Wilkinson 2008a).

SUMMARY

We have only begun to appreciate the complex challenge of how to ensure that children like Jeremy and Sally are appropriately identified and provided with the opportunities and resources to learn, socialize, become independent and responsible and productive members of society. Research indicates that the outcomes for children with ASD can be significantly enhanced by early intensive intervention (Bryson, Rogers, and Fombonne 2003). Thus, it is critically important to identify those children in need of further assessment in order to reduce the time between symptom appearance and formal diagnosis (Goin-Kochel, Mackintosh, and Myers 2006). In this book, the term identification is used as a broad construct that includes both clinical and educational classifications and eligibility-related designations of ASD, including intervention and provision for special education. We will revisit the cases of Jeremy and Sally in Chapter 4 to illustrate a best practice approach to assessment and identification.

In order to derive the most benefit from this guide, readers are encouraged to consider the best practice screening and assessment paradigms described in Chapters 2 and 3 when selecting instruments. Similarly, the interventions and treatments reviewed in Chapters 5 and 6 provide an overview of empirically based interventions and effective special education practices. You are also encouraged to consult the index to locate best practice references in each chapter, the answers to frequently asked questions, and the glossary of common terms. The following chapter focuses on best practice in the screening process and provides a review of validated instruments that can be used by school-based professionals.

Quick Reference

Ten common misconceptions about students with ASD

This child can't have an ASD because he/she:

- is too affectionate
- makes eye contact
- is too social
- has some friends
- has a sense of humor
- is too smart
- didn't have problems in early school years
- doesn't have any stereotypical movements (hand-flapping)
- doesn't seem to have an intense interest in a specific topic
- isn't echolalic (repeats words or phrases).

Quick Reference

Some frequently used (and confused) terms

Pervasive developmental disorder (PDD): A group of five disorders characterized by delays or atypicality in the multiple domains of social development, communication, cognition, and behavior. They include: autistic disorder; Asperger's disorder, pervasive developmental disorder not otherwise specified (PDDNOS), Rett's disorder, and childhood disintegrative disorder.

Autism spectrum disorder (ASD): This term includes autistic disorder, Asperger's disorder, and PDDNOS. Although estimates vary, a majority of children with ASD appear to be higher functioning.

Autism: The most common PDD and less formal term for autistic disorder. Includes strictly defined (classic or Kanner's) autism and milder variants such as high-functioning autism.

High-functioning autism (HFA): The diagnostic criteria for autistic disorder are met, but without intellectual disability and severe impairment in communicative competency.

Asperger syndrome (AS): The same type of deficits in social reciprocity and restricted patterns of behaviors as autistic disorder, but with normal to above intellectual ability and language development. There appear to be few qualitative differences between Asperger syndrome and HFA.

PDDNOS: Pervasive developmental disorder not otherwise specified. A classification used for children who are significantly impaired in their social interactions with either a deficit in communication skills or a pattern of circumscribed behavior, interests, and activities, but who do not meet the diagnostic criteria for another ASD.

Quick Reference

By the numbers

There has been a global increase in the number of children identified with autism over the past decade. Autism is no longer considered a rare condition and is now the fastest-growing development disorder in the United States. Recent estimates by the Centers for Disease Control and Prevention report a prevalence of 1 in 150 for eight-year-old children. Statistics from the United Kingdom also indicate a prevalence of 1 in 160 children under eight years of age. Epidemiological studies of the prevalence of all ASD conditions in Europe and North America indicate a best estimate of 0.6 percent or approximately 1 in 160 of the general population. The explanations for this dramatic increase are multifaceted and include better recognition, consideration of autism as a spectrum disorder, changes in diagnostic criteria, and greater availability of services.

Chapter 2

BEST PRACTICE
IN SCREENING

Screening prevents delays in identification and the timely delivery of intervention services

Based on the information presented in the previous chapter, it is clear that the increased awareness and prevalence of autism, together with the benefits of early intervention, have created an urgent need for school professionals to identify children who may have an autism spectrum condition. Early behavioral intervention is a critical determinant in the course and outcome of autism spectrum disorders (ASDs) (Bryson *et al.* 2003; Rogers and Vismara 2008). Both *IDEA* and the *SEN Code of Practice* focus on the importance of early identification, assessment, and provision of services for students with special educational needs. Behavioral screening is an important first step in this process. Although children with the classic (Kanner's) autism are being identified at an early age, it is not unusual for children with milder forms of autism to go undiagnosed until well after entering school (Brock, Jimerson, and Hansen 2006). For example, a survey of parents in the United Kingdom found that autism was diagnosed on average at 5.5 years and higher functioning ASD such as Asperger syndrome at 11 years. In many instances, parents waited more than five years before a diagnosis was confirmed (Howlin and Asgharian 1999; Howlin and Moore 1997). A recent sample of parents of school-age children with ASD across five countries found an average diagnosis age of 7.5 years for Asperger syndrome and a consistent concern with the timeliness of identification and frustration with the delay in accessing services. Parents were more satisfied with the diagnostic process when they saw fewer professionals to secure a diagnosis and when their children received the diagnoses at younger ages (Goin-Kochel *et al.* 2006). A study examining the timing of identification among children with autism using a population-based sample from an ongoing surveillance effort across 13 sites in the United States found the gap between potential and actual age of identification (for those identified) to be in the range of 2.7 to 3.7 years. Combined with the fact that more than one quarter of cases were never identified as having ASD through age eight, this gap seems characteristic of the weakness in our overall system of screening and identification for ASD (Shattuck *et al.* 2009). Because many children are not identified until well after five years of age, future efforts should place an emphasis on recognition and diagnosis among school-aged children, not just among young children. Accurate differential identification and provision for services are critical since a high proportion of children may be overlooked, misdiagnosed with another psychiatric condition, or present with comorbid psychiatric disorders such as depression and anxiety.

Whatever the reasons for the reported delay in identification, a late diagnosis postpones the timely implementation of intervention services and may contribute to parental distress in coping with an ASD (Goddard, Lehr, and Lapadat 2000; Goin-Kochel *et al.* 2006). It is well established that early interventions for children with developmental disabilities are important in increasing cognitive, linguistic, social, and self-help skills (Dawson and Osterling 1997; Rogers 1998). Assisting parents to develop effective management techniques is also likely to avoid or minimize the potential for secondary behavioral and emotional problems (Howlin 1998; Howlin and Rutter 1987). Importantly, because more capable children with ASD are likely to be educated in mainstream schools and general education classrooms, delayed recognition of their problems can result in the implementation of ineffective or inappropriate teaching methods that fail to address the core social-communication deficits of ASD. Delays in diagnosis and identification also have wide implications for families. It is now accepted that autism is most likely among the most heritable of all childhood disorders and that for any family with a child with ASD, there is considerable risk that other children in the family may have social, language, or other neurocognitive problems (Bailey, Phillips, and Rutter 1996). Family histories of autism or autistic-like behavior or having an older sibling with autism are known risk factors. A delay in identification may result in siblings with the "broader phenotype" being overlooked and as a result, not receive the help needed to address their problems (Howlin and Asgharian 1999). Thus, it is vital that school professionals devote increased attention to the screening and early identification of students who may have symptomatology of an autism-related condition (Brock *et al.* 2006).

BEST PRACTICE
School professionals play a vital role by participating in case finding and screening activities to ensure children with ASD are being identified and provided with the appropriate programs and services.

CATEGORICAL VS. DIMENSIONAL APPROACHES

As discussed earlier, autism is generally diagnosed when a child demonstrates impairments in the domains of social development, communication, and repetitive behavior/obsessive interests. The PDD/ASD subtypes have traditionally been viewed as categorical diagnoses. With a categorical or dichotomous scheme, disorders are either present or absent. For example, the *DSM-IV-TR* and *ICD-10* list specific criteria for each disorder that must be met to receive a diagnostic classification. Similarly, the *IDEA* specifies categories of special education disability. Both are categorical rather than dimensional systems of classification (e.g. a child meets or does not meet criteria) and both focus on a description of behavior rather than function.

There is now considerable debate as to whether autism should be conceptualized as a distinct clinical entity or as a continuum of severity. We know that children with the same diagnostic classification are likely to be heterogeneous and that many childhood disorders, including ASD, fall along a continuum in the general population (Constantino and Gruber 2005). Categorical classification fails to account for these quantitative differences between children with the same core symptoms. According to Wing (2005), the syndromes/disorders comprising ASD are not discrete and separate categories, and the triad of autistic impairments is best understood by using a dimensional approach. Likewise, there is a growing consensus among professionals who work with children with ASD that differences between the higher functioning subtypes are not particularly useful in terms of either intervention or outcome and that autism is more appropriately conceptualized as a spectrum condition rather than an "all-or-nothing" diagnostic entity (Constantino and Todd 2003; Howlin 2005). We also recognize that traits similar to those observed in ASD are not restricted to children with a clinical diagnosis (Skuse *et al.* 2009). This is especially important because even mild degrees of autistic symptomatology can have an adverse effect on a child's adaptive and school functioning. Thus, while categories are much easier to conceptualize, they tend to be of minimal use in actual practice (Wing 2005). The content of this and subsequent chapters reflects the view that social-communication deficits are continuously distributed in the general population of school children and may be associated with varying degrees of functional impairments across school and home contexts.

BEST PRACTICE

All school proessionals should be prepared to participate in the behavioral screening of students who have risk factors and/or desplay warning signs of autism.

SCREENING, DIAGNOSIS, AND ASSESSMENT

Throughout this book, the term *screening* refers to the process of identifying school children most likely to have an ASD and/or developmental delay. *Referral* is the process of initiating an evaluation of a child in this age group. The terms *diagnostic evaluation, diagnosis,* and *classification* refer to the process of assigning a specific diagnostic or special education label whereas *assessment* is used to describe the process of evaluating the child's level of functioning in multiple developmental areas and his or her unique pattern of strengths and weaknesses. Although these functions and procedures are considered separately, in practice, they may take place concurrently. We should keep in mind that screening instruments are not intended to provide diagnoses, but rather to suggest a need for further diagnostic evaluation and intervention planning assessment.

BEST PRACTICE

All school professionals should be able to distinguish between screening, assessment, and diagnosis.

BEHAVIORAL SCREENING

The broader autism phenotype has shifted our attention away from a strict definition of autism to recognition of higher-functioning subtypes of ASD (Wing 2005; Wing and Potter 2002). Population estimates of prevalence may, in actuality, underestimate the importance of autistic characteristics of less severity (Skuse *et al.* 2009). For example, cases are usually determined from assessments based on the initial selection of children who have severe and obvious symptoms. Mild or even moderate deficits in social-communicative competence may be missed, especially if they are associated with coexisting (comorbid) conduct and attention problems.

Developing screening tools to identify the milder variants of autism has been especially difficult because of the varying degrees of symptomatology (Wing 2005). Until recently, there were few validated screening measures available to assist professionals in the identification of students with characteristics of the broader autistic phenotype (Campbell 2005; Lord and Corsello 2005). However, our knowledge of ASD is expanding rapidly and we now have more reliable and valid tools to screen and evaluate children efficiently and with greater accuracy (Yeargin-Allsopp *et al.* 2003). These instruments may be used with children who present with risk factors (e.g. sibling or family history of autism) and/or when parents and teachers or health care professionals observe or identify the presence of "red flags" (e.g.

social, communication and behavioral concerns) of a neurodevelopmental disorder. Both parent and teacher screening tools are ideal for identifying children who are in need of a more comprehensive evaluation. They yield important information from individuals who know the child the best and are relatively easy to administer and score (Wiggins *et al.* 2007).

BEST PRACTICE

Parent and teacher screening tools are ideal instruments to assist with the identification of ASD because they gather important information from people familiar with the student and are easy to administer and score.

Psychometric characteristics

The psychometric characteristics most frequently considered when evaluating screening measures are *sensitivity* and *specificity*. Both are important validity statistics that describe how well a test can identify true cases of a disorder. Sensitivity is the probability that a child who has the condition will screen positive. Specificity is the probability that a child who does not have the condition will screen negative. Sensitivity levels of .80 or higher are generally recommended. This indicates that at least 80 percent of children who truly have a condition or disorder (as determined by a more comprehensive evaluation) should be identified by their scores on the screening measure. Specificity levels of .80 and higher are also recommended, indicating that 80 percent or more of children who do not have the disorder should be identified as not at risk. False negatives (children with a disorder who screen negative) decrease sensitivity, while false positives (children without a disorder who screen positive) decrease specificity. An efficient screening tool should have high sensitivity and minimize false negatives as these are children with likely ASD who remain unidentified (Goin-Kochel *et al.* 2006; Johnson *et al.* 2007; National Research Council 2001). It is also important to understand that a screening instrument's predictive value will depend on the prevalence of the disorder in the population or group under consideration. For example, a screening measure may be expected to have higher positive predictive value and sensitivity when utilized with at-risk children who exhibit signs or symptoms of developmental delay, social skills deficits, or language impairment (Posserud, Lundervold, and Gillberg 2006).

BEST PRACTICE

Early childhood specialists and school professionals should be trained in identifying the "red flags" of ASD and the importance of early referral for screening and assessment.

Screening tools for school-age children

A number of measures have been developed to screen and identify children who are in need of a more comprehensive evaluation. Literature reviews and validity studies were used to locate questionnaires specifically designed to identify the more subtle impairments associated with high-functioning ASD. All measures selected were considered to have sound psychometric properties, to be appropriate for school-age children, and time efficient. Training needs were minimal and required little or no specific instruction to complete. However, interpretation of results presumed familiarity with ASD and experience in administering, scoring, and interpreting psychological tests. While other instruments, [e.g. Gilliam Autism Rating Scale (GARS; Gilliam 1995); Asperger Syndrome Diagnostic Scale (ASDS; Myles, Bock, and Simpson 2001); Gilliam Asperger's Disorder Scale (GADS; Gilliam 2001); and Autism Behavior Checklist (ABC; Krug, Arick, and Almond 1988)], are available, they demonstrate significant weaknesses, including the underidentification of higher-functioning ASD and questions concerning standardization and norming procedures (Campbell 2005; Coonrod and Stone 2005; Lord and Corsello 2005; Ozonoff, Goodlin-Jones, and Solomon 2005). Autism-specific measures for young preschool children such as the Checklist for Autism in Toddlers (CHAT), Modified Checklist for Autism in Toddlers (M-CHAT), and Pervasive Developmental Disorders Screening Test II (PDDST-II) are not included here as they were not designed to screen elementary school-age children.

The following screening tools provide brief, reliable, and valid dimensional measures of autistic traits in children without cognitive delay or learning disability. Table 2.1 lists the specific measures, together with information regarding format, administration time, validity, and applicable age ranges.

BEST PRACTICE

A standardized screening tool should be administered at any point when concerns about ASD are raised by a parent or teacher or as a result of school observations or questions about developmentally appropriate social, communicative, and play behaviors.

Table 2.1 Screening measures for autism spectrum disorders

Measure	Age range	Format (no. of items)	Sensitivity	Specificity	Time to complete
ASSQ (a)	6:0–17:0	Questionnaire—Parent/Teacher (27)	.91	.86	10 minutes
AQ-Child (b)	4:0–11:0	Questionnaire—Parent (50)	.95	.95	10 minutes
CAST (c)	4:0–11:0	Questionnaire—Parent (37)	1.0	.97	10 minutes
CCC-2 (d)	4:0–16:11	Questionnaire—Parent or Professional (70)	.89	.97	10–15 minutes
SCDC (e)	4:0–16:0	Questionnaire—Parent (12)	.88	.91	10 minutes
SCQ (f)	4:0–Adult	Questionnaire—Parent (40)	.85	.75	10 minutes
SRS (g)	4:0–18:0	Questionnaire—Parent/Teacher (65)	.85	.75	10–20 minutes

Note. ASSQ-Autism Spectrum Screening Questionnaire; AQ-Child-Autism Spectrum Quotient: Children's Version; CAST-Childhood Autism Spectrum Test; CCC-Children's Communication Checklist; SCDC-Social Communication Disorders Checklist; SCQ-Social Communication Questionnaire; SRS-Social responsiveness Scale. *Availability:* (a) Appendix: Ehlers *et al.* 1999; b) Appendix: Auyeung *et al.* 2008; (c) Appendix: Scott *et al.* 2002; (d) Purchase: Psych Corp; (e) Appendix: Skuse, Mandy, and Scourfield 2005; (f) Purchase: Western Psychological Services; (g) Purchase: Western Psychological Services.

Source. Adapted with permission from Wilkinson 2009. Copyright 2009 SAGE Publications.

SCREENING TOOLS

Autism Spectrum Screening Questionnaire

The Autism Spectrum Screening Questionnaire (ASSQ; Ehlers, Gillberg, and Wing 1999), formerly known as the Asperger Syndrome and High-Functioning Autism Questionnaire, is a parent and teacher questionnaire comprised of 27 items designed to discriminate between more capable children with ASD and typically developing peers. The ASSQ has been widely used as a screening instrument in the United Kingdom and across northern Europe. The content addresses social interaction (11 items), verbal and nonverbal communication (6 items), restricted and repetitive behaviors (5 items), and motor clumsiness and associated symptoms (5 items). Social items include questions related to difficulties with friendship (e.g. "Wishes to be sociable, but fails to make relationships with peers"), prosocial behavior (e.g. "Lacks empathy"), and social communication (e.g. "Uses language freely but fails to make adjustment to fit social contexts or the needs of different listeners"). The respondent rates behavioral descriptions on a 3-point scale, "not true" (0), "sometimes true" (1), and "certainly true" (2). Two separate cut-off threshold scores are suggested. Parent scores of ≥ 19 and teacher scores of ≥ 22 are recommended as optimal cut-off points for identifying likely ASD cases while minimizing the rate of false positives (Ehlers *et al.* 1999). These threshold scores are comparable to a sensitivity value of .62 for parent ratings and .70 for teacher ratings, and a specificity value of .90 (both parent and teacher ratings) in a clinical sample. Children with these sensitivity levels were 5.5 and 7.5 times more likely to have an ASD than another developmental disorder. A lower cut-off threshold of ≥ 13 for parents and ≥ 11 for teachers increases sensitivity values to .91 and .90, respectively. While this threshold is recommended for use when it is essential to minimize the risk of missing mild autism cases (false negatives), these scores will increase the risk of false positives (Ehlers *et al.* 1999; Posserud *et al.* 2006). A recent validation study found the ASSQ to be an effective screening tool for identifying ASD and the broader autism phenotype in a general population sample (e.g. public schools) of seven to nine-year-old children. Analyses indicated an optimal cut-off score of ≥ 17 on either parent or teacher questionnaire for discriminating between ASD and non-ASD cases. Combining the results for both informants and using this cut-off score provided the most efficient screening results with a sensitivity value of .91 and a specificity value of .86 (Posserud, Lundervold, and Gillberg in press). Research indicates that the ASSQ possesses strong test-retest reliability, acceptable inter-rater reliability, and good internal consistency, and that it significantly differentiates high-functioning ASD from other childhood disorders (Ehlers *et al.* 1999; Posserud *et al.* 2008). A sample of the ASSQ is provided in Table 2.2.

Table 2.2 The Autism Spectrum Screening Questionnaire (ASSQ)

This child stands out as different from other children of his/her age in the following way:

	No	Somewhat	Yes
1. is old-fashioned or precocious	[ ]	[ ]	[ ]
2. is regarded as an "eccentric professor" by the other children	[ ]	[ ]	[ ]
3. lives somewhat in a world of his/her own with restricted idiosyncratic intellectual interests	[ ]	[ ]	[ ]
4. accumulates facts on certain subjects (good rote memory) but does not really understand the meaning	[ ]	[ ]	[ ]
5. has a literal understanding of ambiguous and metaphorical language	[ ]	[ ]	[ ]
6. has a deviant style of communication with a formal, fussy, old-fashioned or "robot like" language	[ ]	[ ]	[ ]
7. invents idiosyncratic words and expressions	[ ]	[ ]	[ ]
8. expresses sounds involuntarily; clears throat, grunts, smacks, crises or screams	[ ]	[ ]	[ ]
9. is surprisingly good at some things and surprisingly poor at others	[ ]	[ ]	[ ]
10. uses language freely but fails to make adjustment to fit social contexts or the needs of different listeners	[ ]	[ ]	[ ]
11. lacks empathy	[ ]	[ ]	[ ]
12. makes naive and embarrassing remarks	[ ]	[ ]	[ ]
13. has a deviant style of gaze	[ ]	[ ]	[ ]
14. wishes to be sociable but fails to make relationships with peers	[ ]	[ ]	[ ]
15. can be with other children but only on his/her terms	[ ]	[ ]	[ ]
16. lacks best friend	[ ]	[ ]	[ ]
17. lacks commons sense	[ ]	[ ]	[ ]

Table 2.2 *continued*

This child stands out as different from other children of his/her age in the following way:

	No	Somewhat	Yes
18. is poor at games: no idea of cooperating in a team scores "own goals"	[ ]	[ ]	[ ]
19. has clumsy, ill coordinated, ungainly, awkward movements or gestures	[ ]	[ ]	[ ]
20. has involuntary face or body movements	[ ]	[ ]	[ ]
21. has difficulties in completing simple daily activities because of compulsory repetition of certain actions or thoughts	[ ]	[ ]	[ ]
22. has special routines: insists on no change	[ ]	[ ]	[ ]
23. shows idiosyncratic attachment to objects	[ ]	[ ]	[ ]
24. is bullied by other children	[ ]	[ ]	[ ]
25. has markedly unusual facial expression	[ ]	[ ]	[ ]
26. has markedly unusual posture	[ ]	[ ]	[ ]

Note. Reprinted with kind permission from Springer and Business Media: *Journal of Autism and Developmental Disorders,* A screening questionnaire for Asperger syndrome and other high-functioning autism spectrum disorders in school-age children, 29, 1999, pp. 139–140, Ehlers, S., Gillberg, C., and Wing, L. Copyright 1999 Kluwer Academic Publishing.

The Autism Spectrum Quotient-Children's Version

The Autism Spectrum Quotient-Children's Version (AQ-Child; Auyeung *et al.* 2008) is a 50-item parent-report questionnaire developed to quantify autistic traits in children 4 to 11 years of age. It was adapted from the adult and adolescent versions of the AQ. The AQ-Child consists of a series of descriptive statements designed to assess five areas associated with autism and the broader phenotype: social skills, attention switching, attention to detail, and communication and imagination, each represented by ten items. Parents rate to what extent they agree or disagree with the statements about their child on a 4-point response scale: "definitely agree" (3); "slightly agree" (2); "slightly disagree" (1); and "definitely disagree" (0). Total AQ scores are represented by the sum of each item score. The minimum score (0) indicates no autistic traits; the maximum score (150) suggests full endorsement on all autistic items. Analyses indicated that using a cut-off score of 76, sensitivity and specificity levels were both .95 in a general population sample of children. The AQ-Child reports good test—retest reliability and high internal consistency. The questionnaire appears to be an efficient and useful indicator of whether a comprehensive diagnostic assessment might be warranted. It is shown in Appendix A.

Childhood Autism Spectrum Test

The Childhood Autism Spectrum Test (CAST; Scott *et al.* 2002), formerly titled the Childhood Asperger Syndrome Test (CAST), is a parent questionnaire based on the *Diagnostic and Statistical Manual of Mental Disorders* (4th edn) *DSM IV* (American Psychiatric Association 1994) and the *ICD-10* core features and behavioral indicators for autism, especially the milder variants such as high-functioning autism and Asperger Disorder. The CAST has a total of 37 items, of which 31 are key items that are summed to yield a total score (maximum possible score of 31). The remaining six items are control questions dealing with general development and are not scored. Social items include questions regarding peer relationships (e.g. "Does s/he join in playing games with other children easily?") and play activities (e.g. "Does s/he prefer imaginative activities such as play-acting or story-telling, rather than numbers or lists of facts?"). The CAST demonstrates a sensitivity value of 1.0 and a specificity value of .97 when using a cut-off score of ≥ 15 in a large general population sample (Williams, Johnson, and Sukhodolsky 2005). Validation studies also report a strong correlation with both the Autism Diagnostic Observation Schedule (ADOS: Lord *et al.* 2001) and the Autism Diagnostic Interview-Revised (ADI-R: Rutter, LeCouteur, and Lord 2003), recognized "gold standard" instruments for the assessment and diagnosis of autism. Research indicates that the CAST has good test—retest reliability and that it is a robust screening tool for identifying possible ASD cases in school-age populations (Allison *et al.* 2007; Williams *et al.* 2006). The CAST is presented in Appendix B.

Children's Communication Checklist-Second Edition

The Children's Communication Checklist-Second Edition (CCC-2; Bishop 2003) is a measure intended to assess communication skills in the areas of pragmatics, syntax, morphology, semantics, and speech of children ages 4:00 to 16:11. Although it was not designed specifically as a screening tool, the CCC-2 has shown utility in identifying children who may require further assessment for an autism spectrum disorder. Initially developed in the United Kingdom, the CCC-2 has also been adapted for use in the United States (Bishop 2006). A Caregiver Response Form is completed by an adult who has regular contact with the child, usually a parent, teacher, therapist, or other professional. The CCC-2 consists of 70 items that are divided into 10 scales, each with 7 items. The first four scales address specific aspects of language and communication skills (content and form). The next four scales assess the pragmatic aspects of communication. The last two scales assess behaviors that are usually impaired in children with autism spectrum disorders. The respondent rates the frequency of the communication behavior described in each item from 0 (less than once a week or never) to 3 (several times a day or always). Interpretation is based on a General Communication Composite (GCC) and Social Interaction Difference Index (SIDI), a metric specifically designed for use in identifying a communication profile that might be characteristic of ASD. Disproportionately depressed communicative competence, coupled with a score of ≥11 on the SIDI suggest a profile of ASD and the need for further evaluation. The CCC-2 reports a sensitivity value of .89 and specificity value of .97 for identifying children with autistic symptomatology and social impairment (Bishop 2006). Previous versions of the CCC-2 have been strongly associated with the ADI-R total score and ICD-10 diagnostic criteria (Charman et al. 2007; Verte et al. 2006).

Social Communication Disorders Checklist

The Social Communication Disorders Checklist (SCDC; Skuse, Mandy, and Scourfield 2005) is a questionnaire, completed by parents, that measures social reciprocity and verbal/nonverbal characteristics similar to those found in ASD. There are 12 items, rated according to whether the corresponding behavior has been observed during the past 6 months; whether the associated statements are "not true," "quite or sometimes true," or "very or often true." Scores of 0–1–2 are assigned, so the maximum possible score is 24. The SCDC questions' content comprises the domains of social reciprocity, nonverbal skills, and pragmatic language usage. The scale was derived from a principal components analysis of a longer instrument and represents a single factor with strong internal consistency. Discriminant validity, measured in clinical population, predicted autism with a sensitivity of .90 and specificity of .69 with an obtained cut-off score of 9 points. Criterion validation showed modest correlations between the SCDC total score and ADI algorithm scores (qualitative abnormalities in reciprocal social interaction, qualitative abnormalities in communication, and restricted, repetitive, and stereotyped patterns of behavior). A recent study of the SCDC with a large general population sample of children found that maximum sensitivity (.88) and specificity (.91) were obtained with a cut-off score of 8 or more. Despite its brevity, the SCDC demonstrates high levels of sensitivity and specificity in relation to independently diagnosed cases of ASD in the general population. The SCDC-measured trait also has high heritability which is similar in magnitude to the heritability of autistic traits measured by other screening scales. A sample of the SCDC is shown in Table 2.3.

Table 2.3 The Social and Communication Disorders Checklist (SCDC)

For each item, please mark the box that best describes your child's behaviour over the past 6 months.

	Not true	Sometimes true	Very/often true
1. Not aware of other people's feelings	[ ]	[ ]	[ ]
2. Does not realise when others are upset or angry	[ ]	[ ]	[ ]
3. Does not notice the effect of his/her behaviour on other members of the family	[ ]	[ ]	[ ]
4. Behaviour often disrupts family life	[ ]	[ ]	[ ]
5. Very demanding of other people's time	[ ]	[ ]	[ ]
6. Difficult to reason with when upset	[ ]	[ ]	[ ]
7. Does not seem to understand social skills, (e.g. persistently interrupts conversations)	[ ]	[ ]	[ ]
8. Does not pick up on body language	[ ]	[ ]	[ ]
9. Does not appear to understand how to behave when out (e.g. in shops, or other people's homes)	[ ]	[ ]	[ ]
10. Does not realise if s/he offends people with her/his behaviour	[ ]	[ ]	[ ]
11. Does not respond when told to do something	[ ]	[ ]	[ ]
12. Cannot follow a command unless it is carefully worded	[ ]	[ ]	[ ]

Do you have any other comments or concerns? (If yes, please describe.)

Note: Reprinted with permission from the *British Journal of Psychiatry*, Skuse, D. H., Mandy, W. P. L. and Scourfield, J. (2005). Measuring autistic traits: Heritability, reliability and validity of the social and communication disorders checklist, p. 572. Copyright 2005, Royal College of Psychiatrists.

Social Communication Questionnaire

The Social Communication Questionnaire (SCQ; Rutter, Bailey, and Lord 2003), formerly known as the Autism Screening Questionnaire (ASQ), was initially designed as a companion screening measure for the ADI-R. The SCQ is a 40-item, parent/caregiver screening measure that identifies the symptomatology associated with disorders on the autism spectrum. Each item is scored 0 or 1 according to a yes/no response format. There are two separate versions available: Lifetime and Current. The Lifetime form is suitable for diagnostic screening purposes and the Current form useful for evaluating changes over time in children previously diagnosed with ASD. Questions include items in the reciprocal social interaction domain (e.g. "Does she/he have any particular friends or best friend?"), the communication domain (e.g. "Can you have a to and fro 'conversation' with him/her that involves taking turns or building on what you have said?") and the restricted, repetitive, and stereotyped patterns of behavior domain (e.g. "Has s/he ever seemed to be more interested in parts of a toy or an object (e.g. spinning the wheels of a car), rather than using the object as intended?"). The SCQ is appropriate for individuals of any chronological age above four years of age. The total score obtained from the Lifetime form is interpreted with reference to a cut-off criterion. The SCQ has been found to have good discriminative validity (Charman *et al.* 2007; Corsello *et al.* 2007). A threshold score of ≥15 is recommended to minimize the risk of false negatives and indicates the need for a comprehensive evaluation. Comparing autism to other diagnoses (excluding mental retardation), this threshold score resulted in a sensitivity value of .96 and a specificity value of .80 in a large population of children with autism and other developmental disorders. A somewhat lower threshold may be considered if other risk factors are reported (e.g. sibling with autism or language impairment). A recent study of the properties of the SCQ in a cohort of children with ASD confirmed the utility of the SCQ as an efficient screener for at-risk groups of school-age children (Chandler *et al.* 2007).

Social Responsiveness Scale

The Social Responsiveness Scale (SRS; Constantino and Gruber 2005) is a brief quantitative measure of autistic behaviors in 4 to 18-year-olds. This 65-item rating scale was designed to be completed by an adult (teacher and/or parent as respondent) who is familiar with the child's current behavior and developmental history. The questionnaire focuses on the child's reciprocal social interactions, a core impairment in all pervasive developmental disorders. The SRS items measure the severity of ASD symptoms in the domains of social awareness, social information processing, reciprocal social communication, social anxiety/avoidance, and stereotypic behavior/restricted interests. Each item is scored from 1 (not true) to 4 (almost always true). Scores are obtained for five treatment subscales: Social Awareness (e.g. "Is aware of what others are thinking or feeling"), Social Cognition (e.g. "Doesn't recognize when others are trying to take advantage of him or her"), Social Communication (e.g. "Avoids eye contact or has unusual eye contact"), Social Motivation (e.g. "Would rather be alone than with others"), and Autistic Mannerisms (e.g. "Has an unusually narrow range of interests"). Interpretation is based on a single score reflecting the sum of responses to all 65 SRS questions. A total raw score of ≥ 75 was associated with a sensitivity value of .85 and specificity value of .75 for any ASD (autistic disorder, Asperger' disorder, or PDDNOS). The SRS demonstrates strong reliability across informants, acceptable internal consistency, and correlates highly with the ADI-R (Constantino *et al.* 2003; Lord and Corsello 2005). The SRS also affords the potential to reliably measure the severity of social impairment in the most common (and subtle) of autistic disorders, PDDNOS (Constantino and Gruber 2005).

BEST PRACTICE
Broad-based screening for school-age children should include tools such as the Autism Spectrum Screening Questionnaire (ASSQ), Autism Spectrum Quotient-Children's Version (AQ-Child), Childhood Autism Spectrum Test (CAST), and Social Communication Disorders Checklist (SCDC).

A MULTISTEP GUIDE FOR SCREENING

These instruments have demonstrated utility as efficient screening questionnaires for identifying children across the broad autism spectrum who are in need of further diagnostic assessment. Figure 2.1 displays a multistep procedure for screening students who demonstrate risk factors and/or warning signs of atypical development or where caregiver/parent concerns strongly suggest the presence of ASD symptoms.

Step 1

The ASSQ, CAST, AQ-Child, or SCDC can be utilized as an initial screen for students who present with elevated developmental risk factors and warning signs of autism. These questionnaires are useful in identifying the presence of the more broadly defined symptoms of higher-functioning ASD in general population settings. However, as with all screening tools, there will be some false negatives. Thus, children who screen negative, but who have a high level of risk and where caregiver and/or teacher concerns highly suggest

ASD symptoms, might be given serious consideration for further screening or assessment (Filipek *et al.* 1999; Johnson *et al.* 2007). All children who exhibit developmental variations and behaviors consistent with an autism-related disorder should continue to be monitored, regardless of screening results.

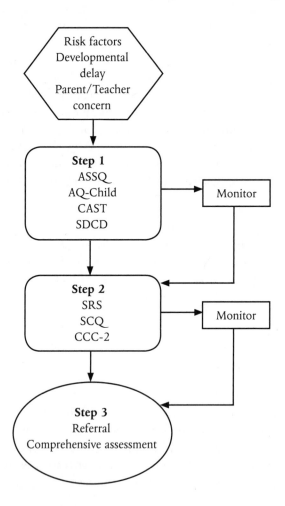

Figure 2.1 Multistep screening process

Step 2

Children who meet the threshold criteria on the ASSQ, CAST, AQ-Child, or SCDC can be screened further with the CCC-2, SCQ, and/or SRS to quantify the degree of ASD symptomatology. These instruments have the ability to measure the approximate level of symptom severity impairment in the domains of reciprocal social behavior, pragmatic language and communication, and stereotypical behavior and restricted range of interests (Bishop 2003; Constantino and Gruber 2005; Rutter, Bailey and Lord 2003). As with the initial screening, students who screen negative, but arouse concerns in the social behavior and communication domains, should continue to be observed and monitored.

Step 3

Students who meet the threshold criteria in step two may then be referred for a comprehensive assessment. Because the CCC-2, SCQ, and SRS are strongly related to the well-established and researched gold standard measures such as the Autism Diagnostic Interview (ADI-R) and the Autism Diagnostic Observation Schedule (ADOS), the results from these screening measures can be used in combination with an interdisciplinary assessment of social behavior, language and communication, adaptive behavior, motor skills, sensory issues, and cognitive functioning to help with intervention planning and determining eligibility for special educational services (Corsello *et al.* 2007; National Research Council 2001; Ozonoff *et al.* 2005a). The assessment should be concerned not only with a diagnosis or classification, but on developing a profile of strengths and weaknesses that can be linked to intervention. Parents should also be actively involved in this process. Lastly, some children who screen positive and are referred for a comprehensive assessment may not necessarily be identified with ASD, but may have another childhood disorder which requires intervention and treatment. Therefore, it is important that evaluators have a range of experience in the diagnosis and assessment of developmental disabilities.

BEST PRACTICE

Gender should be taken into consideration when screening and evaluating students for ASD.

Gender considerations

Gender differences should also be taken into consideration when screening and evaluating children for ASD. Although few studies have examined effects of gender-specific differences on various screening measures, the ASSQ, CAST, SCDC, and SRS have generally reported higher mean scores for boys than girls (Williams *et al.* 2006). For instance, the SRS identifies two separate total raw score cut-offs, with a lower threshold for girls than for boys (Constantino and Gruber 2005). Boys also obtained mean scores 30 percent higher than girls on the SCDC (Skuse *et al.* 2009). Similarly, the ASSQ found higher scores for boys than girls in both the parent and teacher questionnaires, with the greatest difference in reports from teachers (Posserud *et al.* in press). These lower symptom scores for girls may reflect gender differences in autistic traits and expression of the phenotype. Although this phenomenon continues to be studied, a higher cut-off threshold for boys might be considered when screening for autism traits in the general population (Williams *et al.* 2006).

Limitations

These screening instruments can be recommended as reliable and valid tools for identifying children across the broad autism spectrum. However, they are not flawless. As with any screening instrument, some students who screen positive will not be diagnosed with a disorder. On the other hand, some children who are not identified with a likely autism spectrum condition will go on to meet the diagnostic criteria for one. Thus, it is especially important to carefully monitor those students who screen negative so as to minimize misclassification and ensure access to intervention services (Bryson *et al.* 2003). Gathering information from family and school resources during screening will also facilitate identification of possible cases (Posserud *et al.* 2006).

> ### BEST PRACTICE
> Students who screen negative should be carefully monitored so as to minimize misclassification and ensure access to intervention services.

None of the screening measures discussed here can differentiate between the autism spectrum subtypes and are not recommended for differential diagnosis. They may also perform differently in various countries owing to cultural interpretation of the questionnaire items. Likewise, a screening tool's efficiency will be influenced by the practice setting in which it is used. Practitioners must weigh the disadvantages of an inaccurate classification against the consequences of a delayed or missed diagnosis (Goin-Kochel *et al.* 2006). Lastly, autism-specific tools are not currently recommended for the universal screening of typical school-age children (Allison *et al.* 2007; Johnson *et al.* 2007). Focusing on referred children with identified risk-factors and/or developmental delays (second-level screening) will increase predictive values and result in more efficient identification efforts (Coonrod and Stone 2005; Lee, David, Rusyniak, Landa, and Newschaffer 2007).

SUMMARY

Although screening tools may have utility in broadly identifying children with an autism spectrum condition, they are not a substitute for a more thorough assessment. Screening tools are not recommended as stand alone diagnostic instruments and should be used only as part of a more comprehensive diagnostic assessment. Indeed, screening tools should only be used to answer the question "Should this student be referred for a comprehensive assessment?" Interviews and observation schedules, together with a multidisciplinary assessment of social behavior, language and communication, adaptive behavior, motor skills, sensory issues, atypical behaviors, and cognitive functioning are best suited for diagnosis and educational classification (National Research Council 2001; Ozonoff *et al.* 2005a). The next chapter examines the parameters of a comprehensive developmental assessment and provides a review of tests and measures included in a comprehensive assessment battery for ASD.

Quick Reference

Screening, assessment, and diagnosis

Third-party screening questionnaires have been shown to discriminate well between children with and without ASD. It is important to view assessment as a continuing process, rather than a single event. Rating scales should be used with caution and as part of a larger evaluation methodology. Screening measures differ from diagnostic measures in that they typically require less time and training to administer, and the results of screening measures indicate levels of risk for disability rather than providing a diagnosis (Coonrod and Stone 2005). Although screening instruments yield useful information, they cannot substitute for a more thorough diagnostic assessment and validation of the symptomatology identified during the screening process.

Chapter 3

BEST PRACTICE IN ASSESSMENT

Children who screen positive for ASD should receive a comprehensive developmental assessment.

The primary goals of conducting an autism spectrum assessment are to determine the presence and severity of an ASD, develop interventions for educational planning, and collect data that will help with progress monitoring (Shriver, Allen, and Matthews 1999). School professionals must also determine whether an ASD that has been overlooked or misclassified describes coexisting (comorbid) disorders, or identifies an alternative classification. Interviews and observation schedules, together with an interdisciplinary assessment of social behavior, language and communication, adaptive behavior, motor skills, sensory issues, atypical behaviors, and cognitive functioning are recommended best practice procedures (National Research Council 2001; Ozonoff *et al.* 2005a). This chapter describes a comprehensive developmental assessment approach and focuses on the tools and procedures for the assessment and identification of ASD included in recommendations of the American Academy of Neurology (Filipek *et al.* 2000), the American Academy of Child and Adolescent Psychiatry (Volkmar *et al.* 1999), and a consensus panel with representation from multiple professional societies (Filipek *et al.* 1999).

COMPREHENSIVE DEVELOPMENTAL APPROACH

There are several important considerations that should inform the assessment process. First, a developmental perspective is critically important. While the core symptoms are present during early childhood, ASD is a life-long disability that affects the individual's adaptive functioning from childhood through adulthood. Evaluating the child within a developmental assessment framework provides us with a yardstick for understanding the severity and quality of delays or atypicality (Klin *et al.* 2005; Klin and Volkmar

2000). Because ASD affects multiple developmental domains, utilizing an interdisciplinary team constitutes best practice for assessment and diagnosis of ASD. A team approach is essential for establishing a developmental and psychosocial profile of the child in order to guide intervention planning. A team of professionals including, but not limited to, a school or educational psychologist, general and special educators, a speech/language pathologist, occupational therapist, and in some cases a physician, should evaluate the child and collaborate to determine an appropriate classification or diagnosis. The following principles are intended to guide the assessment and evaluation process (Filipek *et al.* 1999, 2000; Klin *et al.* 2005; Klin and Volkmar 2000; Volkmar *et al.* 1999).

- Children who screen positive for ASD should be referred for a comprehensive assessment. Although the screening tools discussed in the previous chapter have utility in broadly identifying children who may have an autism spectrum condition, they are not recommended as stand alone diagnostic instruments or as a substitute for a more inclusive assessment. However, they may be used as components of a more comprehensive diagnostic battery.
- Assessment should involve careful attention to the signs and symptoms consistent with ASD as well as other coexisting childhood disorders.
- When a student is suspected of having an ASD, a review of his or her developmental history in areas such as speech, communication, social and play skills is an important first step in the assessment process.
- A family medical history and review of psychosocial factors that may play a role in the child's development is a significant component of the assessment process.
- The integration of information from multiple sources will strengthen the reliability of the assessment results.
- Evaluation of academic achievement should be included in assessment and intervention planning to address learning and behavioral concerns in the child's overall school functioning.
- Assessment procedures should be designed to assist in the development of instructional objectives and intervention strategies based on the student's unique pattern of strengths and weaknesses.
- Because impairment in communication and social reciprocity are core features of ASD, a comprehensive developmental assessment should include both domains.

> ## BEST PRACTICE
> An interdisciplinary team is preferred for evaluation and intervention planning as there is a need for a broad range of assessment procedures.

The comprehensive developmental assessment approach requires the use of multiple measures including, but not limited to, verbal reports, direct observation, direct interaction and evaluation, and third-party reports (Filipek *et al.* 1999; Shriver *et al.* 1999). Although none of these assessment methods alone comprehensively focus on the *DSM-IV*, *ICD-10* or *IDEA* definitions of autism, together they provide reliable and valid procedures for making diagnostic and educational decisions within a developmental framework. As discussed earlier, assessment is a continuous process, rather than a series of separate actions, and procedures may overlap and take place in tandem. While specific activities of the assessment process will vary and depend on the child's age, history, referral questions, and any previous evaluations and assessments, the following components should be included in a best practice assessment and evaluation of ASD in school-age children (California Department of Developmental Services 2002; Filipek *et al.* 1999; Johnson *et al.* 2007; National Research Council 2001; Ozonoff *et al.* 2005a; Volkmar *et al.* 1999):

- record review
- developmental and medical history
- medical screening and/or evaluation
- parent/caregiver interview
- parent/teacher ratings of social competence
- direct child observation
- cognitive assessment
- academic assessment
- adaptive behavior assessment
- communication and language assessment.

Table 3.1 shows the recommended core measures included in a comprehensive developmental assessment. Although not exhaustive, these tools provide a reliable and valid assessment of the autistic triad. Their selection was based on relevance to identification, differential diagnosis and classification, intervention planning, professional experience, or a combination of these in both the research and practice literature. It should be noted, however, that none of the instruments can reliably differentiate among the ASD subtypes

Table 3.1 Core measures for assessing autism spectrum disorders

Measure	Format	Age range	Time
Direct observation:			
ADOS	Direct Testing	2 years to adult	30 to 50 min
CARS	Observation	2 years to adult	5 to 10 min
Parent/Teacher report:			
ADI-R	Questionnaire	18 months to adult	1 to 2.5 hrs
SCQ	Questionnaire	4 years to adult	10 to 15 min
SRS	Questionnaire	4 to 18 years	10 to 15 min
Achievement:			
WIAT-II	Direct Testing	4 to adult	90 min
WJ-III	Direct Testing	2 to adult	60 to 70 min
KTEA-II	Direct Testing	4.6 years to adult	50 to 80 min
Cognitive:			
DAS-II	Direct Testing	2.6 to 17 years	45 to 60 min
SB-5	Direct Testing	2 to 85	45 to 75 min
WISC-IV	Direct Testing	6 to 16 years	50 to 70 min
WPPSI-III	Direct Testing	2 to 7 years	45 to 60 min
Communication:			
CASL	Direct Testing	3 to 21 years	30 to 45 min
CCC-2	Questionnaire	4 to 16 years	10 to 15 min
PLSI	Questionnaire	5 to 12 years	5 to 10 min
TOPL	Direct Testing	6 to 18 years	45 to 60 min
Adaptive behavior:			
ABAS-II	Rating Scale	Birth to Adult	15 to 20 min
DP-3	Interview	Birth to 12 years	20 to 40 min
VABS-II	Interview	Birth to 18 years	20 to 60 min

Note. ADOS-Autism Disorder Observation Scale; CARS-Childhood Autism Rating Scale; ADI-R-Autism Diagnostic Interview; SCQ-Social Communication Questionnaire; SRS-Social Responsiveness Scale; KTEA-II-Kaufman Test of Educational Achievement; WIAT-II-Wechsler Individual Achievement Test; WJ-III-Woodcock Johnson Psychoeducational Battery; SB-5-Stanford-Binet Intelligence Scales; WISC-IV-Wechsler Intelligence Scale for Children; WPPSI-III Wechsler Preschool and Primary Scale of Intelligence;

Table 3.1 *continued*

CCC-2-Children's Communication Checklist; CASL-Comprehensive Assessment of Spoken Language; PLSI-Pragmatic Language Skills Inventory; TOPL-Test of Pragmatic Language; VABS-II-Vineland Adaptive Behavior Scales; ABAS-II-Adaptive Behavior Assessment System; DP-III-Developmental Profile

(Klinger *et al.* 2003). School professionals are advised to select at least one measure from each area and become familiar with its administration, scoring, and properties. An ASD assessment worksheet is provided in Appendix C to help organize and structure the assessment battery.

> **BEST PRACTICE**
> A comprehensive assessment should include evaluation of multiple domains of functioning in order to differentiate ASD from other conditions and provide a complete profile of the student to facilitate intervention planning.

CORE ASSESSMENT DOMAINS

Record review

The first step in the assessment process is to review the child's early developmental history and current concerns with parents or caregiver. The focus of the record review is to look at past behavior and help determine developmental trends. Sources of information may include previous medical, school, and psychological records. Data from other evaluations or intervention reports (e.g. behavioral, speech/language) are especially valuable sources of information. For example, the parent and child might have had contact with community resources outside of the school setting (e.g. early intervention programs, agencies, private practitioners), which provides an opportunity for collecting additional background information. A review of records might also help to develop a more concise picture of existing concerns.

> **BEST PRACTICE**
> An important step in the core assessment process is to review the student's early developmental/medical history and current concerns with his or her parents. This should include a review of communication, social, and behavioral development.

Developmental/medical history

A comprehensive developmental/medical history, generally in the form of a parent or caregiver interview, is an important foundation component of the assessment process. The parent or caregiver typically serves as the source for obtaining the child's developmental history and information regarding behaviors and milestones. Inquiry should be made as to any history of developmental, learning and/or psychiatric problems in the family. Psychiatric disorders (e.g. depression) have a significant heritability component and this information may be helpful in understanding the child's functioning. Likewise, the interviewer should specifically question the immediate and extended family for autism, intellectual disability, and fragile X syndrome because of their association with ASD. A careful review of medical history should also take into consideration any current or previously prescribed medications, their action and any reported side effects. We should understand that while parents have the greatest amount of information about their child, they tend to have the highest degree of adaptation (or scaffolding) to their child's communication and behavioral profile (Volkmar *et al.* 1999). Likewise, the mild and atypical nature of symptoms of older school-age children with ASD can be complicated by challenges to the long-term memory of a parent, sibling, family member, or other caregiver.

BEST PRACTICE

All students suspected of ASD should have their vision and hearing screened using appropriate methodology and be referred for a formal assessment if concerns are present.

Medical screening/evaluation

Hearing and visual acuity should be routinely checked as part of the assessment process since both are frequent impairments in children with developmental disabilities. The need for additional medical and/or laboratory tests may become obvious, based upon the history and physical examination. In many cases, children under the age of ten may have had significant medical testing. This is particularly true in children with identified with intellectual impairment or learning disability for which the presence of an ASD is being questioned. Similarly, cases where several years of normal development are followed by a marked developmental regression may suggest the need for further medical referral and evaluation (Volkmar *et al.* 1999). With older children, the presence of a seizure disorder should also be questioned, particularly in students with lower cognitive functioning or who demonstrate a noticeable regression in their behavior (Minshew, Sweeney and Bauman 1997).

> **BEST PRACTICE**
> The parent or caregiver interview plays an important role in evaluating a child's developmental history and assessing behaviors associated with ASD.

Parent/Caregiver interview

Formal interview instruments play an important role in evaluating a child's developmental history and assessing behaviors associated with ASD (Lord *et al.* 1997). Familiarity with standardized interview measures and appreciation of the complexities of developmental change are essential for assessment and evaluation purposes. At present, the Autism Diagnostic Interview-Revised (ADI-R; Lord *et al.* 1994) is the most reliable standardized measure that can be used to obtain an early developmental history of autistic behaviors (Lord *et al.* 1994; Rutter, Le Couteur and Lord 2003). The ADI-R has been translated into 11 languages and is considered the "gold standard" parent interview that identifies symptoms closely linked to the diagnostic criteria of the *DSM-IV-TR* and *ICD-10* (Lord and Corsello 2005). It is typically administered by a trained clinician using a semistructured interview format. The items that empirically distinguish children with autism from those with other developmental delays are summed into three functional domains: Language and Communications, Reciprocal Social Interactions, and Restricted, Repetitive, and Stereotyped Behaviors and Interests. The scores on these items discriminate children with autism from those with other disorders, such as severe receptive language disorders (Mildenberger *et al.* 2001) and general developmental delays (Lord *et al.* 1994). As yet, there are no thresholds established for other ASD subtypes (e.g. Asperger's disorder or PDDNOS). The long version of the ADI-R requires approximately two and one-half to three hours for administering and scoring. A shorter version is available which includes only the items on the diagnostic algorithm, takes less time, (approximately 90 minutes), and may be used for clinical assessment (Lord *et al.* 1994). Although the ADI-R is able to identify the likelihood of autism, its validity is highly dependent on the interviewer's training and experience with this disorder. A major disadvantage of the ADI-R in a real-world setting is that it is labor intensive and requires more administration time than most school professionals are able to allocate. It also requires general experience in interviewing and a familiarity with autism in order to be effective. The SCQ (discussed in the previous chapter) may be considered as an alternative measure when time and training opportunities are limited (Naglieri and Chambers 2009). It contains the same questions included on the ADI-R algorithm, presented in a brief yes/no format that parents can complete on their own. Although the SCQ produces subscores that parallel the longer interview form (Reciprocal Social Interaction, Qualitative Abnormalities in Communication, and Restricted, Repetitive, and Stereotyped Patterns of Behavior), the Total Score is the primary, validated indicator of the likelihood that an individual has ASD.

BEST PRACTICE

Parent and teacher ratings are one of the most important sources of information about the student's social responsiveness and social-communication skills.

Parent/Teacher ratings of social competence

Because social impairment is a defining core feature of ASD, the determination of social functioning is fundamental to the assessment and evaluation of the student. It is important to recognize, however, that children with ASD vary widely in their social comprehension and interaction. Social impairments are also common in many other childhood disorders and therefore, must be compared with the pervasive impairment found in ASD. The best practice assessment of social functioning requires data collection from multiple sources. Data can be collected through observation during assessment (e.g. formal testing, interviews, play observations) and via direct observation of the child in naturalistic settings such as school or home. Questionnaires completed by parents and teachers are one of the most vital sources of information about the child's social responsiveness and social-communication skills. For example, the SCQ and SRS described in the last chapter are both well researched and validated instruments that are user-friendly and efficient. The SCQ has high agreement with the more labor-intensive ADI-R and can be an efficient tool to obtain diagnostic information or screen for autistic symptoms (Bishop and Norbury 2002; Naglieri and Chambers 2009). The SRS has also shown utility as a measure of social responsiveness across home and school contexts and may be incorporated into the core assessment battery as well. Popular third party rating scales such as the Gilliam Autism Rating Scale (GARS; Gilliam 1995), the Asperger Syndrome Diagnostic Scale (ASDS; Myles and Simpson 2001), the Gilliam Asperger's Disorder Scale (GADS; Gilliam 2001), and the Autism Behavior Checklist (ABC; Krug *et al.* 1988)] should be used with caution due to significant weaknesses, including the underidentification of higher-functioning ASD and questions concerning standardization and norming procedures (Brock *et al.* 2006; Campbell 2005; Coonrod and Stone 2005; S. Goldstein 2002; Lord and Corsello 2005; Ozonoff *et al.* 2005a; South *et al.* 2002). However, they may be used as a guide for identifying behavioral symptoms within the autistic triad. Of course, we must be mindful that no single rating scale or assessment tool should be used to identify a student with ASD and that they provide only one piece of convergent information used to make a diagnosis or classification determination.

BEST PRACTICE
Direct behavioral observation of the student in both structured and unstructured settings improves accuracy in the identification of ASD.

Direct child observation

Direct observation should take place throughout the assessment and intervention planning process. The specific format can be either formal or informal. The Autism Diagnostic Observation Schedule (ADOS; Lord *et al.* 2001; Lord *et al.* 2000) is considered the "gold standard" for directly assessing and diagnosing autism across ages, developmental levels, and language skills. The ADOS is a semistructured interactive assessment consisting of four different modules, graded according to language and developmental level. The module chosen is based upon the language level of the child or adolescent. The algorithm for the ADOS includes social and communication symptoms, but not the presence of repetitive and stereotyped behaviors. Two empirically defined cut-off scores, one for autistic disorder and the other for ASD (e.g. Asperger's disorder or PDDNOS) are provided. Information obtained on the child's social and language functioning by the ADOS can be especially useful in quantification of ASD domains and in intervention and educational planning (Lord and Corsello 2005). As with the ADI-R, the ADOS is a sophisticated instrument that requires specialized training, background, and experience in the treatment of autism, and practice to be utilized effectively. It is also expensive and time consuming to administer and score, and may not be an ideal measure for use in educational settings.

The Children's Autism Rating Scale (CARS; Schopler, Reichler, and Renner 1988) is a frequently used instrument to assess autism in children. The CARS is a 15-item structured observation instrument appropriate for children over 24 months of age. Each item covers a particular characteristic, ability, or behavior. After observing the child and examining relevant information from parent reports and other records, the examiner rates the child on each item. Items are rated on a 4-point-scale (from normal to severely abnormal) and summed to produce a composite score that ranges from 0 to 60. Scores above 30 are consistent with a diagnosis of autism and are divided into two categories: Mildly-Moderately Autistic (30 to 36) and Severely Autistic (37 to 60). The CARS has good technical qualities and correlates highly with the ADI-R. However, it tends to overidentify autism relative to the ADI-R, occasionally classifying children with intellectual disability as having autism. It is also based on pre-*DSM-IV-TR* conceptualizations of autism (Ozonoff *et al.* 2005; Van Bourgondien, Marcus, and Schopler 1992). Nevertheless, the CARS may be used as an alternative to the ADOS in that it less complicated and time efficient and requires minimal training. Well-informed professionals such as special educators, educational and school psychologists, and speech/ language pathologists who have minimal exposure to autism can be trained to use the CARS effectively. It is important to keep in mind that although ratings can be made from a parent interview, classroom observation, or case history review, this instrument does not produce a diagnosis or classification (Schopler *et al.* 1988).

Techniques to supplement these instruments are necessary in order to obtain additional information in the core domains. Informal measures such as the ASD Observation Checklist shown in Appendix D can be used as part of the assessment process when observing, interviewing the parent/teacher, and/or directly interacting with the student. The ASDC provides a framework for observing and recording behaviors in each of the core developmental areas. Specific behaviors include: reciprocal turn-taking; shared attention; social reciprocity; eye contact; repetitive behaviors; pretend play; spontaneous giving/showing; social language; and use of toys and objects. When using informal observation measures, it is very important to have an understanding of the way children respond at various ages and developmental levels, both children with ASD and their typical peers.

BEST PRACTICE

The measurement of cognitive ability is critical for making a determination of ASD and for intervention planning purposes. Evaluation of cognitive functioning in both verbal and nonverbal domains is necessary to develop a complete diagnostic profile of the student.

Cognitive assessment

A critical domain of the core assessment is intellectual or cognitive functioning. Establishing the level of cognitive ability is important for both classification and intervention planning purposes. For example, the level of intellectual functioning is associated with the severity of autistic symptoms, skill acquisition and learning ability, and level of adaptive functioning, and is one of the best predictors of long-term outcome (Harris and Handleman 2000; Stevens *et al.* 2000; Venter, Lord, and Schopler 1992). Because the IQs of children with ASD have the same properties as those obtained by other children aged five years and older, they are reasonable predictors of future educational performance (Klinger, O'Kelley, and Mussey 2009; Sattler and Hoge 2006). Thus, an appropriate measure of IQ is considered to be an essential component of the core assessment battery.

The primary goal of conducting an intellectual evaluation includes establishing a profile of the child's cognitive strengths and weaknesses in order to facilitate educational planning and to help determine the presence of any cognitive limitations that might warrant eligibility for special educational services. Assessment of cognitive strengths and weaknesses is particularly important because of the characteristically uneven profile of skills demonstrated by children with ASD. It is important that the individual test chosen (1) be appropriate for both the chronological and the mental age of the child, (2) provides a full range of standard scores, and (3) measures both verbal and nonverbal skills (Filipek *et al.* 1999). Of course, the use of any single score to describe the intellectual abilities of a child with ASD is clearly inappropriate. It also needs to be emphasized that there are no specific cognitive profiles that can reliably differentiate children with ASD from children with other disorders (Klinger *et al.* 2009; Sattler and Hoge 2006; Volkmar *et al.* 1999). In addition, the cognitive measures described in this section are not appropriate for children who have little or no useful speech or whose structural language is severely impaired. Nonverbal instruments such as the Leiter International Performance Scale-Revised (LIPS-R; Roid and Miller 1997) should be used with children who are nonverbal or older children with severely limited vocabulary and language skills (e.g. ability to communicate with only single words). In this circumstance, the LIPS-R may be an appropriate measure as it requires no verbal instructions from the examiner or verbal responses from the child.

Although there is no single best measure of intellectual functioning for children with ASD, the Wechsler Scales of intelligence are the most commonly used measure of intelligence and are often considered the "gold standard" in the evaluation of intellectual functioning across age groups. The Wechsler Intelligence Scale for Children-Fourth Edition (WISC-IV; Wechsler 2003) is the latest edition of the Wechsler Intelligence Scales for children of 6 to 16 years old and the most widely used intelligence test in schools. The WISC-IV provides a Full Scale IQ and Composite Indexes that yield information about specific cognitive abilities (Verbal Comprehension Index, Perceptual Reasoning Index, Working Memory Index, and Processing Speed Index). The

Wechsler Preschool and Primary Intelligence Scale-Third Edition (WPPSI-III; Wechsler 2002a) is used with two age groups: ages 2.6 to 3.11 and 4.0 to 7.3. The WPPSI-III provides a Verbal IQ, Performance IQ, Full Scale IQ, Processing Speed Quotient, and General Language Composite. Earlier studies using the Wechsler Intelligence Scale for Children, Third Edition (WISC-III; Wechsler 1991) found that some children with autism exhibited uneven subtest profiles with the Performance IQ (PIQ) significantly higher than Verbal IQ (VIQ). However, this finding is not universal for children with ASD. As noted earlier, intelligence test profiles should never be used for diagnostic confirmation or differential diagnosis of ASD subtypes (Klinger et al. 2009; Lincoln, Allen, and Kilman 1995; Ozonoff et al. 2005a; Siegel, Minshew, and Goldstein 1996). However, when a specific intellectual profile is evident, this can have an important implication for how the child learns best and what intervention activities may be most effective.

The Stanford-Binet Intelligence Scales, Fifth Edition (SB-5; Roid 2003) is a well known and popular instrument for measuring intelligence in individuals from 2 to 85 years of age. The SB-5 contains separate sections for Verbal IQ (based on five verbal subtests) and Nonverbal IQ (based on five nonverbal subtests). Factor scores can be calculated for Fluid Reasoning, Knowledge, Quantitative Reasoning, Visual-spatial Processing, and Working Memory, which can be useful for identifying strengths and weaknesses in children with ASD. The SB-5 may be an appropriate IQ test for assessing older children with developmental delay or mild intellectual disability, or as an outcome measure to assess intervention effectiveness over time.

The Differential Abilities Scales (DAS-II; Elliott 2007) is also an option for evaluating cognitive ability in children with ASD. The DAS-II assesses both intellectual and academic skills. It can be administered to children across a wide chronological and mental age range (2.5 through 17 years), making it appropriate for repeat administrations, to track progress, and for research projects in which the developmental range of participants may vary considerably. Especially helpful for the ASD population is the option of out-of range testing (e.g. administration of tests usually given to children of a different age). Norms for school-age children are available for the preschool battery, permitting use of the test with older children with significant intellectual limitations. The DAS-II also provides a Special Nonverbal Composite (SNC) score which summarizes the nonverbal domains. The SNC is particularly useful when testing children with ASD who are verbal but may have a mild to moderate language impairment.

Many school-age children are already placed in special education programs and may have had a recent psychoeducational evaluation. There may also be occasions where cognitive and academic performance is not a direct concern. For example, a child may be functioning at or above grade level and not have academic or learning challenges. Rather, concerns might center on significant problems in behavioral and/or social functioning. In this circumstance, other assessment domains (e.g. adaptive, communication, behavioral/emotional) may be the primary focus of attention. When records of standardized testing indicate stable cognitive abilities over time or when a more extensive battery is not needed, instruments such as the Reynolds Intellectual Assessment Scales (RIAS; Reynolds and Kamphaus 2003) or the Wechsler Abbreviated Scales of Intelligence (WASI; Wechsler 1999) may provide sufficient data for assessment purposes.

> ### BEST PRACTICE
> Assessment of academic ability is important for the purposes of educational decision making and intervention planning. Areas of strength and weakness can often go unrecognized.

Academic assessment

The assessment of academic ability is necessary for the purposes of educational decision making and planning. An evaluation of academic functioning will often reveal a profile of strengths and weaknesses. For example, it is not unusual for students with ASD to have precocious reading skills (sometimes called hyperlexia) and ability to decode words at a higher level than others of the same age and functional ability while at the same time having poor comprehension and difficulties with abstract language. For other students, calculation skills may be well developed, whereas mathematical concepts are delayed. Reading and other academic strengths can be used to compensate for weaknesses, as when a written schedule is provided to facilitate transitions (Bryan and Gast 2000) or when written directions are used to improve compliance. The good memory of children with ASD may also mean that spelling lists and multiplication tables will be learned more easily (Mayes and Calhoun 2003).

For school-age children, the most frequently used general achievement tests include the Woodcock-Johnson III NU Tests of Achievement (WJ III NU; Woodcock, McGrew and Mather 2007), the Wechsler Individual Achievement Test-Second Edition (WIAT-II; Wechsler 2002b), and the Kaufman Test of Educational Achievement-Second Edition (KTEA-II; Kaufman and Kaufman 2004). The WJ III, WIAT-II, and KTEA-II are useful tools for assessing current school performance across a number of curriculum areas. The WJ III NU is a comprehensive achievement battery designed to assess five curriculum areas: reading, oral language, mathematics, written language, and academic knowledge. A total of 22 subtests are included in the standard and extended batteries which are combined to produce a number of cluster scores (e.g. Broad Reading, Reading Comprehension, Math Calculation Skills, Broad Written Language). The WIAT-II is a general achievement test that contains nine subtests. Three assess reading (Word Reading, Pseudoword Decoding, Reading Comprehension), two math (Numerical Operations, Math Reasoning,), two written language (Spelling, Written Expression), and two oral language (Listening Comprehension, Oral Expression). These subtests yield five composite scores: Reading, Mathematics, Written Language, Oral Language and a Total Score. The KTEA-II is also an individually administered battery that provides an assessment of key academic skills. Composite scores are available for Reading, Math, Written Language, Oral Language, Comprehensive Achievement and six Reading Related subtests (e.g. Phonological Awareness, Nonsense Word Decoding, and Decoding Fluency).

BEST PRACTICE
Adaptive functioning should be assessed for all students, as this domain is pivotal in the identification of ASD and/or coexisting intellectual disability. Discrepancies between cognitive ability and adaptive behavior can help identify objectives and strategies for intervention and treatment.

Adaptive behavior assessment

This domain is a fundamental component of the core ASD assessment battery. Assessment of adaptive behavior should always accompany intellectual testing, because identification of an intellectual disability cannot be made unless performance is compromised on both standardized tests of intelligence and measures of adaptive functioning. Measuring adaptive behavior is also important for setting appropriate goals in treatment and intervention planning, and has been used in many longitudinal and intervention outcome studies of ASD (Freeman *et al.* 1999; Szatmari *et al.* 2003).

Adaptive functioning is an indication of the extent to which the child is able to use his or her ability to adapt to environmental demands (Klin, Sparrow *et al.* 2000). Often with ASD, the social and communication domains are measured significantly below estimated intellectual ability (Liss *et al.* 2000). For example, many higher functioning children with ASD, while scoring in the normal range and above on IQ tests, are functionally impaired because they are unable to translate their cognitive abilities into efficient adaptive behavior. Research indicates that children with ASD consistently demonstrate adaptive behavior levels (e.g. social skills) lower than their measured intellectual ability, and that this pattern is most evident for more capable children on the autism spectrum (Bolte and Poustka 2002).

The most widely used adaptive measure with children suspected of ASD is the Vineland Adaptive Behavior Scales-II (VABS-II; Sparrow, Balla, and Cicchetti 2005). The scales of the VABS-II are organized within a three domain structure: Communication, Daily Living, and Socialization. An Adaptive Behavior Composite score summarizes functioning in these domain areas. A Motor Skills Domain and an optional Maladaptive Behavior Index are also available to provide further information about a child's functioning. The VABS-II is completed during a semistructured interview with a parent or teacher. It is appropriate for individuals from birth to adulthood and offers four forms to gather in-depth information: the Survey Interview Form; Parent/ Caregiver Rating Form; Expanded Interview Form; and Teacher Rating Form. All VABS-II forms assist with diagnosing and classifying intellectual and other disorders, such as autism, Asperger syndrome, and developmental delays.

The Developmental Profile-Third Edition (DP-3; Alpern, Boll, and Shearer 2007) can also be used as an efficient measure of development and adaptive behavior in several critical domains. Designed to evaluate children from birth through age 12 years, 11 months, the DP-3 evaluates children's functioning in five key areas. A General Development score is provided, as well as scale scores in the following domains: (a) Physical, (b) Adaptive Behavior, (c) Social-Emotional, (d) Cognitive and (e) Communication. While a parent interview is the preferred method of administration, the DP-3 offers an alternative Parent/Caregiver Checklist that is helpful when a face-to-face meeting is not possible. The Checklist can be completed, without professional supervision, by the child's parent or other caregiver who is knowledgeable about the child's functioning.

The Adaptive Behavior Assessment System-Second Edition (ABAS-II; Harrison and Oakland 2003) may also be an appropriate option when time is a constraint, as it can be administered via questionnaire-checklist procedures, rather than an interview, in approximately 15 to 20 minutes. The ABAS-II is a valid and reliable instrument designed to measure the adaptive behavior skills of infants, children, and adults from birth to 89 years of age (Sattler and Hoge 2006). The test yields four composite scores (Conceptual, Social, Practical, and General Adaptive). Research indicates that, overall, the VABS-II and the ABAS-II provide similar levels of overall adaptive functioning for individuals aged 5 to 20 (Sparrow *et al.* 2005).

BEST PRACTICE
A thorough speech-language-communication evaluation should be conducted for all students referred for a comprehensive assessment. Deficits in pragmatic language functioning may not be detected on formal language tests and require nontraditional assessment procedures.

Communication and Language Assessment

The assessment of communication skills is a vital component of a comprehensive ASD assessment. The level of expressive language, together with IQ, is a good predictor of long-term outcome, so it is an especially important domain to measure in terms of intervention planning (Marans 1997; Stone and Yoder 2001; Twachtman-Cullen 1998). A best practice communication assessment should provide information about the child's communicative abilities in both the verbal and nonverbal domains, and should not be limited to the formal, structural aspects of language (e.g. articulation and receptive/expressive language functioning). Particular attention should be given to the pragmatic, social communicative functions of language (e.g. turn taking, understanding of inferences and figurative expressions) as well as to the nonverbal skills needed to communicate and regulate interaction (e.g. eye contact, gesture, facial expression, and body language). Although standardized measures provide important information about specific parameters of speech and language, they provide only limited information about social-pragmatic skills which are typically difficult to identify in more capable children with ASD (Wetherby, Schuler and Prizant 1997). Thus, a variety of strategies should be used, including direct assessment, naturalistic observation and interviewing significant others, including parents and educators, who are valuable sources of information (Prizant and Wetherby 1993; Stone and Caro-Martinez 1990).

A variety of traditional instruments, such as the Peabody Picture Vocabulary Test-Fourth Edition (PPVT-4; Dunn and Dunn 2007), Expressive One-Word Picture Vocabulary Test (EOWPVT; Brownell 2000), and Clinical Evaluation of Language Fundamentals-Fourth Edition (CELF-4; Wiig, Secord, and Semel 2003) have been used to measure the receptive and expressive language skills of school-age children with ASD. However, experience indicates that many children with ASD demonstrate age-appropriate skills on traditional tests of language, including articulation, fluency, vocabulary, syntax and reading (Minshew, Goldstein and Siegel 1995).

As a group, higher functioning students with ASD tend to demonstrate strength in formal language, but a weakness is pragmatic and social skills (Landa 2000; Tager-Flusberg, Paul, and Lord 2005). As a result, they often fail to qualify for speech-language services because they present strong verbal skills and large vocabularies, and score well on formal language assessments. Nevertheless, significant and severe deficits in the ability to communicate and interact with others can limit their participation in mainstream academic settings and community activities (Klin, Sparrow *et al.* 2000). Moreover, pragmatic deficits tend to become even more obvious and problematic as social and educational demands increase with age (Paul and Wilson 2009).

Assessments to identify pragmatic language deficits are not as well developed as tests of language fundamentals. Few standard measures are available to asess these skills in higher functioning children with ASD. Valid norms for pragmatic development and objective criteria for pragmatic performance are also limited (Young *et al.* 2005). Available standardized instruments that focus specifically on pragmatic language include the Test of Pragmatic Skills (TPS; Shulman 1985), the Comprehensive Assessment of Spoken Language (CASL; Carrow-Woolfolk 1999), the Test of Pragmatic Language, 2nd Edition (TOPL-2; Phelps-Terasaki and Phelps-Gunn 2007), the Test of Language Competence (TACL; Wiig and Secord 1989), the Children's Communication Checklist-Second Edition (CCC-2; Bishop 2003) and the Pragmatic Language Skills Inventory (PLSI; Gilliam and Miller 2006). The CCC-2 and PLSI are third party checklists and have the advantage of sampling pragmatic skills in the child's natural environment. Of course, these instruments should not be used in isolation to make decisions regarding classification and intervention planning. Results from other instruments, direct observations, and parent interviews provide valuable information for identifying a pragmatic language disorder.

ADDITIONAL DOMAINS OF ASSESSMENT

Children with ASD often demonstrate additional problems beyond those associated with the core domains. Thus, other areas should be included in the assessment battery depending on the referral question, history, and core evaluation results. These may include:
• sensory processing
• executive function and attention
• motor skills
• family system
• coexisting behavioral/emotional problems.
A list of additional assessment tools is displayed in Table 3.2.

BEST PRACTICE
Sensory challenges can have a negative effect on the student's current functioning and ability to benefit from intervention, and may be a focus of attention.

Table 3.2 Assessment tools for additional domains

Measure	Format	Age range	Time
Behavioral/ Emotional problems:			
BASC-2	Checklist	2 to 21 years	5 to 10 min
CBCL	Checklist	6 to 18 years	10 to 20 min
TRF	Checklist	6 to 18 years	10 to 20 min
CDI	Self-Report	7 to 17 years	15 min
RCMAS-2	Self-Report	6 to 19 years	10 to 15 min
Executive function and attention:			
BRIEF	Questionnaire	5 to 18 years	10 to 20 min
Conners 3	Questionnaire	6 to 18 years	10 to 20 min
WRAML2	Direct Testing	5 to 90 years	45 min
Family system:			
PSI-3	Questionnaire	≥12 years	20 to 25 min
Motor:			
VMI	Direct Testing	2 to Adult	10 to 15 min
BOT-2 (Short Form)	Direct Testing	4 to 21	15 to 20 min
Sensory processing:			
SP (Short Form)	Questionnaire	3 to 10 years	10 min
SP (Teacher)	Questionnaire	3 to 11 years	15 min

Note: BASC-2 Behavior Assessment System for Children; CBCL-Child Behavior Checklist; TRF-Teacher's Report Form; CDI-Children's Depression Inventory; RCMAS-Revised Children's Manifest Anxiety Scale; BRIEF-Behavior Rating Inventory of Executive Function; Conners 3-Connors Third Edition; PSI-Parenting Stress Index; SP-Sensory Profile; VMI-Test of Visual Motor Integration; BOT-2 Bruininks-Oseretsky Test of Motor Proficiency; SP-Sensory Profile

Sensory processing

Unusual sensory responses are present in many children with ASD and are often one of the earliest indicators of autism in childhood (Baranek 2002; Crane, Goddard, and Pring 2009; O'Neill and Jones 1997). Although sensory issues are considered a "nontriadic" characteristic and often overlooked in many ASD assessment procedures, attention to sensory problems can be an important component of a screening or evaluation (Dunn 2001; Harrison and

Hare 2004). One of the most widely used tools to assess sensory processing is the Sensory Profile (SP; Dunn 1999). The SP is a caregiver questionnaire which measures children's (3–10 years of age) responses to certain sensory processing, modulation, and behavioral/emotional events in everyday life. A short version (Short Sensory Profile) is available for screening. The Sensory Profile School Companion, a school-based measure, is also available to evaluate a child's sensory processing skills and their affect on classroom behavior. This measure can be used in conjunction with the Sensory Profile to provide a comprehensive evaluation of sensory behavior across home and school contexts (Cook and Dunn 1998; Crane *et al.* 2009; Dunn 2001; Kern *et al.* 2007).

> ## BEST PRACTICE
> Deficits in executive function, memory, and attention can affect the student's learning and classroom performance and may warrant assessment.

Executive function and attention

Research evidence suggests that deficits in executive function may be an important feature of ASD (Hill 2004; Ozonoff, South, and Provencal 2005b; Pennington and Ozonoff 1996; Ozonoff 1997). *Executive function* is a broad term used to describe the higher-order cognitive processes such as response initiation and selection, working memory, planning and strategy formation, cognitive flexibility, and inhibition of response. Executive functions include many of the skills required to prepare for and execute complex behavior, such as planning, inhibition, organization, self-monitoring, cognitive flexibility, and set-shifting. Markers of executive dysfunction include difficulty in initiating action, planning ahead, inhibiting inappropriate responses, transitioning, and poor self-monitoring.

The Behavioral Rating Inventory of Executive Function (BRIEF; Gioia *et al.* 2000) is a parent- or teacher-rated questionnaire for children aged 5 to 18 years that can be used to assess executive functioning in children with ASD. The BRIEF is comprised of eight subscales representing specific domains of executive functioning: Inhibit, Shift, Emotional Control, Initiate, Working Memory, Plan/Organize, Organization of Materials and Monitor. Because executive functions are important to school success, the inclusion of the BRIEF as an additional measure enables us to assess impaired multi-task performance, document the impact of executive function deficits on real-world functioning, and to plan educational accommodations (Clark, Prior, and Kinsella 2002). There is some research to suggest that the BRIEF profile of children with ASD is one of elevated scores on all subscales, particularly the Shift subscale which measures cognitive flexibility and transitioning (Gioia *et al.* 2002).

The Wide Range Assessment of Memory and Learning, Second Edition (WRAML2; Sheslow and Adams 2003) is a direct assessment of memory function that can be useful in evaluating learning and school-related problems of children with ASD. This comprehensive measure includes a Core Battery and supplemental subtests that provide index scores for General Memory, Verbal Memory, Visual Memory, Working Memory, and Attention and Concentration. A brief four subtest Memory Screening Form that correlates highly with the full test is also available.

School-age children with ASD frequently demonstrate symptoms associated with attention-deficit/hyperactivity disorder (ADHD) (Ghaziuddin 2002; Goldstein, Johnson, and Minshew 2001). Research indicates that ADHD is a common initial diagnosis for many children with ASD. These symptoms may include inattention, impulsivity, hyperactivity, and other features such as low frustration tolerance, poor self-monitoring, temper and anger management problems, and mood changes in the classroom (Loveland and Tunali-Kotoski 1997; Towbin 2005). Although current diagnostic practice discourages a diagnosis of both ASD/PDD and ADHD, recent research suggests that attention deficits can play an important role in the treatment and intervention planning for children with ASD. Thus, an assessment of ADHD characteristics may be included when inattention and/or impulsivity are indicated as presenting problems. Measures such as the Conners Third Edition (Conners 3; Connors 2008) can be used to assess attention-deficit/hyperactivity disorder (ADHD) and related problems in children. Short and long versions of parent, teacher, and self-report forms are available for children, aged 6 years through 18 years. The short version of the Connors 3 is particularly useful when time is limited or when a screening is needed.

BEST PRACTICE

Given the importance of visual-motor processing and motor skills in learning and classroom performance, this area may be included as a component of a comprehensive assessment battery.

Motor skills

Motor skills are often less affected in autism than are other developmental skills. However, many children with ASD have problems in fine and/or gross motor functioning and visual-motor integration. For example, some students may demonstrate atypical motor development, poor coordination, or deficits in praxis (motor planning, execution, and sequencing). Given the importance of visual-motor processing and motor skills to learning, this domain might be an additional component of an assessment battery. The Beery—Buktenica Developmental Test of Visual-Motor Integration-Fifth Edition (VMI; Beery, Buktenica, and Beery 2004) evaluates graphic and motor skills, perceptual accuracy, and eye-hand coordination. The Short Format and Full Format of the VMI tests present drawings of geometric forms arranged in order of increasing difficulty that the child is asked to copy. The Full Format can be administered either individually or to a group in about 15 minutes. The VMI also provides supplemental Visual Perception and Motor Coordination tests, which use the same stimulus forms as the Short and Full Format tests. These optional assessments are designed to be administered after results from the Short or Full Format test show the need for further testing, and to help compare an individual's test results with relatively pure visual and motor performances (one or both of the supplemental tests may be used).

A comprehensive measure of gross and fine motor skills may be completed with the Bruininks-Oseretsky Test of Motor Proficiency, Second Edition (BOT-2; Bruininks and Bruininks 2006). The BOT-2 provides composite scores in four motor areas and one comprehensive measure of motor proficiency. Separate measures of gross and fine motor skills are included, making it possible to obtain meaningful comparisons of performance in two areas. Special education professionals and occupational therapists can use the BOT-2 to assess motor proficiency, ranging from normal development to moderate motor-skill deficits. Although the complete form requires 45 to 60 minutes, the short form can be completed in 15 to 20 minutes.

> ### BEST PRACTICE
> The identification of parenting stress and parent–child relationship problems can alert the assessment team to the need for additional family support or counseling.

Family system

Parents are often overwhelmed by the challenges of a child with ASD (Estes *et al.* 2009). For example, research has shown that parents of children with autism exhibit a characteristic stress profile which includes anxiety related to the child's uneven intellectual profiles, deficits in social relatedness, disruptive behaviors and long-term care concerns (Bebko, Konstantareas, and Springer 1987; R.L. Koegel *et al.* 1992; Osborne *et al.* 2008). Mothers, in particular, appear to face unique challenges related to the characteristics of ASD. In a recent study, mothers of children diagnosed with autism reported higher levels of stress than mothers of typically developing children on 13 of 14 subscales of the Parenting Stress Index (Hoffman *et al.* 2009). Because autism impairs social relatedness and adaptive functioning, parent stress can directly influence the parent or caregiver's ability to support the child with disabilities (Estes *et al.* 2009). Targeting problem behaviors may help reduce parenting stress and thus increase the effectiveness of interventions. The identification of parenting stress and parent–child relationship problems can also alert the assessment team to the need for additional support or counseling.

An instrument with established psychometric properties that has been used with the ASD population is the Parenting Stress Index-Third Edition (PSI-3; Abidin 1995). The PSI is designed as a screening and diagnostic instrument that measures the degree of stress in the parent–child system. It consists of 120 items and takes 20 to 30 minutes for the parent to complete. The PSI yields a Total Stress Score, plus scale scores for both Child and Parent Characteristics, which pinpoint sources of stress within the family. A Short Form is also available and can be completed in 10 to 15 minutes. It is useful when time with the parent is limited, or as a progress monitoring tool.

BEST PRACTICE

A screening of potential coexisting (comorbid) behavioral/emotional issues, such as anxiety and depression, should be conducted to determine the need for a more detailed evaluation (possibly including referral to specialists).

Coexisting behavioral/emotional problems

Over the course of development, children with ASD may develop problems with sleep, appetite, mood, anxiety, activity level, anger management, and aggression. Research indicates that children with ASD have a high risk for meeting criteria for other disorders, such as Attention Deficit/Hyperactivity Disorder (ADHD), disruptive behavior disorders, mood, and anxiety disorders, all which contribute to overall impairment (Ghaziuddin 2002; Ghaziuddin, Weidmer-Mikhail, and Ghaziuddin 1998). Depression is one of the most common coexisting (comorbid) syndromes observed in individuals with ASD, particularly higher functioning children (Lainhart and Folstein 1994). Anxiety is also frequently reported (Kim *et al.* 2000). These problems should be assessed whenever significant behavioral issues (e.g. inattention, mood instability, anxiety, sleep disturbance, aggression) become evident or when major changes in behavior are reported (Koegel and Koegel 1995; Quill 1995). Coexisting disorders should also be carefully investigated when severe or worsening symptoms are present and are not responding to traditional methods of intervention (Lainhart 1999).

Assessment of coexisting behavior/emotional problems is challenging, because we have no autism-specific tools designed for this purpose (Deprey and Ozonoff 2009). However, popular self-report measures such as the Children's Depression Inventory (CDI: Kovacs 1992) and the Revised Manifest Anxiety Scale-Second Edition (RCMAS-2; Reynolds and Richmond 2008) can be used to assess symptoms of anxiety and depression in school-age children and adolescents. The CDI is a 27-item measure designed to assess cognitive, affective, and behavioral symptoms of depression in children 7 to 17 years of age. It has five scales: Negative Mood, Interpersonal Problems, Ineffectiveness, Anhedonia, and Negative Self-Esteem. The CDI requires a first-grade reading level and takes approximately 15 minutes to complete. It can be useful to quickly screen children for depression and related problems. The RCMAS-2 is a brief measure of the level and nature of anxiety in 6- to 19-year-olds. The test is composed of 49 items covering the following scales: Physiological Anxiety; Worry; Social Anxiety; Defensiveness; and an Inconsistent Responding index. The RCMAS-2 can be completed in 10 to 15 minutes. Items are written at a second-grade reading level. An Audio CD is provided for younger children and those with reading or attention problems. The RCMAS-2 can be used to provide information on many problems, including stress, test anxiety, school avoidance, and peer and family conflicts. It is important to recognize, however, that these instruments do not have a normative database for ASD and lack empirical investigation.

Behavior rating scales can also provide important information about emotional/behavioral problems in children with ASD. The Achenbach System of Empirically Based Assessment (ASEBA) is a widely used behavior rating system for identifying coexisting internalizing and externalizing problems across home and school contexts. Although it does not provide an autism factor per se, studies have suggested that certain patterns, such as elevated scores on the Social Problems and Thought Problems scales, may be associated with ASD (Bolte, Dickhut, and Poustka 1999; Duarte et al. 2003). The ASEBA includes both the Child Behavior Checklist/6-18 (CBCL/6-18; Achenbach and Rescorla 2001) which obtains reports from parents, close relatives, and/ or guardians regarding children's competencies as well as the Teacher Report Form (TRF; Achenbach and Rescorla 2001), designed to obtain teachers' reports of children's academic performance, adaptive functioning, and behavioral/emotional problems. Ratings from the CBCL/6-18 and TRF are scored in the areas of Aggressive Behavior; Anxious/Depressed; Attention Problems; Rule-Breaking Behavior; Social Problems; Somatic Complaints;

Thought Problems; and Withdrawn Behavior. The ASEBA also includes scales related to *DSM-IV* diagnostic categories; Affective Problems, Anxiety Problems; Somatic Problems; Attention Deficit/Hyperactivity Problems; Oppositional Defiant Problems; and Conduct Problems.

Another broad-based measure for assessing coexisting problems in children with ASD is the Behavioral Assessment System for Children-Second Edition (BASC-2; Reynolds and Kamphaus 2004). The BASC-2 is a comprehensive set of rating scales and forms including the Teacher Rating Scales (TRS), Parent Rating Scales (PRS), Self-Report of Personality (SRP), Student Observation System (SOS), and Structured Developmental History (SDH). The self-report form measures "sense of inadequacy" and "sense of atypicality," and may be helpful for understanding the problems of children with ASD who can provide a valid report (Ozonoff, Provencal, and Solomon 2002). The BASC-2 may also prove useful for measuring the effects of intervention and treatment in children with ASD (Ozonoff, Provencal, and Soloman 2002).

SUMMARY

In this chapter, we reviewed the components of both a core assessment battery and additional domains for children suspected of ASD. These components have been shown to be relevant to the evaluation, identification, diagnosis, intervention planning, and outcome measurement of ASD in scientifically based investigations. However, few studies have directly compared the various instruments, so we have no definitive guide to selecting among the different assessment tools. Moreover, due to evolving changes in the definition of autism and development of new measures, instruments used in the assessment process must be reviewed and evaluated frequently (Eaves, Campbell, and Chambers 2000). For example, newly published instruments such as the second edition of the CARS (CARS2: Schopler, Van Bourgondien, Wellman and Love, 2010) and the Autism Spectrum Ratings Scales (ASRS: Goldstein and Naglieri, 2009) promise to enhance best practice and intervention for ASD. Assessment and diagnosis are only of value when they provide access to the delivery of appropriate intervention and educational services. The next chapter illustrates the application of the comprehensive developmental approach to the cases of our students, Jeremy and Sally.

Quick Reference

No single test is diagnostic of ASD

There are no specific biological or test markers to determine ASD. Although ASD is a neurobiological disorder; the diagnosis is made by behavioral criteria. No single measure provides a definitive diagnosis: data from an instrument must be interpreted in context as a component of the diagnostic process. The risk of under- and overdiagnosing ASD is minimized by utilizing information from multiple sources. Caution must be used when using any cut-off score to indicate a diagnosis or disability because this determination is not solely dependent on an absolute score or scores, but rather on whether the measured traits result in impairments in everyday functioning or adaptive behavior and the need for specialized services. Intellectual test profiles should never be used for diagnostic confirmation or differential diagnosis of ASD subtypes.

Chapter 4

CASE EXAMPLES: JEREMY AND SALLY

Just as no two typical students are exactly alike, no two students with ASD have the same behavioral profile.

We now return to the students introduced in Chapter 1. For illustrative purposes, the results of a hypothetical evaluation are presented for Jeremy and Sally, as they might be presented in a summary report and narrative. A brief interpretive discussion follows the results of each component to illustrate the best practice assessment for children with ASD outlined in the last chapter.

JEREMY

Reason for referral

Jeremy was referred for an individual psychoeducational evaluation to assess strengths and weaknesses in the areas of intellectual functioning, academic achievement, and social/emotional development. He was initially referred to the school's support team to assist with developing interventions to address problems with inattention, social relatedness, task completion, and disruptive behavior in the classroom. Following a positive screening, Jeremy was referred for a comprehensive evaluation to determine the presence of ASD and develop an intervention plan.

Assessment methods

Review of Records
Wechsler Intelligence Scale for Children-Fourth Edition (WISC-IV)
Woodcock-Johnson III Normative Update Tests of Achievement (WJ III NU)
Social Responsiveness Scale (SRS)
Social Communication Questionnaire (SCQ)
Direct Observation

Pragmatic Language Skills Inventory (PLSI)
Vineland Adaptive Behavior Scales-Second Edition (Vineland-II)
Beery-Buktenica Developmental Test of Visual-Motor Integration-Fifth Edition (VMI-V)
Behavior Rating Inventory of Executive function (BRIEF)
Behavior Assessment System for Children – 2nd Edition (BASC-2)

Background information/Developmental history

Background information obtained from an interview with Jeremy's mother indicates that Jeremy was enrolled in a private preschool at three years of age. Presenting problems at that time included difficulty following directions, transitioning, and maintaining on-task behavior. Jeremy was also reported to have problems relating and playing cooperatively with other children. He was observed to talk repetitively about certain topics and seldom participated in group activities. At home, he was described as argumentative and often had temper tantrums when required to follow household rules. Developmental milestones were achieved within normal expectations, including crawling at 6 months, walking at 11 months, and speaking his first words at 12 months. Jeremy's mother reports that the family history is positive for attention and learning problems. Although Jeremy's challenging behavior has been in evidence since early childhood, his parents became even more concerned upon entrance to kindergarten where he was described as disruptive and oppositional. Although improvement has been noted, Jeremy continues to experience significant social and behavioral challenges in his current classroom. Both vision and hearing exams were completed during the past year, with both reported to be within normal limits. An annual physical examination indicated no specific health related issues or concerns.

Behavior observation

Jeremy was easily engaged in the testing activities. His affect was continually elevated throughout the session. Although able to follow directions adequately, Jeremy experienced difficulty maintaining reciprocity in conversation. He was verbally interactive and responsive, but often provided tangential and inappropriate responses. Eye contact was initially intermittent, but reasonably good when directly engaged by the examiner. Although Jeremy demonstrated some inattentiveness, rapport and attention were considered adequate for testing purposes. The results of the current assessment should be considered a valid and reliable estimate of Jeremy's current intellectual, academic, and social/behavioral functioning.

Cognitive functioning

Wechsler Intelligence Scale for Children-Fourth Edition: (WISC-IV)

Scale	Composite	Percentile Rank	Confidence Interval
Verbal Comprehension Index (VCI)	95	37	89–102
Perceptual Reasoning Index (PRI)	127	96	117–132
Working Memory Index (WMI)	94	34	87–102
Processing Speed Index (PSI)	109	73	99–117
Full Scale IQ (FSIQ)	108	70	103–113

Verbal Comprehension	Scaled Score	Perceptual Reasoning	Scaled Score
Similarities	9	Block Design	13
Vocabulary	11	Picture Concepts	16
Comprehension	7	Matrix Reasoning	14

Working Memory	Scaled Score	Processing Speed	Scaled Score
Digit Span	9	Coding	11
Letter—Number Sequencing	9	Symbol Search	12

The results of the current assessment indicate that Jeremy is functioning in the average range of general intellectual ability. He earned a Full Scale IQ (FSIQ) of 108 on the Wechsler Intelligence Scale for Children-Fourth Edition (WISC-IV). Jeremy's FSIQ score places him at the 70th percentile compared to same-age peers. There is a 95 percent probability that his true FSIQ score falls in the 103–113 range. Jeremy's overall functioning is difficult to summarize due to a significant difference between his Verbal Comprehension (VCI=95) and his Perceptual Reasoning (PRI=127) Index scores. This difference is clinically significant and may be expected to occur in less than 1 percent of the normative population.

Jeremy's verbal reasoning abilities, as measured by the Verbal Comprehension Index (VCI), are in the average range and above those of 37 percent of his peer group. The VCI is designed to measure verbal reasoning and concept formation. Jeremy's performance reflects a diverse set of verbal abilities. He demonstrated greatest weakness on comprehension tasks requiring the ability to provide solutions to everyday problems and explicate the underlying reasons for social rules or convention.

Jeremy's nonverbal reasoning abilities, as measured by the Perceptual Reasoning Index (PRI), are in the superior range and above those of approximately 97 percent of his peers. The PRI is designed to measure fluid reasoning in the perceptual domain with tasks that assess nonverbal concept formation, visual perception and organization, simultaneous processing, visual-motor coordination, and learning. Jeremy demonstrated significant strength with subtest measures requiring visual information processing and abstract categorical reasoning skills.

Jeremy's ability to sustain attention, concentrate, and exert mental control is in the average range. He performed better than approximately 34 percent of his peer group. Jeremy's abilities in this cognitive domain are a relative weakness compared to his nonverbal reasoning skills. A weakness in working memory may make the processing of complex information more time consuming for Jeremy and result in more frequent errors on a variety of learning tasks. Jeremy's ability to process simple or routine visual materials without making errors is in the average range. He performed better than approximately 73 percent of his peer group on processing speed tasks.

Achievement

Woodcock-Johnson III Normative Update Tests of Achievement (WJ III NU)

Subtests	Standard Score	Percentile Rank
Letter—Word Identification	119	90
Reading Fluency	123	93
Passage Comprehension	100	49
Broad Reading	114	83
Calculation	115	85
Math Fluency	118	88
Applied Problems	114	82
Broad Mathematics	118	89
Math Calculation Skills	117	87

Academic achievement, as compared to that of other students of the same age, was assessed with the Woodcock-Johnson III Normative Update Tests of Achievement. When compared to others at his age level, Jeremy's standard scores are high average in Broad Reading, Broad Mathematics and Math Calculation Skills. A review of Jeremy's achievement test profile indicates exceptional word identification skills and ability to read with fluency. In comparison, a relative weakness was noted with reading comprehension tasks. Jeremy does not appear to demonstrate a deficit in academic skill development or the presence of a specific learning disability.

Social competence (Teacher/Parent reports)

Social Responsiveness Scale: (SRS)

Subscale	T-Score (Parent Report)	T-Score (Teacher Report)
Social Awareness	72	69
Social Cognition	82	77
Social Communication	79	85
Social Motivation	58	80
Autistic Mannerisms	90	83
Total Score	82	85

The Social Responsiveness Scale (SRS) was completed by Jeremy's mother and classroom teacher to assess Jeremy's level of social awareness, social information processing, capacity for reciprocal social communication, social anxiety, and atypical mannerisms. Jeremy's profile reflects clinically significant scores across settings. Parent and teacher reports are positive for problems in social information processing and social communication. Jeremy's mother also reports a relatively high score on items indicating a narrow range of interests and stereotypical behaviors. Endorsements included "behaves in ways that seem strange," "thinks and talks about the same thing over and over," and "can't seem to get his mind off something once he starts thinking about it." Jeremy's Total Scores suggest a severe interference in everyday social interactions and are strongly associated with a clinical diagnosis of autistic disorder, Asperger' disorder, or more severe cases of PDDNOS. In most clinical and educational settings, *SRS* scores at or above $76T$ from two separate informants provide very strong evidence of the presence of a clinically diagnosable autism spectrum condition.

Social Communication Questionnaire (SCQ)-Lifetime:

The Social Communication Questionnaire (SCQ) was completed by Jeremy's mother to assess behaviors associated with impairment in communication and social skills. Jeremy's overall *SCQ* score exceeds the recommended threshold of 15, suggesting impairment in reciprocal social interaction, communication, and restricted, repetitive and stereotyped patterns of behavior (including circumscribed interests and unusual preoccupations).

Direct observation

Jeremy was observed in multiple settings throughout the school day, including his classroom and playground. The Autism Spectrum Disorders Checklist (Appendix D) was used to guide the observation process. Jeremy demonstrated several behaviors associated with impairment in social interaction, including significant difficulty maintaining and sustaining reciprocity with his peers. He was often inappropriately intrusive and appeared to have little sense of other children's boundaries. Although there was no evidence of speech abnormalities or echolalia, Jeremy had difficulty using tone and volume appropriately and frequently engaged in excessive conversation about specific topics without regard for other children's interests. He was also observed to make inappropriate comments to both peers and adults. Although no repetitive or stereotyped motor movements were observed, Jeremy presented with a somewhat awkward gait and demonstrated mild difficulties with graphomotor tasks. He also appeared to be highly disorganized and had difficulty with activities involving multiple steps. Challenging behavior was readily observed when required to terminate a preferred activity and transition between learning centers, most notably anger and frustration, tantruming and refusal.

Pragmatic language

Pragmatic Language Skills Inventory: (PLSI)

Subscale	Standard Score	Percentile Rank
Classroom Interaction	7	16
Social Interaction	8	25
Personal Interaction	5	5
Pragmatic Language Index (PLI)	82 (below average)	12

The Pragmatic Language Skills Inventory (PLSI) was completed by Jeremy's classroom teacher to provide information relative to Jeremy's social communication skills. Endorsements in the areas of Classroom Interaction, Social Interaction, and Personal Interaction indicate relatively poor interaction skills compared to average students of the same age. Qualitative analysis of his response form indicates difficulty "understanding the meaning of simple similes, metaphors, and idioms," "maintaining a topic or keeping a topic going," "recognizing when the teacher is cuing a routine," "knowing when to talk and when to listen," "taking turns in conversation," and "understanding what causes people not to like him or her." Jeremy's overall Pragmatic Language Inventory (PLI) score falls within the below average range and reflects significant limitations in pragmatic language skills.

Adaptive behavior

Vineland Adaptive Behavior Scales-Second Edition: (Vineland-II)

Domain	Standard Score	Percentile	Adaptive Level
Communication	114	82	Adequate
Daily Living Skills	100	50	Adequate
Socialization	86	18	Moderately Low
Motor Skills	91	27	Moderately Low
Adaptive Behavior Composite	97	42	Moderately Low

The Vineland Adaptive Behavior Scales-Second Edition (Vineland-II) was completed by an interview with Jeremy's mother to assess Jeremy's ability to master personal and social demands in the home setting. The Vineland-II assesses adaptive behavior in three domains: Communication, Daily Living Skills and Socialization. It also provides a composite score that summarizes a student's performance across all domains. A review of Jeremy's profile indicates relative strength in the Communication skills domain. Greatest weakness was observed in the Socialization domain, where Jeremy's adaptive level was considered moderately low in both the Interpersonal and Coping skills subdomains. A comparison of Jeremy's Communication and Socialization standard scores indicates a significant and meaningful difference between scores, with this difference occurring in only one percent of the normative population. Jeremy's Adaptive Behavior Composite score of 97 classifies his general adaptive functioning as moderately low compared to children of the same age. Jeremy's repertoire of adaptive skills is generally below his measured cognitive development.

Visual-motor

Beery-Buktenica Developmental Test of Visual-Motor Integration-Fifth Edition: (VMI-V)
Percentile Rank: 58
Standard Score: 103

The Beery-Buktenica Developmental Test of Visual-Motor Integration-Fifth Edition (VMI-V) was utilized to assess Jeremy's ability to integrate visual and motor skills. His standard score of 103 and corresponding percentile rank of 58 are consistent with age appropriate performance in this developmental area. Although characterized by impulsivity and disorganization, Jeremy's overall VMI performance does not suggest functional impairment or a delay in visual-motor perception.

Executive function

Behavior Rating Inventory of Executive Function: (BRIEF)

	Parent		Teacher	
Scale/Index	T-Score	Percentile	T-Score	Percentile
Inhibit	65	91	89	99
Shift	67	96	66	92
Emotional Control	64	92	78	98
Behavioral Regulation Index	68	94	82	98
Initiate	79	99	69	94
Working Memory	60	87	83	99
Plan/Organize	72	95	77	96
Organization of Materials	66	94	60	87
Monitor	69	97	74	96
Metacognition Index	72	95	76	96

The Behavior Rating Inventory of Executive Function (BRIEF) was completed by Jeremy's mother and classroom teacher to assess Jeremy's ability to initiate, plan, organize, and sustain problem-solving working memory. Analysis of his profile indicates significant elevations across the Behavioral and Metacognition domains. Jeremy's profile reflects marked difficulty with metacognitive problem-solving, including organizing and planning strategies, systematic problem-solving, cognitive flexibility, and holding information in working memory. Jeremy demonstrates significant problems in basic executive inhibitory control and cognitive flexibility in both home and school contexts. The most salient area of impairment includes behaviors associated with transitions, problem-solving flexibility, the ability to alternate attention and change of focus. Jeremy's overall test results indicate a significant global executive dysfunction despite his level of cognitive ability.

Behavioral/Emotional functioning

Behavior Assessment System for Children—2nd Edition: (BASC-2)

Clinical Scales	T-Score	T-Score
	(Parent)	(Teacher)
Hyperactivity	65	68
Aggression	72	74
Conduct Problems	61	66
Anxiety	62	65

Behavior Assessment System for Children—2nd Edition: (BASC-2)

Clinical Scales	T-Score (Parent)	T-Score (Teacher)
Depression	68	58
Somatization	53	58
Atypicality	76	83
Learning Problems	NA	73
Withdrawal	69	71
Attention Problems	76	73
Adaptive Scales:		
Adaptability	29	25
Social Skills	28	30
Leadership	42	45
Activities of Daily Living	44	N/A
Study Skills	N/A	27
Functional Communication	35	40
Composites:		
Externalizing Problems	67	77
Internalizing Problems	62	67
School Problems	N/A	73
Behavioral Symptoms Index	66	71
Adaptive Skills	40	26

Jeremy's teacher completed the Teacher Rating Scales (TRS) to provide information regarding Jeremy's adaptive and problem behaviors in the classroom. Her ratings indicate clinically significant concerns in the composite domains of Externalizing Problems, Behavioral Symptoms, School Problems, and Adaptive Skills. At-risk concerns were also endorsed in the area of Internalizing problems. Jeremy's Clinical Scales indicate that his verbal aggression and inappropriate behavior, poor academic engagement, difficulty interacting with peers, and inattentiveness are especially concerning and problematic. Jeremy's teacher reported that Jeremy frequently argues when he does not get his own way, is easily upset and angered, and has many conflicts with his classmates. Jeremy's low scores on the Adaptive Scales represent significant problems in adjusting to change, communication effectiveness, social interaction, and organizational skills.

The Parent Rating Scale (PRS) was completed by Jeremy's mother to provide a measure of Jeremy's adaptive and problem behaviors in community and home settings. Like Jeremy's teacher, she endorsed concerns with

Jeremy's aggressive behavior, atypicality, and attention. Jeremy's Adaptive Scales reflect ongoing concerns with his inappropriate behavior, poor social skills, and communication problems. Jeremy's mother reported that Jeremy frequently complains about not having friends and often says, "Nobody likes me." Jeremy's TRS and PRS scores indicate significant behavior and adaptive problems across both school and home settings. Children with similar scores have impaired social and communication skills, poor behavioral and academic adjustment, and have an increased risk for more substantial behavior problems and poor outcomes.

Summary and recommendations

Jeremy was referred for an individual psychoeducational evaluation to assess strengths and weaknesses in the areas of intellectual functioning, academic achievement, and social-emotional development. The results of the current assessment indicate that he is functioning in the average range of general intellectual ability. Jeremy earned a Full Scale IQ (FSIQ) score of 108 on the Wechsler Intelligence Scale for Children-Fourth Edition (WISC-IV). His overall cognitive ability cannot be easily summarized due to a significant disparity between verbal and nonverbal measures. Jeremy's reasoning abilities on verbal tasks are generally in the average range (VCI=95), while his nonverbal reasoning abilities are significantly higher and in the superior range (PRI=127). This difference is statistically significant and clinically meaningful, and expected to occur in less than 1 percent of the normative population. Jeremy demonstrates relative strength with cognitive tasks that are more easily adapted to nonverbal and visual-spatial strategies, compared to those involving verbal comprehension and pragmatic language skills. The results of the Woodcock-Johnson III Normative Update Tests of Achievement indicate that when compared to others at his age level, Jeremy's performance is high average in Broad Reading, Mathematics and Math Calculation Skills. Hs current levels of academic performance indicate a notable precociousness in word identification skills and reading fluency. In contrast, reading comprehension was measured at a lower level.

Broad-based behavior rating scales completed both at home and school confirm significant problems in social skills development, functional communication, attention, adaptability, and overall behavior. Observation and ratings on autism-specific scales also indicate moderate-to-severe impairment in reciprocal social behavior and responsiveness across home and school contexts. In addition, Jeremy has significant difficulty in managing the executive function domains of working memory, planning and organization, and the ability to inhibit and self-monitor his behavior.

Jeremy's impairment and atypicalities presented in the communication, socialization, and behavioral domains are descriptive of the autistic triad and warrant further intervention and treatment. He demonstrates a consistent pattern of qualitative difficulties initiating and sustaining connected relationships with peers and adults appropriate for his developmental level. Jeremy also displays a pattern of restricted and stereotyped patterns of behavior, interest and activities. Likewise, coexisting (comorbid) externalizing problems adversely affect his educational performance, social adjustment, and classroom productivity.

In terms of educational planning, Jeremy will require a focus on social skills, interactive appropriateness, and communication effectiveness. His educational needs are best met in a classroom that provides a highly structured setting and support via a smaller class size, greater structure, a multimodal approach to instruction, and a focus on communication and social effectiveness. Jeremy's problems in social relatedness may be addressed through the use of social stories, social skills instruction in the classroom, and activities designed to enhance peer interaction and cooperation. Strategies should focus on relating and communicating with peers and adults (initiating, maintaining, turn-taking) both at home and at school. Jeremy may be assigned a "peer buddy" identified for a specific time/activity, and social routines taught and practiced in a daily context. Classroom instruction should include an emphasis on visually structured strategies and activities such as a work system, written instructions, checklists, and other visual methods. Those who work with Jeremy should also be aware of common stressors which may include unstructured situations, such as transitions and changes in routine. Jeremy is also in need of an individual behavior support plan to address his externalizing behavior problems. This should include a functional behavior assessment (FBA) to guide intervention planning. A comprehensive speech/language evaluation should be completed to obtain further qualitative and quantitative information regarding Jeremy's communication status. The assessment team should integrate the results of the current evaluation, together with multiple sources of information, to determine the appropriate goals and objectives to meet Jeremy's educational needs.

SALLY

Reason for referral

Sally was referred for an individual psychoeducational evaluation to assess strengths and weaknesses in the areas of intellectual functioning, academic achievement, and behavioral adjustment. Referral information indicates a long standing history of social and behavioral challenges in the classroom and at home. Following positive screening results, Sally was referred for a comprehensive evaluation to assist in determining the appropriate educational program and services.

Assessment methods

Parent Interview/Review of Records
Wechsler Intelligence Scale for Children-Fourth Edition (WISC-IV)
Woodcock-Johnson III Normative Update Tests of Achievement
Children's Communication Checklist-Second Edition (CCC-2)
Social Responsiveness Scale (SRS)
Childhood Autism Rating Scale (CARS)
Sensory Profile (SP)
Beery-Buktenica Developmental Test of Visual-Motor Integration-Fifth Edition (VMI-V)
Adaptive Behavior Assessment System-Second Edition (ABAS-II)
Childrens Depression Inventory (CDI)
Child Behavioral Checklist (CBCL)
Teacher's Report Form (TRF)
Parenting Stress Index—Short Form (PSI)

Parent interview/Background information

Background information obtained from the parent interview and school records indicates that Sally received a preschool evaluation at age 3 years 10 months. Concerns at that time included problems in the areas of social skills, transitioning, and atypical sensory experiences. A review of Sally's social and developmental history indicates health problems, including sleep difficulties, stomach problems, allergies, and frequent colds. Early motor and speech/language developmental milestones were considered to have been met within broad normal limits. Sally walked alone at 12 months, spoke her first word at 11 months, and used phrases by 36 months. According to her mother, Sally demonstrated sensory defensiveness in response to loud sounds, rough textures, and sticky foods. She was considered very "shy" in social situations, made limited use of eye contact, and seemed to have little interest in interacting with her peers. Sally's family history is positive for depression and mental health concerns.

Reports from Sally's preschool teacher described Sally as a very quiet and immature child who did not actively participate in classroom activities, but rather seemed to prefer solitary play. She was also observed to "fixate or obsess on one thing" for extended periods of time and talked only when spoken to by other children. Some oppositional behavior was reported when required to follow teacher directions and participate in play groups. Cognitive ability was considered normative, with a Full Scale IQ of 105 obtained on the Wechsler Primary Scale of Intelligence-Third Edition (WPPSI-III). Expressive and receptive vocabulary skills were commensurate with measured intellectual ability. Pre-academic skills indicated relative strength in visual memory and readiness skills. Although a relative weakness in social skills and language processing was indicated, Sally was considered to have the cognitive and academic readiness skills needed to function satisfactorily in a general education classroom. As a result, she was not considered eligible to receive special educational services. At the time of referral, sensory screenings indicated that both vision and hearing were within normal limits.

Behavior observations

Sally was cooperative and attentive throughout the testing session. Although initially reticent, interaction and spontaneity increased as she became more comfortable with the testing environment. However, she continually presented with a flat and restricted range of affect. Although Sally completed all tasks presented, she initiated few interactions and made eye contact only when directly engaged by the examiner. There were no stereotypic behaviors or circumscribed interests observed during the testing session. Difficulties were noted with expressive language, with responses limited to short phrases and brief responses. Prompting and encouragement were required to maximize test results. The results of the current assessment should be viewed within the context of Sally's behavioral presentation.

Cognitive functioning

Wechsler Intelligence Scale for Children-Fourth Edition: (WISC-IV)

Scale	Composite	Percentile Rank	Confidence Interval
Verbal Comprehension Index (VCI)	98	45	91–105
Perceptual Reasoning Index (PRI)	106	66	98–113
Working Memory Index (WMI)	91	27	84–99
Processing Speed Index (PSI)	91	27	83–101
Full Scale I.Q. (FSIQ)	97	42	92–102

Verbal Comprehension	Scaled Score	Perceptual Reasoning	Scaled Score
Similarities	12	Block Design	10
Vocabulary	12	Picture Concepts	10
Comprehension	5	Matrix Reasoning	13

Working Memory	Scaled Score	Processing Speed	Scaled Score
Digit Span	8	Coding	7
Letter—Number Sequencing	9	Symbol Search	10

The results of the current assessment indicate that Sally is functioning in the average range of general intellectual ability. She earned a Full Scale IQ (FSIQ) score of 97 on the Wechsler Intelligence Scale for Children-Fourth Edition (WISC-IV). Sally's FSIQ score places her at the 42nd percentile compared to same age peers. The chances are approximately 95 out of 100 that her true IQ falls in the 92–102 range. Although Sally performed somewhat better on nonverbal reasoning tasks, there is no significant and meaningful difference between her Verbal Comprehension (VCI) and Perceptual Reasoning (PRI) Index scores.

Sally's verbal reasoning abilities, as measured by the Verbal Comprehension Index (VCI), are in the average range and above those of 45 percent of her peer group. Sally's performance on the VCI reflects a varied set of verbal abilities. She demonstrated average performance with vocabulary items, but a marked weakness on comprehension tasks that require the ability to provide solutions to everyday problems and explain the underlying reasons for social rules or convention.

Sally's nonverbal reasoning abilities, as measured by the Perceptual Reasoning Index (PRI), are in the average range and above those of approximately 61 percent of her peers. The PRI is designed to measure fluid reasoning in the perceptual domain with tasks that assess nonverbal concept formation, visual perception and organization, simultaneous processing, visual-motor coordination, and learning. Sally demonstrated relative strength with tasks assessing nonverbal reasoning and problem-solving skills.

Sally's ability to sustain attention, concentrate, and exert mental control is in the average range. However, she performed better than only 27 percent of her peer group in this area. Sally's working memory abilities are a weakness relative to her nonverbal reasoning abilities. This may make the processing of complex information more time consuming for her. Sally's ability to process simple or routine visual materials without making errors is also in the average range. She performed better than approximately 27 percent of her peer group on processing speed tasks. Sally demonstrated greatest weakness with tasks involving fine-motor coordination, short-term memory, and psychomotor speed and accuracy.

Achievement

Woodcock-Johnson III Normative Update Tests of Achievement: (WJ III NU)

Subtests	Standard Score	Percentile Rank
Letter—Word Identification	107	68
Reading Fluency	96	66
Passage Comprehension	90	25

Woodcock-Johnson III Normative Update Tests of Achievement: (WJ III NU)

Subtests	Standard Score	Percentile Rank
Broad Reading	100	51
Calculation	103	58
Math Fluency	93	30
Applied Problems	105	63
Broad Mathematics	103	57

Academic achievement, compared to that of other students of the same age, was assessed with the Woodcock-Johnson Pschoeducational Battery-III NU Tests of Achievement. When compared to her age group, Sally's performance is average in overall reading and mathematics. Analysis of her test profile indicates relative strength with rote memory tasks such as word identification and weakness with reading comprehension and math fluency. In general, Sally's achievement test results are consistent with measured intellectual ability and do not indicate the presence of a learning disability.

Pragmatic language

Children's Communication Checklist-Second Edition: (CCC-2)

Scale	Scaled Score	Percentile
Speech	12	75
Syntax	10	50
Semantics	12	75
Coherence	8	25
Initiation	9	37
Scripted Language	8	25
Context	8	25
Nonverbal Communication	1	.1
Social Relations	3	1
Interests	8	25

	Standard Score	Percentile	Confidence Interval
General Communication Composite (GCC)	90	25	84–97

The Children's Communication Checklist-Second Edition (CCC-2) was completed by Sally's teacher during the screening process to provide information relative to Sally's overall communication competence. Sally's overall communication score indicates a weakness compared to her measured cognitive ability. Although structural language skills in the areas of content and form are adequate, Sally's test performance reflects a marked weakness in pragmatic language. Analysis of her communication profile indicates greatest weakness in nonverbal communication and social relations.

Social competence (Teacher/Parent reports)

Social Responsiveness Scale: (SRS)

Subscale	T-Score (Parent Report)	T-Score (Teacher Report)
Social Awareness	52	55
Social Cognition	65	80
Social Communication	64	94
Social Motivation	75	65
Autistic Mannerisms	78	62
Total Score	70	67

The Social Responsiveness Scale (SRS) was completed by Sally's mother and classroom teacher to assess Sally's levels of social awareness, social information processing, and capacity for reciprocal social communication, social anxiety/ avoidance, and atypical mannerisms. Sally's Total Scores are in the mild-to-moderate range and suggest deficits in reciprocal social behavior that are clinically significant and may result in functional impairment in everyday social situations. These scores are typical for children with higher functioning autism spectrum conditions, such as Asperger syndrome and PDDNOS. An analysis of Sally's SRS profile indicates significant elevations in the areas of social cognition, motivation, and communication. Positive endorsements were noted for "is socially awkward," "overly sensitive to sounds, textures, or smells," and "has trouble keeping up with the flow of conversation."

Social Communication Questionnaire (SCQ)-Lifetime
The Social Communication Questionnaire (SCQ) was completed by Sally's mother to further assess behaviors associated with impairment in social-communication skills. Sally's overall SCQ score of 24 is clinically significant, indicating deficits in the reciprocal social interaction, communication, and restricted, repetitive, and stereotyped patterns of behavior (including circumscribed interests and unusual preoccupations) domains.

Direct observation

Childhood Autism Rating Scale: (CARS)
Based on direct observation and parent/teacher interview, the CARS was completed to assist in assessing the presence of characteristics associated

with ASD. Sally's Total CARS score is 32.5, indicating functioning in the mildly to moderately autistic range. Atypicalities were observed in the areas of interpersonal relationships, verbal and nonverbal communication, auditory responsiveness, and adaptation to environmental change.

Sensory processing

Short-Sensory Profile: (SSP)

Domain	Difference
Tactile Sensitivity	Definite
Taste/Smell Sensitivity	Definite
Movement Sensitivity	Typical
Unresponsive/Seeks Sensation	Definite
Auditory Filtering	Definite
Low Energy/Weak	Typical
Visual/Auditory Sensitivity	Definite
Total	Definite

The Short Sensory Profile (SSP) was completed by Sally's mother to determine whether Sally is experiencing clinically important levels of sensory problems. A review of Sally's profile indicates that she has definite sensory difficulties in the areas of Tactile Sensitivity, Taste/Smell Sensitivity, Auditory Filtering, and overall sensory functioning. Endorsements were noted for "appears not to hear what you say," "does not respond when name is called," "responds negatively to unexpected or loud noises," "is bothered by bright lights," "touches people and objects," and "will only eat certain tastes."

Visual-motor

Beery-Buktenica Developmental Test of Visual-Motor Integration-5th Edition: (VMI-V)
Percentile Rank: 25
Standard Score: 90

The Beery-Buktenica Developmental Test of Visual-Motor Integration-Fifth Edition (VMI-V) was utilized to assess Sally's ability to integrate visual-motor skills. Her standard score of 90 and corresponding percentile rank of 25 suggest a relative weakness in this developmental area. Qualitatively, Sally's performance reflects mild difficulty with motoric expression and control.

Adaptive behavior

Adaptive Behavior Assessment System—Second Edition: (ABAS-II)

Parent Rating Summary

Skill Areas	Scaled Score	Percentile
Communication (Com)	3	1
Community Use (CU)	6	9
Functional Academics (FA)	3	1
Home Living (HL)	10	50
Health and Safety (HS)	11	57
Leisure (LS)	6	22
Self-Care (SC)	5	5
Self-Direction (SD)	9	37
Social (Soc)	3	1

Composite	Standard Score	Percentile Rank	Qualitative Range
Conceptual	72	3	Borderline
Social	75	5	Borderline
Practical	82	12	Below Average
GAC	80	9	Below Average

The ABAS-II was completed by Sally's mother to assess Sally's adaptive behavior functioning in everyday situations. The General Adaptive Composite score (GAC) summarizes performance across all skill areas. Sally obtained a GAC score of 80, placing her current overall level of adaptive behavior in the below average range. Sally's Functional Academics, Communication and Social skills scores are significantly lower than her average scores across all skill areas, representing a significant weakness within her profile. Sally's adaptive behavior can be described as significantly lower than is typical for her age and cognitive level.

Behavioral/Emotional functioning

Children's Depression Inventory: (CDI)

Scale	T-Score	Percentile
Negative Mood	64	91
Interpersonal Problems	57	89
Ineffectiveness	64	91
Anhedonia	55	74

Children's Depression Inventory: (CDI)

Scale	T-Score	Percentile
Negative Self-Esteem	62	91
Total CDI Score	64	90

Sally completed the CDI to provide self-report information relative to depressive symptomatology and mood problems. Sally's total score of 64 is elevated to a clinically significant level. Her scores on the Negative Mood, Interpersonal Problems, Ineffectiveness, and Negative Self-Esteem are also above average relative to her gender and age group. She endorsed items such as "I have trouble sleeping," "I have some friends but wish I had more," "I am sad many times," "I feel like crying everyday," "I do not like being with people many times."

Achenbach Child Behavior Checklist: (CBCL) (TRF)

Empirically Based Scales	T-Score	Percentile	T-Score	Percentile
Anxious/Depressed	70	>97	73	>97
Withdrawn/Depressed	80	>97	74	>97
Somatic Complaints	53	62	57	76
Social Problems	65	93	76	>97
Thought Problems	66	95	63	90
Attention Problems	62	89	55	69
Rule-Breaking behavior	52	58	55	69
Aggressive Behavior	63	90	64	92
Internalizing Problems	63	90	72	>98
Externalizing Problems	60	84	63	90
Total Problems	63	90	67	96
DSM-Oriented Scales				
Affective Problems	73	>97	72	>97
Anxiety Problems	77	>97	67	96
Somatic Problems	50	<50	50	<50
ADHD Problems	52	58	62	89
Oppositional Defiant Problems	59	81	61	87
Conduct Problems	52	58	55	69

The Child Behavior Checklist (CBCL) was completed by Sally's mother to obtain her perceptions of Sally's competencies and problems. She reported that although Sally has an intense interest in several activity areas, she has no close friends and interacts with peers less than once a week outside of school. Sally's Total Competence score is in the clinical range below the 10th percentile for parents' ratings of girls 6 to 11 years of age. On the CBCL problem scales, Sally's Total Problems, Internalizing, and Externalizing scores are all in the borderline clinical range (84th to 90th percentiles). Her scores on the Somatic Complaints, Attention Problems, Rule-Breaking Behavior, and Aggressive Behavior syndromes are in the normal range. Her scores on the Anxious/Depressed and Withdrawn/Depressed syndromes are in the clinical range above the 97th percentile. Her scores on the Social Problems and Thought Problems syndrome scales are in the borderline clinical range (93rd to 97th percentiles). These results indicate that Sally's mother reported more problems than are typically reported by parents of girls 6 to 11 years of age, particularly anxious, withdrawn and depressed behavior, social problems, and thought problems. On the DSM-oriented scales, Sally's scores on the Anxiety Problems, Somatic Problems, Attention Deficit/Hyperactivity Problems, Oppositional Defiant Problems, and Conduct Problems scales are in the normal range. Her scores on the Affective Problems and Anxiety Problems scales are in the clinical range (above the 97th percentile). These results suggest that Sally may be at risk for coexisting anxiety or mood disorders.

The Teacher Report Form (TRF) was completed by Sally's teacher to obtain her perceptions of Sally's adaptive functioning and problems in the classroom. Sally's teacher rated Sally's performance in two academic subjects at somewhat below grade level, and one subject at grade level. She also rated Sally as working less hard, behaving less appropriately, learning somewhat less, and much less happy compared to typical students of the same age. Sally's Total Adaptive Functioning score is in the clinical range below the 10th percentile. On the TRF problem scales, Sally's Total Problems and Internalizing scores are both in the clinical range above the 90th percentile. Her Externalizing score is in the borderline clinical range (84th to 90th percentiles). Her scores on the Somatic Complaints, Attention Problems, Thought Problems, Rule-Breaking Behavior, and Aggressive Behavior syndromes are in the normal range. Her scores on the Anxious/Depressed, Withdrawn/Depressed, and Social Problems syndromes are in the clinical range above the 97th percentile. These results indicate that Sally's classroom teacher reported more problems than are typically reported by teachers of girls 6 to 11 years of age, particularly problems of anxiety, withdrawn or depressed behavior, and social problems. On the DSM-oriented scales, Sally's scores on the Somatic Problems, Attention Deficit/Hyperactivity Problems, Oppositional Defiant Problems, and Conduct Problems scales are in the normal range. Her score on the Affective Problems scale is in the clinical range (above the 97th percentile). Her score on the Anxiety Problems scale is in the borderline clinical range (93rd to 97th percentiles). These results further suggest that Sally may be experiencing symptoms associated with internalizing problems such as anxiety and depression.

Family system

Parenting Stress Index—Short Form

Scale	Raw Score	Percentile
Defensive Responding	28	99
Parental Distress (PD)	43	95
Parent–Child Dysfunctional Interaction (P-CDI)	37	99
Difficult Child (DC)	43	95
Total Stress	123	99

The Parenting Stress Index (PSI) was completed by Sally's mother. She endorsed a total level of stress in the clinical range. Results suggest that Sally's mother may not be able to cope effectively and feel anxious, depressed, and overwhelmed by the demands of parenting. Her high level of reported stress may be a function of both her own temperament and Sally's impairments. She appears to be highly distressed by Sally's behavior and may need assistance in understanding and managing her daughter's social problems.

Summary and recommendations

Sally was referred for an individual evaluation to assess strengths and weaknesses in the areas of intellectual functioning, academic achievement, and social/behavioral adjustment. The results of the current assessment indicate that Sally is functioning in the average range of general intellectual ability. She earned a Full Scale IQ (FSIQ) score of 97 on the Wechsler Intelligence Scale for Children-Fourth Edition (WISC-IV). Sally's FSIQ score places her at the 42nd percentile compared to same age peers. Although Sally performed somewhat better on nonverbal reasoning tasks, there is no significant and meaningful difference between her Verbal Comprehension (VCI) and Perceptual Reasoning (PRI) Index scores. She demonstrated a relative weakness with verbal comprehension tasks involving social judgment and reasoning, working memory abilities, and the ability to process visual information with speed and accuracy. The results of the Woodcock-Johnson III Normative Update Tests of Achievement indicate that when compared to others at her age level, Sally's performance is average in both Broad Reading and Math. Some weakness was noted with reading comprehension.

Observation and behavioral rating scales indicate problems in the areas of social responsiveness and communication, and pragmatic language functioning. Sally demonstrates a mild-to-moderate impairment in reciprocal social behavior and responsiveness across home and school contexts. Her social communication (pragmatic) functioning is also positive for concerns related to social relationships and nonverbal communication skills. Test results suggest that Sally is experiencing definite sensory difficulties in the areas of taste/smell, visual/auditory sensitivity, and auditory filtering which may interfere with everyday performance. Sally's social behavior and communication skills, including expressive vocabulary, listening, conversation and nonverbal communication are areas of weakness within her everyday adaptive functioning. Broad-based behavior rating scales completed both at home and school indicate clinically elevated problems in the areas of anxiety or depression, problems in social relationships, and cognitive inflexibility. Although we cannot conclude from Sally's CDI score that she is clinically depressed, the intensity and frequency of reported depressive symptoms may be significant enough to impair her adaptive functioning. Sally's mother reports a high level of stress in the parent-child relationship and with Sally's adjustment difficulties within the family system.

Sally's impairment and atypicalities presented in the communication, socialization, and behavioral domains are consistent with an educational classification of ASD. She demonstrates a persistent pattern of qualitative impairment in social interaction manifested by a lack of social communication and reciprocity, and a failure to develop peer relationships appropriate to her developmental level. Sally also demonstrates restricted and stereotyped patterns of behavior, interest and activities (e.g. sensory difficulties and unusual sensory functioning).

Sally will require small-group and individualized services in language and social communication within a setting that provides support and exposure to typically developing peers. Strategies should be initiated to address social skills and reciprocal social behavior, in particular, motivation to engage in social-interpersonal behavior and the interpretation of social cues. Educational planning should also focus on adaptive behavior concerns in the areas of communication, socialization, and daily living skills. Special attention should be given to the socialization domain, especially interpersonal relationships. The use of social stories may help Sally to comprehend the exchange of information in conversation and enhance her social understanding and engagement. It is also important that Sally understand and be aware of the unwritten rules of social interaction (hidden curriculum). A comprehensive speech/language assessment is recommended to clarify her communication competence and pragmatic language functioning. Consultation from an occupational therapist might also be helpful in formulating accommodations for Sally's sensory issues and visual-motor weakness. Cognitive behavioral programs such as "Exploring Feelings" may be utilized to address concerns related to anxiety and internalizing behavior issues. In terms of external resources, Sally's parents should be referred to the appropriate community organizations and agencies for parenting assistance and support. Lastly, the interdisciplinary assessment team should integrate the results of the current evaluation with multiple sources of assessment information to determine the most appropriate special education classification and provision for services.

DISCUSSION OF CASE EXAMPLES

Jeremy and Sally's evaluations illustrate many of the concepts and methods relevant to the assessment of students suspected of having ASD described in the last chapter. First and foremost, they demonstrate the best practice application of a comprehensive developmental approach to the evaluation of multiple domains of functioning. These sample reports also show, in addition to Sally and Jeremy's history and reports of autistic traits and symptoms, how these behaviors are assessed with multimethod measures across home and school settings.

While both Sally and Jeremy's impairment and atypicalities presented in the communication, socialization, and behavioral domains are in keeping with an educational classification of ASD, there are important similarities and differences in their cognitive and behavioral profiles. For example, Jeremy's cognitive profile is more obviously identified with the so called "autistic" pattern of significantly greater visual-spatial abilities compared to lower comprehension skills on IQ measures. Although Sally's test performance also reflects an uneven cognitive profile, she does not exhibit the widely discrepant scores traditionally associated with autism. However, both demonstrate deficits with cognitive tasks requiring verbal reasoning and comprehension of social situations, as well as knowledge of conventional standards of social behavior. Working memory abilities are also a weakness for both students.

Jeremy and Sally's reports also illustrate how the behavioral expression of the autism phenotype can vary. For example, while the most salient feature of both profiles is impairment in social reciprocity, Sally's behavioral profile is one of withdrawal and depression while Jeremy's presents with externalizing behaviors such as verbal aggression and oppositionality. Sally's behavioral profile provides an example of how it is often the absence of expected behavior (communication and social interaction) rather than atypical behavior that may characterize ASD. Both Sally and Jeremy have a consistent profile of adaptive functioning characteristic of children with ASD, specifically delays and impairments in the social skills domain relative to age and cognitive ability. Both cases show how coexisting (comorbid) internalizing and externalizing problems can have a negative effect on educational performance and productivity. Sally's case provides an especially good example of how a combination of even mild autistic symptomatology and other psychological liabilities such as depressive symptomatology can impair social developmental functioning and school performance. Sally's case also illustrates how the identification of parental stress can be relevant to improving outcomes for children with ASD. Both case examples show the importance of focusing on social-communication competence and pragmatic skills, in addition to traditional language assessments. Finally, we might apply Wing's (2005) subgrouping scheme to our students. Sally demonstrates characteristics of the "passive group" of children with ASD, while Jeremy's profile contains many features of the "active-but-odd" group of students. In the next chapter, we will examine some of the scientifically based and controversial interventions and treatments for ASD.

Quick Reference

An identification process for ASD

1. Collect information from parents, using reliable and valid checklists, about current concerns and past functioning.
2. Use norm referenced and ASD-specific instruments, together with traditional psychometric measures to assess the student's strengths and weaknesses.
3. Integrate information from multiple sources and developmental domains.
4. Apply this information to *DSM-IV* and *IDEA* criteria.
5. Consider and rule out other explanations for symptoms.

Chapter 5

BEST PRACTICE FOR INTERVENTION AND TREATMENT

Supporting students with ASD requires individualized and effective intervention strategies.

There are no interventions or treatments that can cure autism, and there are very few which have been scientifically shown to produce significant, long-term benefits. However, there is a vision shared worldwide on how to approach the treatment for ASD (Autism Europe 2008). While children with ASD share a common diagnostic label, each has individual needs. Because of these differences, an individualized approach is needed that addresses the core deficits of the disorder (e.g. communication, social, sensory, academic difficulties) and that matches each child's unique needs and family preferences. At the present time, the most effective treatment is a comprehensive and intensive program consisting of educational interventions, developmental therapies, and behavior management with a focus on reducing symptom severity and improving the development course of the child.

Numerous studies have described the benefits of early identification and intervention for children with developmental disabilities and, particularly, for children on the autistic spectrum (Dawson and Osterling 1997; Harris and Delmolino 2002; National Research Council 2001; Smith 1999). Indeed, there is strong empirical support for the use of intensive behavioral programs for young children with ASD, even though the specific teaching strategies and curricula content are often the focus of debate (Dawson and Osterling 1997; Gresham and MacMillan 1998; Lovaas 1987; Ozonoff and Cathcart 1998; Rogers 1998; Sheinkopf and Siegel 1998). While the components of intervention programs might vary, it is generally agreed that program intensity combined with early identification can lead to substantial improvement in child functioning (Harris 1994; Sheinkopf and Siegel 1998).

Intervention approaches and nontraditional therapies for ASD are routinely discussed by researchers, parents, and professionals. There are many approaches that promise cures or, at the very least, dramatic improvement and recovery. While anecdotal reports indicate that some strategies are successful for a few, there is no single scientifically based approach that is effective for all children with ASD. However, we do know that many students can make progress and adapt to the classroom setting if provided with the appropriate interventions and behavioral supports (Jordan 2003; Kunce 2003). While the research on the effectivess of intervention strategies for children with autism is still in a formative stage, any method should be effective, practical, transportable, and facilitate generalization of acquired skills. In this chapter, some of the more well-known interventions and treatments for ASD are briefly described. These include strategies typically designed to improve academic and communication skills, promote social integration, and decrease disruptive behavior. Controversial treatments are also discussed and critiqued.

BEST PRACTICE

Although no professional can be an expert on every method and make a detailed study of the literature, we should be cautious about accepting at face value widely reported interventions and treatments that are often presented as self-evident facts and infrequently challenged.

INTERVENTION AND TREATMENT

Supporting children with ASD requires individualized and effective intervention strategies. Table 5.1 displays effectiveness ratings for selected interventions and treatments. They should be considered a "snapshot" in time and are intended to reflect the scientific evidence published in peer-reviewed journals. Each intervention is rated for effectiveness, both positive and negative, providing a classification which identifies the level of scientific evidence which supports or does not support its use. For example, interventions that are "well established" have strong empirical support in the scientific literature. Interventions having an "emerging and effective" level of support are considered promising and have become or are emerging as important features of many programs. However, they require additional objective verification. Those with a lack of empirical data (no evidence) do not infer that the intervention or treatment is ineffective, but rather that efficacy has not been objectively demonstrated or validated. Lastly, those rated as having "negative evidence" may cause harm and are not recommended for use.

It is important to note that there is considerable overlap between the many different treatment approaches. For example, strategies based on applied behavioral analysis (ABA) are an integral part of many interventions, such as early intensive behavioral intervention (EIBI), picture exchange communication system (PECS), and pivotal response treatment (PRT). The success of the intervention depends on the interaction between the age of the child, his or her developmental level and individual characteristics, the strength of the treatment and competency of the interventionalist. These ratings are not intended as an endorsement or a recommendation as to whether or not a specific intervention is suitable for a particular child with ASD. Each child is different and what works for one may not work for another. A brief description of each intervention or treatment follows.

Table 5.1 Quality ratings for interventions

Well established
Early Intensive Behavioral Intervention (EIBI)

Effective evidence
Positive Behavioral Support (PBS)
Picture Exchange Communication System (PECS)
Cognitive Behavioral Therapy (CBT)
Peer-Mediated Strategies

Emerging and effective evidence
Social Stories
TEACCH
Visual Schedule/Support
Incidental Teaching
Pivotal Response Treatment (PRT)
Social Skills Training

No evidence
Sensory Integration Therapy (SI)

Negative evidence/Not recommended
Auditory Integration Training (AIT)
Facilitated Communication (FC)

BEST PRACTICE
Different approaches to intervention have been found to be effective for children with autism, and no comparative research has been conducted that demonstrates one approach is superior to another. The selection of a specific intervention should be based on goals developed from a comprehensive assessment.

Early intensive behavioral intervention (EIBI)

Early intensive behavioral intervention (EIBI) is considered a central feature of intervention programming for children with autism. EIBI programs are among the most and best researched of the psychoeducational interventions. Positive effects of early intervention programs have been demonstrated in both short-term and long-term studies. EIBI programs are based on applied behavior analysis (ABA), a behavioral approach used to treat children with autism that is well supported in the research literature (Stone 2006). Perhaps the best-known technique within EIBI is called discrete trial training. This method involves breaking behaviors down into subcategories and teaching each subcategory through repetition, positive reinforcement, and prompts that are gradually removed from the program as the child progresses. ABA can also be thought of as an inclusive term that encompasses a number of concepts and techniques used in the assessment, treatment, and prevention of behavioral problems. For example, the principles of ABA are incorporated within many specific interventions and programs (e.g. discrete trial training, incidental teaching, PRT, and PEC).

EIBI programs have typically focused on preschool and young children. Research now suggests that school-age children with ASD may benefit as much as younger children from this approach and that EIBI programs can be successfully adapted to school settings (Eikeseth et al. 2002). Although there is little professional disagreement that EIBI is an effective treatment, on average, for children with autism, we should be mindful that it does not produce significant changes in all areas of children's functioning or result in similar gains for all children. Moreover, EIBI may not be appropriate for all children. While EIBI is an important and effective intervention approach, there is no evidence to indicate that it results in "recovery" or normal development (Shea 2004).

> BEST PRACTICE
>
> Positive behavioral support has been shown to be an effective proactive approach to eliminate, minimize, and prevent challenging behavior.

Positive behavioral support (PBS)

The problem behaviors of children with ASD are among the most challenging and stressful issues faced by schools and parents. The current best practice in treating and preventing unwanted or challenging behaviors utilizes the principles and practices of positive behavioral support (PBS). PBS has been demonstrated to be effective with individuals with a wide range of problem behavior and disability labels. Although used successfully both in the classroom and school-wide, PBS is not a specific intervention per se, but rather an approach that has evolved from traditional behavioral management methods. PBS refers to a set of research-based strategies that are intended to decrease problem behaviors by designing effective environments and teaching students appropriate social and communication skills (Koegel, Robinson, and Koegel 2009; Sugai et al. 2000). The objective of PBS is to decrease potentially problematic behavior by making environmental changes and teaching new skills rather than focusing directly on eliminating the problem behavior. An essential component of PBS is a functional behavior assessment (FBA) to help determine the events that influence and maintain the student's challenging behavior. This is followed by the development of a positive intervention plan for teaching appropriate, functional and communicative skills that serve as replacement behaviors (Carr et al. 2002).

Research indicates that PBS can be effective for eliminating and preventing problem behaviors of children with ASD (Dunlap et al. 2008; Johnston et al. 2006; Odom et al. 2003; Rathvon 2008; Sprick and Garrison 2008). For example, a review of published research studies found that in cases where PBS strategies were used, there was as much as an 80 percent reduction in challenging behavior for approximately two-thirds of the outcomes studied (Horner et al. 2002). The IDEA has endorsed PBS as a preferred form of intervention for managing the challenging behavior of students with disabilities. We will discuss FBA and development of behavior intervention plans (BIP) in the next chapter.

BEST PRACTICE

PECS can increase a student's ability to function and communicate in the classroom.

Picture exchange communication system (PECS)

The picture exchange communication system (PECS) is an augmentative and alternative communication system (AAC) used primarily with children who are nonverbal or who use speech with limited effectiveness to assist them in acquiring functional communication skills (Bondy and Frost 1994, 2001). PECS has received international recognition and incorporates both ABA and developmental-pragmatic principles. The method does not require complex or expensive materials and can be easily implemented by educators and family members. PECS uses pictures and other symbols to develop a functional communication system by teaching students to exchange a picture of a desired item for the actual item. Studies show that PECS is effective in teaching communications that involve single words or short phrases and in providing students who have little or impaired speech with a functional means of communication (Sulzer-Azaroff *et al.* 2009). Research also indicates that PECS can improve behavior problems. Although not specifically designed to reduce aggression, there is some evidence to suggest that PECS increases social-communication behavior and may help to reduce maladaptive behaviors (Charlop-Christy *et al.* 2002; Sulzer-Azaroff *et al.* 2009). A recent meta-analysis of 13 published single subject studies examined the effectiveness of PECS and found that PECS produced increases in functional communication, decreased problem behaviors, and increased speech in many participants (Hart and Banda 2009).

Cognitive behavioral therapy (CBT)

Cognitive behavioral therapy (CBT) has been shown to be of value in addressing many of the coexisting problems experienced by individuals with ASD. The term cognitive behavioral therapy or CBT is not a distinct therapeutic technique, but rather a general term for a classification of therapies with similarities (e.g. rational emotive behavior therapy, rational behavior therapy, rational living therapy, and cognitive therapy). There is a strong evidence base for the use of CBT interventions for depression and anxiety in both ASD and non-ASD populations (Velting, Setzer, and Albano 2004). CBT provides a more structured approach than other types of psychotherapy, relies less on insight and judgment than other models, and focuses on practical problem-solving. Thus, it has applicability to children with ASD who typically have deficits and distortions in thinking about thoughts and feelings and therefore, may be considered an "autism-friendly" approach (Attwood 2006; Baron-Cohen 2008b; Ozonoff *et al.* 2002a). There is also some research evidence to support the effectiveness of interventions that incorporate cognitive behavioral strategies in targeting social skills for more capable children with ASD such as Asperger syndrome and high-functioning autism (Attwood 2005; Hare 1997, 2004; Lopata, Thomeer, Volker, and Nida 2006; Reaven *et al.* 2009). As with all complex interventions, professionals who implement CBT-related strategies should be appropriately trained and experienced. Some cognitive behavioral approaches may also be too complex for many younger children with ASD and may be more appropriate for intermediate and secondary age students (9 to 12 years).

Peer-mediated strategies

Peer-mediated procedures are an intervention approach for addressing social interaction deficits among young children with autism (Kamps *et al.* 1998; McConnell 2002; Odom *et al.* 2003; Owen-DeSchryver *et al.* 2008; Rogers 2000). In peer-mediated interventions, typically developing children are taught to interact with children with ASD and to encourage the use of desired communicative and social behaviors. These procedures include a range of interventions designed to increase peer social initiations and social and communicative interactions, including social skills training, modeling, and instructional interventions such as peer-mediated incidental teaching and structured peer tutoring (Kamps *et al.* 2002). An important benefit of peer-mediated interventions is their ability to promote generalization and maintenance of skills, as opposed to adult-managed interventions, which may not often generalize. Peer-mediated strategies are also proactive, require little teacher planning time, and can be easily adapted to the classroom. The available research evidence on peer-mediated strategies indicates that having trained peers promotes both acceptance of the child with ASD and skill development in all children. Peer-mediated strategies have been shown to be a successful method of building social responsiveness and increasing interactions (DiSalvo and Oswald 2002; Owen-DeSchryver *et al.* 2008; Weiss and Harris 2001; Williams *et al.* 2005). Both incidental teaching and pivotal response training have been used with peer-mediated strategies and recognized as successful multicomponent intervention strategies for facilitating the inclusion of children with autism in general education classrooms (Harrower and Dunlap 2001).

Social stories

A social story describes a situation, skill, or concept in terms of relevant social cues, perspectives, and common responses in a specifically defined style and format. They are designed to help the individual learn how others perceive various social actions and to facilitate the understanding of important social cues and the unwritten rules (or hidden curriculum) of social interaction. Social stories can take many forms. For example, some are written on sheets of paper, others are written in booklets, while some are recorded on audio or video. The author of the story may read it to the child, record it so that it can be played back as needed, or the student may read it themselves. There is evidence from a large number of case studies that the social story approach (combined with other interventions) can be effective in reducing unwanted behavior and increasing social interaction for some children with ASD (Attwood 2006; Gray 1998; Ozonoff *et al.* 2002a). However, it is unclear from published research whether this approach alone is responsible for durable changes in key social behaviors. This suggests that social stories should not be the only social skills intervention for children with ASD and that other strategies (e.g. prompting, reinforcement schedules) implemented together with social stories may be required to produce the desired change in behaviors (Sansosti, Powell-Smith, and Kincaid 2004). Thus, this intervention should be considered an emerging and effective approach when used as part of a multicomponent intervention in clinical or classroom settings (Norris and Dattilo 1999; Ozdemir 2008; Sansosti *et al.* 2004; Spencer, Simpson, and Lynch 2008).

TEACCH

TEACCH is an acronym for the **T**reatment and **E**ducation of **A**utistic and **C**ommunication-**H**andicapped **C**hildren. It is the term given to describe the various activities carried out by Division TEACCH, a university-based statewide program of services for children and adults with autism in North Carolina. TEACCH (Mesibov, Schopler, and Hearsey 1994; Schopler, Mesibov, and Hearsey 1995) is an intervention approach designed to take advantage of the visual and rote memory strengths of children with ASD in order to help them develop language, cognitive, imitative, and social skills (Ozonoff *et al.* 2002a). The program emphasizes structured teaching in multiple settings with the involvement of several teachers. TEACCH is perhaps the best known special education program for children with autism, and is used worldwide. Several hundred research studies have been conducted by or in collaboration with Division TEACCH. Although the outcomes of children who participate in the TEACCH interventions have not been examined as rigorously as EIBI, there is scientific evidence to indicate that the TEACCH program can provide significant benefits to many students with ASD (National Research Council 2001; Schopler 2005). Larger, systematic and controlled studies are needed in order to more effectively evaluate the immediate and long-term outcomes of the TEACCH program.

> BEST PRACTICE
>
> Interventions and programs should capitalize on children's natural tendency to respond to visual structure, routines, schedules, and predictability.

Visual schedules/Supports

A visual schedule is a form of visual support, consisting of a set of pictures that communicates a series of activities or the steps of a specific activity. A schedule can be created using photographs, pictures, written words, physical objects, or any combination of these items. A daily or across-task schedule shows the child all of the activities he or she will undertake during a single day. A within-task (or mini-schedule) illustrates all of the steps the student needs to take to complete a specific activity. Because school-age children with autism routinely experience new learning environments and a lack of consistency in classroom routines, picture schedules provide a way to engage in appropriate task-related behaviors with minimal adult prompting (Bryan and Gast 2000).

Successful implementation of visual schedules has been shown to decrease challenging behaviors, to improve transitioning, and to teach daily living skills to children with autism (McClannahan and Krantz 1999; Morrison *et al.* 2002; Pierce and Schreibman 1994, 1997). Visual schedules have also been used to enhance on-task behavior as well as to improve the ability of children with ASD to follow classroom schedules (Bryan and Gast 2000). Visual schedules and supports have become an accepted and integral part of most comprehensive programs for children with ASD.

Incidental teaching

Incidental teaching is a form of teaching in which a teacher takes advantage of naturally occurring events or situations to provide learning opportunities for the student. Although the classroom environment is organized around a set of preplanned learning objectives, the student's individual preferences are given consideration. For example, when the child demonstrates an interest in an item or activity, the teacher encourages that interest by questioning or prompting the student. There is a reasonable amount of scientific evidence to indicate that this approach holds promise as a way of providing naturalistic teaching strategies to both teachers and parents, and for promoting the social language skills of children with ASD (Ledford *et al.* 2008; National Research Council 2001). There is also research to suggest that combining incidental teaching and discrete trial training may result in increases in spontaneous speech, appropriate social responding, and functional communication skills. (Charlop-Cristy and Carpenter 2000; McGee and Daly 2007; National Research Council 2001).

Pivotal response treatment (PRT)

Pivotal response treatment or training (PRT) is an approach in which certain aspects of a child's development are considered to be pivotal or critical. A primary objective of PRT is to shift children with autism toward a more typical developmental path by focusing on a broad number of behaviors. This includes targeting motivational variables, incorporating choice, increasing responsiveness to multiple cues, and teaching self-management skills and self-initiations. The interventionalist concentrates on altering these pivotal areas in order to modify the behaviors that depend on them, such as language, social responsiveness, and challenging behavior. PRT uses both a developmental approach and ABA procedures to provide learning opportunities in the child's natural environment (Koegel, Koegel, and Carter 1999; Koegel *et al.* 2006). The outcome research for pivotal response training is promising and has shown positive effects on language and communicative interaction, and social engagement and play for children with ASD (Bryson *et al.* 2007; Pierce and Schreibman 1995, 1997). There is also research to suggest that a pivotal behavior such as self-management can have a positive effect on social behaviors and in reducing challenging behaviors such as disruptive and off-task behavior (Koegel *et al.* 1999; Koegel and Koegel 2006; McConnell 2002; National Research Council 2001; Wilkinson 2005, 2008b). PRT is sometimes incorporated within other models and approaches. For example, an interesting development in peer-mediated strategies has been the use of peer-implemented pivotal response training for building social skills (Weiss and Harris 2001).

BEST PRACTICE
Social skills interventions have the potential to produce noticeable effects in the social interactions and social relationships of children with autism, if appropriately designed and delivered.

Social skills training

Severe impairment in social reciprocity is the core, underlying feature of ASD. Socialization deficits are a major source of impairment, regardless of cognitive or language ability and do not diminish over the course of development (Carter *et al.* 2005). Distress often increases as children approach adolescence and the social milieu becomes more complex and difficult (Tantam 2003). Evidence accumulating in the empirical literature indicates that, in general, social skills interventions are likely to be appropriate for primary school-age children with either high-functioning autism (HFA) or Asperger's disorder (Bellini *et al.* 2007; Charlop-Christy and Kelso 1999; Gray 1998; Hall 1997; McConnell 2002). Commonly used approaches include individual and group social skills training, providing experiences with typically developing peers, and peer-mediated social skills interventions, all targeting the core social and communication domains. Child-specific social skills interventions frequently include: teaching to increase knowledge and develop social problem solving skills; differential reinforcement to improve social responding; structured social skills training programs; adult-mediated prompting, modeling, and reinforcement, and various behavior management techniques such as self-monitoring.

While interventions based on the principles of ABA have been shown to improve functional communication and reduce problematic behaviors in children with ASD (Hanley, Iwata, and Thompson 2001; Lovaas 1987), interventions that target social deficits have not received the same level of attention (Weiss and Harris 2001). However, there is emerging evidence to support traditional and newer naturalistic behavioral strategies and other approaches to social skills programming for young children with ASD (McConnell 2002). For example, there is some objective research to suggest that group-based social skills training and peer-mediated (teaching typical children to engage their peers with ASD) approaches may be useful interventions (Barnhill *et al.* 2002; Barry *et al.* 2003; McConnell 2002; Solomon, Goodlin-Jones, and Anders 2004; Tse *et al.* 2007; White, Koening, and Scahill 2007; Yang *et al.* 2003). It should be noted that a recent meta-analysis of single-subject designs examining the effectiveness of school-based social skills interventions for children and adolescents with ASD found that they produced low treatment and minimal generalization effects across participants and settings (Bellini *et al.* 2007). Nevertheless, the research database suggests that social interactive training is an effective and promising technique for promoting communication and social skills when used as a component of an overall educational curriculum for children with ASD (Hwang and Hughes 2000; Weiss and Harris 2001).

Sensory integration therapy (SI)

Unusual sensory responses are relatively common in children with ASD. However, there is little rigorous research on intervention techniques designed to address these sensory symptoms (National Research Council 2001). Sensory integration (SI) therapy is often used individually or as a component of a broader program of occupational therapy for children with ASD. The goal of SI therapy is to remediate deficits in neurologic processing and the integration of sensory information to allow the student to interact with the environment in a more adaptive manner. The efficacy of SI therapy has not been demonstrated objectively. While sensory activities may be helpful as part of an overall educational program, there are few high quality studies examining the efficacy of occupational therapy for children with ASD (Myers, Johnson, and Council on Children with Disabilities 2007; National Research Council 2001). At present, we have no reliable and convincing empirical evidence that sensory-based treatments (including vision therapy) have specific effects. Although SI is often recommended for inclusion in intervention plans and services for children with ASD, this intervention is best described as unvalidated (no evidence).

> ### BEST PRACTICE
> Relying on ineffective and potentially harmful treatments puts the child at risk and uses valuable time that could be utilized in more productive educational or remedial activities.

Auditory integration training (AIT)

Controversial therapies and interventions continue to be a significant part of the history of children and youth with ASD, perhaps more so than any other childhood disorder (Simpson and Zionts 2000). Auditory integration training (AIT) was developed to treat individuals with auditory processing difficulties, particularly hypersensitivity to sound. This technique involves the repeated exposure to different sounds in an effort to "retrain" the ear and improve the way the brain processes information. The underlying theory of AIT is that distortions in hearing or auditory processing may contribute to behavioral and learning problems. AIT has been investigated more than any other sensory approach to intervention. Although the opinion on the usefulness of AIT is at best mixed, the research evidence is generally not supportive of either its theoretical basis or its effectiveness in improving the behavior and functioning of individuals with autism and other sensory problems (Baranek 2002; Simpson and Zionts 2000; Stone 2006). There are no controlled scientific studies to support claims of cure or recovery or improved language, attention, social responsiveness, and academic performance from AIT. Lastly, AIT is not endorsed by the American Academy of Pediatrics and should be considered as ineffective and cannot be recommended (Dawson and Watling 2000; National Research Council 2001).

Facilitated communication (FC)

Facilitated communication (FC) is a form of augmentative alternative communication (AAC). It involves a communication partner, typically called a facilitator, who physically supports the individual so that he or she can point to pictures, symbols, letters and/or words using a computer keyboard or letter/picture books in order to communicate. FC assumes that many of the difficulties faced by individuals with autism are the result of a movement disorder rather than social or communication deficits. There is a significant body of research evidence to show that FC is ineffective as an intervention method for ASD (National Research Council 2001). Systematic and controlled research on FC does not provide support the use of this intervention. A large amount of the research indicates that it is the facilitator who produces the information, not the individual with autism. For these reasons FC is not an appropriate intervention for children with ASD (Simpson 2005; National Research Council 2001). Several professional associations (e.g. American Speech-Language-Hearing Association; American Academy of Child and Adolescent Psychiatry; American Psychological Association) have formally opposed the use of FC as a therapeutic treatment (Gresham, Beebe-Frankenberger, and MacMillan 1999).

> ### BEST PRACTICE
> No one methodology is effective for all children with autism. Generally, it is best to integrate approaches according to a student's individual needs and responses.

EDUCATIONAL APPROACHES

Although there continues to be debate about which interventions and treatments are the most effective for children with ASD, there is a movement towards combining elements of different approaches (National Autistic Society 2003; Tutt, Powell, and Thorton 2006). For example, the National Autistic Society (NAS) in the United Kingdom has developed a framework for understanding and responding to the needs of children with ASD. The acronym for this framework is SPELL or Structure, Positive (approaches and expectations), Empathy, Low arousal, Links. The SPELL approach emphasizes the importance of organizing intervention and educational planning on the basis of the individual and unique needs of each child. It reflects high quality practice in educating children with ASD and focuses on the general principles associated with the effective management of the autistic triad of impairments (National Autistic Society 2006). Understanding the perspective of the student, providing structure to support learning and communication, giving attention to sensory issues, and using positive behavior supports to build on the strengths of the student are all key components of an effective intervention or educational program. Although there is no consensus on a unifying theory of autism, best practice requires an individualized approach that addresses the core deficits of ASD. Both the National Autistic Society and American Autism Society (ASA) advocate for a framework that addresses these deficit areas, focuses on long-term outcomes, and considers the unique needs and developmental level of each child.

> ### BEST PRACTICE
> School professionals should strongly encourage parents to thoroughly investigate any CAM treatment approach or nontraditional therapy prior to its use with their children.

COMPLEMENTARY AND ALTERNATIVE TREATMENTS

Autism is a disorder with no known cause or cure. Parents and advocates of children with ASD will understandably pursue interventions and treatments that offer the possibility of helping the student, particularly if they are perceived as unlikely to have any adverse effects. Unfortunately, families are often exposed to unsubstantiated, pseudoscientific theories, and related clinical practices that are ineffective and compete with validated treatments, or that have the potential to result in physical, emotional, or financial harm. The time, effort, and financial resources spent on ineffective treatments can create an additional burden on families. Professionals and parents should use caution with treatments that: are based on overly simplified scientific theories; make claims of recovery and/or cure; use case reports or anecdotal data rather than scientific studies; lack peer-reviewed references or deny the need for controlled research studies, or are advertised to have no potential or reported adverse effects (Myers *et al.* 2007). School professionals play an important role in helping parents and other caregivers to differentiate empirically validated treatment approaches from treatments that are unproven and potentially ineffective and/or harmful.

Often referred to as CAM, or complementary and alternative medicine, these treatments commonly lack scientific evidence supporting their safety or effectiveness in treating the symptoms of ASD. Although growing in popularity, CAM treatments such as elimination diets, dietary supplements, and biological agents can have negative side effects and are not generally supported by scientific research. Several nutritional interventions are widely used by parents, most notably restriction of food allergens (e.g. yeast-free diet, gluten-and casin-free (GF-CF) diet) and dietary supplements such as vitamins (e.g. A, C, B-6 and magnesium, fatty acids, and DMG). There is a lack of objective scientific evidence to indicate that these CAM therapies improve the symptoms of ASD (Baron-Cohen 2008b; Myers *et al.* 2007; Ozonoff *et al.* 2002a; Stone 2006). Because CAM therapies have not been adequately evaluated, evidence-based recommendations for their use are not feasible (Myers *et al.* 2007).

The most common elimination diet used to treat children with ASD is the gluten-free and casein-free diet (GF-CF). At the present time, there is little scientific evidence to support a link between diet and autism. Moreover, there are many potential risks to withdrawing normal or regular foods, especially from young children. Because some children with ASD have restricted diets and are "picky" eaters, exclusion diets may reinforce repetitive, rigid eating patterns, add to the social impairment of ASD, and increase the risk of nutritional deficiencies.

All vitamins and minerals can be hazardous in incorrect doses, and some may interact dangerously with medications already being taken. There is strong evidence, based on two scientifically valid and reliable scientific trials, that the food supplement DMG is not an effective treatment for improving social, language or other functioning in ASD (Stone 2006). Biological agents such as chelation/heavy metal detoxification and secretin therapy are scientifically unproven treatments and must be approached with considerable caution as there are reports of negative effects in some studies examining the use of these agents (Stone 2006; Baron-Cohen 2008b).

> ### BEST PRACTICE
> Medication has the potential to improve symptom functioning and the ability to benefit from other types of interventions.

PSYCHOPHARMACOLOGICAL TREATMENT

Medications should not be considered to be "first-line" interventions for children with ASD (National Research Council 2001) and are not a substitute for psychoeducational intervention, which is currently the benchmark intervention for autism (Filipek, Steinberg-Epstein, and Book 2006; Howlin 2005). Although prescription medications do not address the core symptoms of autism, problems such as hyperactivity, inattention, aggression, repetitive or compulsive behaviors, self-injury, anxiety or depression, and sleep problems may respond to a medication regimen. Medication may also have the potential to improve the ability of the individual to benefit from other types of interventions, as well as relieve family stress and enhance adaptability. For example, medical management of hyperactivity and impulsivity can help improve school functioning. Similarly, managing social anxiety and depression may increase participation in a social skills group or structured teaching program. While a comprehensive review of medications is beyond the scope of this chapter, they are briefly discussed.

The most commonly prescribed medications are selective serotonin reuptake inhibitors or SSRIs such as Prozac, Zoloft, and Paxil; stimulants such as Concerta, Metadate, Methylin, Ritalin, and Adderall, and atypical neuroleptics such as Risperdal and Abilify, both with United States Food and Drug Administration (FDA) approved labeling for the symptomatic treatment of irritability (including aggressive behavior, deliberate self-injury, and temper tantrums) in children and adolescents with ASD. As with all medications, professionals and parents must be aware of the potential side effects and contraindications of autism medications. We are in need of large scale methodologically adequate trials to examine outcomes with ASD.

BEST PRACTICE
Regardless of the method, school professionals and interventionists should make a concerted effort to collect data related to intervention integrity (fidelity).

TREATMENT INTEGRITY

Treatment integrity or fidelity refers to the accuracy and consistency with which each component of a treatment or intervention plan is implemented as intended. It is an important link between the use and effectiveness of interventions in school settings and one of the key aspects of scientific investigation (Elliott and Busse 1993). Identifying an empirically supported intervention or treatment for ASD is a necessary but insufficient provision for producing behavior change (Wickstrom *et al.* 1998). Intervention plans implemented with poor integrity make it difficult for us to draw accurate inferences about the effects of individual strategies. In other words, a lack of treatment integrity information compromises our knowledge of what interventions (or components) are responsible for improvement. For example, absent or weak treatment effects might be the result of the poor integrity of interventions, despite their demonstrated empirical support. Unfortunately, this construct has largely been ignored in research and practice (Gresham, Gansle, and Noell 1993; Lane *et al.* 2004). A recent review of published behavioral intervention research studies with children with autism found that only 18 percent actually assessed and reported treatment integrity data (Wheeler *et al.* 2006). According to Gresham (1989), the failure of studies to provide treatment integrity information makes it particularly difficult to conclude whether an intervention was ineffective because of the intervention or because the strategy was poorly implemented. Therefore, school professionals are encouraged to collect data when implementing interventions so as to distinguish between ineffective treatments and potentially effective interventions implemented with poor integrity (Gresham 1989; Gutkin 1993). The reader is referred to Wilkinson (2006) for a review of methods that can be used to assess and monitor treatment integrity in school settings.

> **BEST PRACTICE**
> Empirically supported strategies such as self-management have shown considerable promise as a method for teaching students with ASD to be more independent, self-reliant, and less dependent on external control and continuous supervision.

RESEARCH TO PRACTICE

This section provides a real-world example of an empirically based intervention implemented in the classroom to reduce the challenging behavior of our student Jeremy. Self-management is a pivotal response treatment (an emerging and effective intervention) strategy and a component of positive behavioral support that has been shown to facilitate the generalization of adaptive behavior, promote autonomy, and produce broad behavioral improvements across various contexts for many children with ASD (Koegel and Koegel 2006; Koegel *et al.* 1999; Lee, Simpson, and Shogren 2007). Self-management procedures are cost efficient and can be especially effective when used as a component of a comprehensive intervention program (e.g. functional assessment, social groups, curricular planning, sensory accommodations, and parent-teacher collaboration) for ASD (Koegel *et al.* 1999; Kunce 2003; Myles and Simpson 2003).

> **BEST PRACTICE**
> Self-management can be useful in facilitating the inclusion of students with ASD and other disabilities in regular education settings.

Self-management

One of the salient features of students with ASD is an absence of, or a poorly developed set of, self-management skills. This includes difficulty directing, controlling, inhibiting, or maintaining and generalizing behaviors required for adjustment both in and outside of the classroom without external support and structure from others (Adreon and Stella 2001; Myles and Simpson 2002; Ozonoff, Dawson, and McPartland 2002a; Tantam 2003). Many children with ASD do not respond well to typical top down approaches involving the external manipulation of antecedents and consequences (Myles and Simpson 2003). Empirically supported strategies such as self-management have shown promise as a method for teaching students to be more independent, self-reliant, and less dependent on external control and continuous supervision

(Callahan and Rademacher 1999; Ganz 2008; Koegel *et al.* 1999; Koegel, Koegel, Hurley, and Frea 1992; Lee *et al.* 2007; Odom *et al.* 2003; Wilkinson 2008b).

Teaching students to engage in a positive behavior in place of an undesirable one can have the collateral effect of improving academic performance. Self-management provides students with an opportunity to participate in the development and implementation of their behavior management programs, an important consideration for high-functioning students with ASD (Myles and Simpson 2003). Self-management interventions can also help minimize the potential for the power struggles and confrontations often encountered with the implementation of externally-directed techniques (Myles and Simpson 2003; Simpson and Myles 1998).

Self-management generally involves activities designed to change or maintain one's own behavior. In its simplest form, students are instructed to 1. observe specific aspects of their own behavior and 2. provide an objective recording of the occurrence or nonoccurrence of the observed behavior (Cole and Bambara 2000; Koegel, Koegel, and Parks 1995; Shapiro and Cole 1994). This self-monitoring procedure involves providing a cue or prompt and having students discriminate whether or not they engaged in a specific behavior at the moment the cue was supplied. Research indicates that the activity of focusing attention on one's own behavior and the self-recording of these observations can have a positive reactive effect on the behavior being monitored (Cole, Marder, and McCann 2000). The box below lists the steps for developing and implementing a self-management plan in the classroom. They are described in greater detail below and should be modified as needed to meet the individual needs of the student.

Summary of steps for developing a self-management plan

1. Identify preferred behavioral targets.
2. Determine how often the student will self-manage his/her behavior.
3. Meet with the student to explain the self-management procedure.
4. Prepare a student self-recording sheet.
5. Model the self-management plan and practice the procedure.
6. Implement the self-management plan.
7. Meet with the student to determine whether goals were attained.
8. Provide the rewards when earned.
9. Incorporate the plan into a school–home collaboration scheme.
10. Fade the intervention.

Step 1: Identify preferred behavioral targets

The initial step is to identify and operationally define the target behavior(s). This involves explicitly describing the behavior so that the student can accurately discriminate its occurrence and nonoccurence (Koegel *et al.* 1995). For example, target behaviors such as "being good" and "staying on task" are broad and relatively vague terms, whereas "raising hand to talk" and "eyes on paper" are more specific. When developing operational definitions, it is also useful to provide exact examples and nonexamples of the target behavior. This will help students to recognize when they are engaging in the behavior(s).

While self-management interventions can be used to decrease problem behavior, it is best to identify and monitor an appropriate, desired behavior rather than a negative one. Describe the behavior in terms of what students are supposed to do, rather than what they are not supposed to do. This establishes a positive and constructive alternative behavior. Here are some examples of positive target behaviors:

- Cooperate with classmates on group projects by taking turns.
- Follow teacher directions and raise hand before speaking.
- Sit at desk and work quietly on the assignment.

Step 2: Determine how often the students will self-manage his/her behavior

An interval method is usually recommended for monitoring off-task behavior, increasing appropriate behavior and compliance, and decreasing disruptive behavior (Cole *et al.* 2000). Typically, the interval will depend on the student's characteristics, such as age, cognitive level, and severity of behavior. Some students will need to self-monitor more frequently than others. For example, if the goal is to decrease a challenging behavior that occurs frequently, then the student will self-monitor a positive, replacement behavior more often. Teachers may wish to establish interval lengths based on their students' individual ability levels and degree of behavioral control.

Once the frequency of self-monitoring is determined, a decision is made as to the type of cue that will be used to signal students to self-observe and record their behavior. In classroom settings, this generally involves the use of a verbal or nonverbal external prompt. There are several types of prompts that can be used to signal students and help teachers monitor their own instructional time in the classroom: verbal cue; silent cue, such as a hand motion; physical prompt; timing device with a vibrating function; kitchen timer; watch with an alarm function; or prerecorded cassette tape with a tone. The type of cue will depend on the ecology of the classroom and the students' individual needs and competencies (Koegel *et al.* 1995). Regardless of the prompt selected for the student, it is important that it be age appropriate, unobtrusive, and as nonstigmatizing as possible.

Step 3: Meet with the student to explain the self-management procedure

Active student participation is a necessity as it increases proactive involvement in the plan (Myles and Simpson 2003; Shapiro and Cole 1994). Once the target behavior has been defined and frequency of self-monitoring decided, discuss the benefits of self-management, behavioral goals, and specific rewards or incentives for meeting those goals with the student. Providing the student with a definition of behaviors to increase and decrease, as well as commenting on the benefits of managing one's own behavior will increase the likelihood of a successful intervention. Students might be told "self-management means being responsible for your own behavior so that you can succeed in school and be accepted by others." Asking students to select from a menu of reinforcers or identify at least three preferred school-based activities also helps to ensure that the incentives are truly motivating and rewarding.

Step 4: Prepare a student self-recording sheet

The most popular self-management recording method in school settings is the creation of a paper-and-pencil checklist or form. This form lists the appropriate academic or behavioral targets students will self-observe when they are cued at a specified time interval. For example, a goal statement such as "Was I paying attention to my seatwork?" would be included as a question to which the student records a response. When developing the form, it is important to consider each student's cognitive ability and reading level. For students with limited reading skills, pictures can be used to represent the target behaviors or response to the goal statement/question. Figure 5.1 provides an example of a self-recording sheet with behavioral goal questions.

Step 5: Model the self-management plan and practice the procedure

The use of modeling, practice, and performance feedback is critical in training students to self-manage their behavior (Cole *et al.* 2000; Koegel *et al.* 1995). After the target behaviors and goals are identified, frequency of self-monitoring determined, and the data recording form developed, the self-management process is demonstrated for the student. This includes modeling the procedure and asking students to observe while the teacher simulates a classroom scenario. Students are encouraged to role-play both desired and undesired behaviors at various times during practice, and to accurately self-observe and record these behaviors. The teacher also practices rating the target behavior to become familiar with the self-monitoring form and make students aware that others are checking their monitoring. Accuracy is determined by comparing student ratings with those of the teacher made on the same self-recording form. Students are provided with feedback on their progress and, when necessary, given further opportunity to practice. Students practice until they demonstrate mastery of the procedure by meeting a minimum criterion for accuracy (e.g. 80% accuracy for two out of three consecutive instructional sessions).

Name:			
Date:	**My Self-Monitoring Form**		
Today in class . . . 	Was I paying attention to my assigned work?	Y	N
	Was I following the classroom rules?	Y	N
	Was I paying attention to my assigned work?	Y	N
	Was I following the classroom rules?	Y	N
	Was I paying attention to my assigned work?	Y	N
	Was I following the classroom rules?	Y	N
	Was I paying attention to my assigned work?	Y	N
	Was I following the classroom rules?	Y	N
	Was I paying attention to my assigned work?	Y	N
	Was I following the classroom rules?	Y	N

Total number of Y (yes) = _____   My Goal = _____

Signed: _____   _____   _____
              Student   Teacher   Parent

Figure 5.1 Self-recording sheet

Source: Adapted from Wilkinson 2008b.

Step 6: Implement the self-management plan

Once reliability with the self-monitoring procedure is firmly established, the students rate their behavior on the self-recording sheet at the specified time interval in the natural setting. For example, students might be prompted (cued) to record their behavior at 10-minute intervals during independent or small group instruction in their general education classroom. When cued, the student responds to the self-observation question (e.g. Was I paying attention to my seat work?) by placing a plus "+" (yes) or minus "-" (no) on the recording sheet. Students may also be required to maintain a designated level of accuracy (e.g. no more than one session per week with less than 80% accuracy) during implementation of the self-management procedure. If the level is not maintained, booster sessions are provided to review target behavior definitions and the self-monitoring process (Cole *et al.* 2000).

Step 7: Meet with the student to determine whether goals were attained

A brief conference is held with the student each day to determine whether the behavioral goal was met and to compare teacher and student ratings. Students are rewarded from their reinforcement menus or with the agreed upon incentives when the behavioral goal is met for the day. If the behavioral goal is not reached, students are told they will have an opportunity to earn their reward during the next day's self-monitoring session. When the students' ratings agree with their teacher (e.g. 80% of the time), they are provided with verbal praise for accurate recording. Accuracy checks can occur more frequently at the beginning of the intervention and be reduced once the target behavior is established.

It is important to remember that the teacher's ratings are always the accepted standard. It is not unusual, especially at the beginning of a self-management plan, for the teacher and student to have honest disagreements about the accuracy of the ratings. If this occurs, it is best to initiate a conference with the student to help clarify the target behavior and attempt to resolve the conflict. Occasionally, students may continue to argue with the teacher about the ratings. If this problem persists, then the self-monitoring procedure is discontinued, as it is unlikely to be an effective intervention.

Step 8: Provide the rewards when earned

An important component of self-management is the presence of a reward. Although self-monitoring can be effective without incentives, goal-setting and student selection of reinforcement makes the intervention more motivating and increases the likelihood of positive reactive effects (Shapiro and Cole 1994). Therefore, it is critically important that the agreed upon incentives be provided when students have met their daily behavioral goal.

Step 9: Incorporate the plan into a school-home collaboration scheme

Parents play an essential role in developing and implementing behavior management plans students with ASD (Kunce 2003; Ozonoff *et al.* 2002a). The self-recording sheet is sent home each day for their signature to ensure that the student receives positive reinforcement across settings. It is usually best to have a phone or personal conference with parents before beginning the intervention to explain the purpose of self-monitoring and explain how they can positively support the intervention at home (such as using their child's special interest as a reward).

Step 10: Fade the intervention

The procedure may gradually be faded once the desired behavior is established in order to reduce reliance on external cueing. This typically involves extending the interval between prompts or reducing the number of intervals. The target behaviors are continuously monitored to determine compliance with the procedures and the need to readjust the fading process. The ultimate goal is to have students self-monitor their behavior independently and without prompting (Shapiro and Cole 1994). Once students achieve competency with self-management, they can apply their newly learned self-regulation skills to other situations and settings, thereby facilitating generalization of appropriate behaviors in future environments with minimal or no feedback from others (Koegel *et al.* 1995).

Case example: Jeremy

In the first chapter we were introduced to Jeremy, a seven-year-old student with a history of difficulty in the areas of appropriateness of response, task persistence, attending, and topic maintenance. Challenging social behaviors reported by Jeremy's teacher included frequent off-task behavior, arguing with adults and peers, temper tantrums, and noncompliance with classroom rules. Among Jeremy's strengths were his well-developed visualization skills and memory for facts and details. Several interventions had been tried, but without success, including verbal reprimands, time-out, and loss of privileges. Jeremy's teacher decided to implement a self-management intervention in an effort to reduce Jeremy's challenging classroom behavior.

Behavior ratings completed by Jeremy's teacher indicated that Jeremy was disengaged and noncompliant more than 60 percent of the time during independent seatwork and small group instruction. She identified on-task behavior and compliance with classroom rules as the target behaviors. The self-management procedure consisted of two primary components: 1. self-observation and 2. self-recording. Self-observation involved the covert questioning of behavior (e.g. Was I paying attention to my assigned work?) and self-recording the overt documentation of the response to this prompt on a recording sheet. Jeremy was told "self-management means accepting responsibility for managing and controlling your own behavior so that you can accomplish the things you want at school and home." He was also given an example of the target behaviors to be self-monitored. "On-task" behavior was defined as: seated at own desk; work materials on desk; eyes on teacher, board, or work, and reading or working on an assignment. "Compliant" was defined as following classroom rules by: asking relevant questions of teacher and neighbor; raising hand and waiting turn before speaking; interacting appropriately with other students, and following adult requests and instructions. Jeremy was trained to accurately self-observe and record the target behaviors. His teacher read the goal questions on the self-recording form and provided examples of behavior indicating their occurrence or nonoccurrence. She also modeled the behaviors Jeremy needed to increase and demonstrated how to use the self-recording form to respond to the behaviors observed. Jeremy then practiced self-monitoring the target behaviors until he demonstrated proficiency with the procedure.

Following three days of training, the self-monitoring procedure was incorporated into Jeremy's daily classroom routine. A self-recording form was taped to the upper right-hand corner of his desk. Because he was the only student who was self-monitoring in the class and other students might be disturbed by a verbal cue, his teacher physically cued Jeremy by tapping the corner of his desk at 10-minute intervals during approximately 50 minutes of independent and small-group instruction. When cued, Jeremy covertly asked himself "Was I paying attention to my assigned work?' and "Was I following my teacher's directions and classroom rules?" He then marked the self-recording sheet with a "plus" (yes) or "minus" (no), indicating his response to the questions regarding the target behaviors. Jeremy and his teacher then held a brief meeting to determine whether his behavioral goal was met for that day, compare ratings, and sign the self-recording sheet. Jeremy was provided with the agreed-upon rewards when he met his behavioral goal and provided with verbal praise for accurately matching his teacher's ratings. When he met his daily behavioral goals, Jeremy could make a selection from a group of his preselected incentives such as additional computer game time and access to a preferred game or activity before school dismissal. The self-recording sheet was then sent home for his parent's signature, so they could review Jeremy's behavior and provide a reward contingent upon meeting his behavioral goals. The self-monitoring intervention continued for approximately three weeks during which time Jeremy's teacher continued to collect performance data. She also completed a treatment integrity checklist each day to ensure that all components of the self-monitoring intervention were implemented as planned.

When his teacher determined that Jeremy's task engagement and compliant behavior had increased to 90 percent, the procedure was slowly faded by increasing the intervals between self-monitoring cues (e.g. 10 minutes, 15 minutes, and 20 minutes). Jeremy's teacher continued to monitor the target behaviors to determine whether additional support (e.g. booster sessions) was needed to maintain his performance. The goal of the final phase of the plan was to eliminate the prompts to self-monitor and instruct Jeremy to keep track of his "own" behavior. Home—school communication continued via a daily performance report to help maintain his self-management independence and positive behavioral gains. Periodic behavioral ratings by Jeremy's teacher indicated that task engagement and compliant behavior remained at significantly improved levels several weeks after the self-monitoring procedure was completely faded.

LIMITATIONS

Despite the potential uses and benefits of self-management, this strategy is not without some limitations. Self-management procedures are intended to complement, not replace, positive behavioral support strategies already in place in the classroom. They are not static and inflexible procedures, but rather a framework in which to design and implement effective interventions (Shapiro and Cole 1994). For example, the self-monitoring plan described in Jeremy's case vignette represents only one of the many possible ways that self-management procedures can be utilized in the classroom. School professionals are encouraged to use their creativity in applying the components of self-management to their own classroom situations.

Shifting from an external teacher-managed approach to self-management can present some obstacles. As with other interventions, self-management strategies can fail due to student and teacher resistance, poor training, and/or a lack of appropriate reinforcement (Cole *et al.* 2000). Successful implementation of self-management procedures requires that students be motivated and actively involved in the self-monitoring activities. Likewise, teachers considering implementation of a self-management intervention will need to invest the time required to identify behavior needs, establish goals, determine reinforcers, and teach students how to recognize, record, and meet behavioral goals. In order for self-management to be an effective intervention, the procedures must be acceptable to all parties and implemented with integrity. If not fully supported, it is better to focus on a more suitable behavior management approach.

Self-management interventions are not appropriate for every child with ASD. Some procedures will meet the needs of individual students better than others. For example, seriously challenging behaviors may require a comprehensive approach using multiple intervention techniques. You may also find that students react differently to self-management procedures. A number of students will find being in control a motivating and reinforcing activity. For others, self-management procedures may actually prove to be a time-consuming distraction (Cole *et al.* 2000; Shapiro and Cole 1994). As with any behavioral intervention, a thorough understanding of the student's problem and needs should precede and dictate selection of a specific behavior management strategy.

> **BEST PRACTICE**
>
> Advocacy should not interfere with being a scientist. School professionals should focus on empirically based strategies and outcomes and not attempt to prove that one intervention is better than another.

SUMMARY

With a few exceptions, the evidence base for interventions for students with ASD is in the formative stage. Robust, impartial research is needed to determine which interventions are most effective and with which students. While children with ASD share a number of similar behavioral and other characteristics, every child is unique. Intervention approaches must be sensitive to their uniqueness and individuality. Reports from several panels and organizations are in agreement on the following points (Dawson and Osterling 1997; Filipek *et al.* 2000; Iovannone *et al.* 2003; Myers *et al.* 2007; National Research Council 2001; Sandall *et al.* 2005; Volkmar *et al.* 1999).

- Children with autism should participate in a comprehensive intervention program as soon as they are identified.
- All interventions and treatments should be based on sound theoretical constructs, robust methodologies, and empirical studies of effectiveness.
- Medical treatments are not a substitute for behavioral and educational interventions, which are currently the benchmark interventions for autism (Filipek *et al.* 2006; Howlin 2005; National Research Council 2001). However, medication may be effective for some children with ASD if they display challenging behaviors such as aggression or hyperactivity that can interfere with school learning and adjustment.
- Research indicates that in the absence of other interventions with established efficacy, early intensive behavioral intervention (EIBI) should be the preferred approach for children with autism (Eldevik *et al.* 2009; National Research Council 2001; Rogers and Vismara 2008).
- There is a lack of scientific evidence to support the use of complementary and alternative therapies (CAM) such as elimination diets and vitamin therapy for ASD (Myers *et al.* 2007).
- Sensory interventions, including SI, sensory stimulation approaches, and AIT have not been objectively validated for use with ASD.

- Intervention research cannot predict, at the present time, which particular intervention approach works best with which children. No single approach, intervention strategy, or treatment is effective for all children with ASD, and not all children will receive the same level of benefit.
- Parents and family members should to be involved in the intervention; including setting goals and priorities for their child's treatment and supporting their child's newly acquired skills in home and community activities (National Research Council 2001).
- Evidence is accumulating in the empirical literature that, at least under some conditions, children with ASD can benefit reliably from social skills training interventions when implemented appropriately. We also know enough about promoting social interaction development that it should be a standard component of any educational intervention program for children with ASD (Bellini *et al.* 2007; McConnell 2002).
- Data is not available on the differential responsiveness of children with AS and high-functioning autism (HFA) to specific interventions (Carpenter, Soorya, and Halpern 2009). Treatments for impairments in pragmatic (social) language and social skills are the same for both groups of children.

Quick Reference

Questions to ask about ASD interventions and treatments

- Is there reliable evidence to support the effectiveness of the intervention?
- Has it been scientifically validated?
- What is the rationale or underlying purpose of the intervention/ treatment?
- Does the intervention/treatment focus on one particular aspect or is it a general comprehensive approach?
- Is there excessive media publicity surrounding the intervention/ treatment?
- How successful has the intervention been for children in the general classroom and how have they performed?
- How will the treatment/intervention be integrated into the child's educational program? (Do not become preoccupied with an intervention to the extent that the curriculum and social skills are ignored).
- Is there a risk that the treatment will result in harm to the child?
- What assessment procedures are involved?
- Do school personnel have experience with the intervention? What training is required?
- How are activities planned and organized? Are there predictable daily schedules and routines?

Source: National Institute of Mental Health (2004).

Chapter 6

BEST PRACTICE
IN SPECIAL NEEDS
EDUCATION

The IEP should be the vehicle for planning and implementing educational objectives and services.

Mental health professionals, educators, and policy makers throughout the international community recognize that educational programs are essential to providing effective services to children with ASD. Educational provision is considered to be the most effective treatment for children with autism. However, educators are faced with some unique challenges. Children with autism have intellectual and academic profiles that can differ to a large degree. No two children are alike. As a result, no one program exists that will meet the needs of every child with autism. Additionally, children with autism learn differently than typical peers or children with other types of developmental disabilities. To meet the needs of the individual child, it is critical to examine the child's strengths, weaknesses, and unique needs when determining the appropriate educational placement and developing a program of special services. This chapter is based, to a large extent, on the report of the United States Committee on Interventions for Children with Autism for a discussion of the key components of a comprehensive, individualized program for a child with autism (National Research Council 2001). Readers are referred to this excellent resource for an overview of educational goals, evidence-based interventions, policy, legal, and research issues in the education of children with autism.

BEST PRACTICE

Children with any identified ASD, regardless of severity, should be eligible for special educational services under the category of autism spectrum disorders, as opposed to other terminology used by school systems (e.g. other health impaired, developmentally delayed, neurologically impaired).

SPECIAL EDUCATION LAW

Individuals with Disabilities Education Act (IDEA)

There has been a global increase in legislation and policies concerning the development and implementation of special educational services for children with ASD (Volkmar 2005). Although there are differences in international perspectives, there continues to be a movement toward earlier identification, treatment, and the inclusion of children with ASD in mainstream schools. As previously discussed, the specific criteria for autism differ among the various diagnostic and classification systems. Unlike the *DSM-IV-TR*, which is intended as a diagnostic and classification system for psychiatric disorders, the *IDEA* is federal legislation enacted to ensure the appropriate education of children with special educational needs. The *IDEA* also recognizes only a limited number of disability categories. The definitions of these categories, including autism, are controlling in terms of determining eligibility for special educational services in US schools (Individuals with Disabilities Education Improvement Act 2004). As defined by *IDEA* 2004, the term "child with a disability" means a child: "with mental retardation, hearing impairments (including deafness), speech or language impairments, visual impairments (including blindness), serious emotional disturbance, orthopedic impairments, autism, traumatic brain injury, other health impairments, or specific learning disabilities; and who, by reason thereof, needs special education and related services". The definitions of all 13 disability categories are included in Appendix E. According to the *IDEA* regulations, the definition of autism is as follows:

(c)(1)(i) Autism means a developmental disability significantly affecting verbal and nonverbal communication and social interaction, generally evident before age 3, that adversely affects a child's educational performance. Other characteristics often associated with autism are engagement in repetitive activities and stereotyped movements, resistance to environmental change or change in daily routines, and unusual responses to sensory experiences. The term does not apply if a child's educational performance is adversely affected primarily because the child has an emotional disturbance, as defined in this section.

(ii) A child who manifests the characteristics of "autism" after age 3 could be diagnosed as having "autism" if the criteria in paragraph (c) (1)(i) of this section are satisfied.

The *IDEA* shares a number of features with the *DSM-IV*. Both are categorical rather than dimensional systems of classification (e.g. a child meets or does not meet criteria). They focus on the description rather than the function of behavior and have been used in legal decision making regarding special education placement and clinical treatment. Both definitions of autism include deficits in the autistic triad of social reciprocity, communication, and restricted pattern of behavior/interests. The *DSM-IV* conceptualizes a pervasive developmental disorder (PDD) as a clinically significant syndrome or pattern associated with disability or impairment in one or more important areas of functioning (American Psychiatric Association 2000). Appendix F shows the *DSM-IV-TR* diagnostic criteria for autistic disorder, Asperger' disorder, and pervasive developmental disorder not otherwise specified (PDDNOS). The *IDEA* definition also requires that the core behaviors of autism impair or have a negative impact on the child's educational performance. Of course, all spectrum disorders are characterized by significant functional impairments and it is rare that a child with ASD will not need special education and related services (National Research Council 2001). Therefore, the National Research Council (2001) recommends that all children identified with ASD be made eligible for special educational services under the *IDEA* category of autism. An important difference between the two systems of classification involves the age of student. Unlike the *DSM-IV*, which requires onset of symptoms prior to age three, *IDEA* does not preclude a diagnosis or classification at a later age. This is especially important because many capable children with ASD are not diagnosed in early childhood and can be identified for special education at later ages. At the present time, the educational definition of autism is sufficiently broad and operationally acceptable to accommodate both the clinical and educational descriptions of higher-functioning ASD such as Asperger syndrome and PDDNOS.

Despite the similarities between the two systems, school professionals should be aware that while the *DSM-IV* is considered the primary authority in the fields of psychiatric and psychological diagnoses, the *IDEA* definition is the controlling authority with regard to eligibility decisions for special education (Fogt, Miller, and Zirkel 2003; Mandlawitz 2002). While the *DSM-IV* criteria are professionally helpful, they are neither legally required nor sufficient for determining educational placement. School professionals should make sure that children meet the criteria for autism as outlined by *IDEA* and use the *DSM-IV* to the extent that the diagnostic criteria include the same core behaviors (e.g. difficulties with social interaction, difficulties with communication, and the frequent exhibition of repetitive behaviors or circumscribed interests). We should remember that when it comes to special education, it is state and federal education codes and regulations (not *DSM IV-TR*) that drive eligibility decisions (Fogt *et al.* 2003).

IDEA and SEN

As with *IDEA* in the United States, the concept of special educational needs (SEN) in many countries differs from that of a clinical or psychiatric perspective. For example, in England, the *SEN Code of Practice* (Department for Education and Employment 2001) specifies that children have special educational needs if they have a *learning difficulty* which requires that special educational provision be made for them. Children are considered to have a *learning difficulty* if they a) have a significantly greater difficulty in learning than the majority of children of the same age; or b) have a disability which prevents or hinders them from making use of educational facilities generally provided for children of the same age in schools within the area of the local education authority; and c) are under compulsory school age and fall within the definition at (a) or (b) above or would so do if special educational provision was not made for them (Department for Education and Employment 2001). In order to meet the continuum of students' special educational needs, a graduated approach is utilized that provides an increasing level of service designed to meet each student's unique needs. A legally binding Statement of Need may be formulated if the student is determined to have a special educational need requiring ongoing support beyond that which is generally provided in the school attended. The *SEN Code of Practice* does not define specific categories of special educational need per se. However, children generally have needs which fall into at least one of the following four areas: 1. communication and interaction; 2. cognition and learning; 3. behavior, emotional and social development, and 4. sensory and/or physical functioning (Department for Education and Employment 2001). Individual students may have needs which overlap two or more areas. The range of difficulties will typically include children with speech and language delay, impairments, or disorders; specific learning difficulties, such as dyslexia and dyspraxia; hearing impairment, and those who demonstrate features within the autistic spectrum.

> ## BEST PRACTICE
> The IEP is the cornerstone for the education of a child with ASD. It should identify the services a student needs so that he/she may grow and learn during the school year.

Individualized Education Program (IEP)

Federal law in the United States entitles all students with disabilities to a free appropriate public education (FAPE). Both the *IDEA* in the United States and the *SEN Code of Practice* in the United Kingdom require that when a child is identified as having special educational needs, he or she is provided with an individualized education program (or plan) that specifies the services the student will receive during the school year. Under the *SEN Code of Practice*, strategies employed to enable the child to progress are recorded within an Individual Education Plan (IEP) and include information about the short-term targets set for the child, teaching strategies and the provision to be implemented, time frame for the plan to be reviewed, and the outcome of the services.

Special education law in both the United States and United Kingdom recognizes that students with autism have special needs beyond that of academic functioning. In addition to outlining academic objectives and goals, the IEP includes interventions, modifications, behavioral supports, related services, and learning opportunities designed to assist the child throughout school and with transition to adulthood. The ongoing assessment of the child's progress in meeting his or her IEP objectives is required and a lack of objectively documented progress over a three-month period should be taken as an indication of the need to assess the effectiveness of program (National Research Council 2001).

> ## BEST PRACTICE
> A comprehensive IEP should be based on the student's strengths and weaknesses. Goals for a student with ASD usually include the areas of communication, social behavior, challenging behavior, and academic and functional skills.

Content of the IEP

The key to any child's education program lies in the objectives specified in the IEP and the manner in which they are addressed. Parents, teachers, and support professionals play a key role in the development, implementation, and evaluation of the child's IEP. All share in the responsibility for monitoring the student's progress toward meeting specific academic, social, and behavioral goals and objectives in the IEP. Although the type and intensity of services will vary, depending on the student's age, cognitive and language levels, behavioral needs, and family priorities, the IEP should address all areas in which a child needs educational assistance (Fouse 1999; Twachtman-Cullen and Twachtman-Reilly 2003). These include academic and nonacademic goals if the services will provide an educational benefit for the student. All areas of projected need, such as social skills, functional skills, and related services (occupational, speech/language, or physical therapy), are incorporated in the IEP, together with the specific setting in which the services will be provided and the professionals who will provide the service. The content of an IEP must include the following (Individuals with Disabilities Education Improvement Act 2004):

- a statement of the child's present level of educational performance (both academic and nonacademic aspects of his or her performance)
- specific goals and objectives designed to provide the appropriate educational services. This includes a statement of annual goals that the student may be expected to reasonably meet during the coming academic year, together with a series of measurable, intermediate objectives for each goal
- appropriate objective criteria, evaluation procedures, and schedules for determining, at least annually, whether the child is achieving the specific objectives detailed in the IEP
- a description of all specific special education and related services, including individualized instruction and related supports and services to be provided (e.g. counseling, occupational, physical, and speech/language therapy; transportation) and the extent to which the child will participate in regular educational programs with typical peers
- the initiation date and duration of each of the services to be provided (including extended school year services)
- if the student is 16 years of age or older, the IEP must include a description of transitional services (coordinated set of activities designed to assist the student in movement from school to post-school activities).

Appendix G provides a sample of IEP goals and objectives. Tips on writing and developing measurable IEP goals for learners with autism are available from the Life Journey through Autism series (Myles *et al.* 2005); Twachtman-Cullen and Twachtman-Reilly (2003); Fouse (1999), and other resources listed in Appendix H.

SPECIAL PROGRAMS AND SERVICES

> ## BEST PRACTICE
> Communication deficits are a core feature of ASD and an important component in special education programming.

Communication and language skills

Because language and communication deficits are a core feature of ASD, speech/language therapy is an important component of special educational programming (Attwood 2006; National Research Council 2001; Stone 2006; Stone and Yoder 2001; Twachtman-Cullen 1998). School professionals must be aware of the multifaceted nature of communication and the challenges associated with teaching children to be competent communicators. Given the relationship between language skills and other academic and social domains, comprehensive language treatment programs are likely to make a significant impact on long-term outcomes, such as academic achievement, adaptive behavior, and social development. Thus, effective interventions designed to teach social-communication skills should be included in the programs of all students with ASD (H. Goldstein 2002).

Although many children with ASD have some delay in the development of speech (articulation and grammar), the problems are primarily in the area of pragmatic (social) language, semantics (meaning), and prosody (voice characteristics). Children with pragmatic language deficits may fail to use appropriate nonverbal communication skills, such as eye contact, and have impairments in comprehension, or generally have difficulty communicating with others. Services provided by a speech/language pathologist are usually appropriate to address these deficits in social communication. However, traditional, "pull-out" service delivery models frequently lack the required intensity. Speech/language pathologists are likely to be most effective when they collaborate with teachers, other support personnel, families, and the student's peers to promote functional communication in natural settings (classroom).

> ## BEST PRACTICE
> Educational programs for children with ASD should incorporate appropriately structured physical and sensory environments within the context of functional educational goals to accommodate any unique sensory processing patterns.

Occupational therapy

Although not all children with ASD have sensory issues, these types of difficulties, when present, may interfere with performance in many developmental and functional domains across home and school contexts. Best practice guidelines indicate that when needed, educational programs for children with ASD should integrate an appropriately structured physical and sensory milieu in order to accommodate any unique sensory processing patterns. Research on the efficacy of occupational therapy for children with ASD, as noted earlier, is inconclusive. Although sensory integration (SI) therapy is often used in isolation, the interventions to address sensory-related problems should not substitute for the core educational curricula and when utilized, should be viewed as supplementary activities integrated at various levels into the student's individualized educational program (IEP). Comprehensive educational programming may also benefit from consultation with knowledgeable professionals (e.g. occupational therapists, speech/language therapists, physical therapists, adaptive physical educators) to provide guidance about potential interventions for children whose sensory processing or motoric difficulties interfere with educational performance.

> **BEST PRACTICE**
>
> Social skills training should be a central component of educational programming for students with ASD. The type of skill deficit (performance versus skill acquisition) should be considered when developing a social skills intervention plan.

Social skills training

Impairment in social functioning is a predominant feature of ASD that is well documented in the literature (Attwood 2006; Myles *et al.* 2005; Rogers 2000). Social skills deficits include difficulties with initiating interactions, maintaining reciprocity, taking another person's perspective, and inferring the interests of others. Research evidence suggests that when appropriately planned and delivered, social skills training programs have the potential to produce positive effects in the social interactions of children with ASD (Rao, Beidel, and Murray 2008). Unfortunately, few children with ASD receive consistent and intensive social skills programming in school (Hume, Bellini, and Pratt 2005). This is problematic, especially considering that social impairments may result in negative outcomes, such as poor academic achievement, social failure, isolation, and peer rejection. (Bellini 2006; La Greca and Lopez 1998; Tantam 2000; Welsh *et al.* 2001). Likewise, social skills deficits interfere with the ability to establish meaningful social relationships, which often leads to withdrawal and coexisting (comorbid) anxiety and depression. Because social skills are critical to successful social, emotional, and cognitive development and long-term outcomes, best practice indicates that social skills programming should be an integral component of educational programming for all children with ASD (National Research Council 2001).

Social skills training involves teaching specific skills (e.g. maintaining eye contact, initiating conversation) through behavioral and social learning techniques (Cooper, Griffith, and Filer 1999; McConnell 2002). Goals typically include skill acquisition, performance, generalization and maintenance of prosocial behaviors, and the reduction or elimination of competing behaviors. Social skills training approaches have been reported to be an effective component of treatment programs for many childhood disorders, including childhood social phobia (Spence, Donovan, and Brechman-Toussaint 2000) and specific learning disabilities (Forness and Kavale 1999). Most often, schools are expected to assume the responsibility of delivering social skills training programs to children with social skills deficits, because these impairments significantly interfere with social relationships and have an adverse effect on academic performance (Welsh *et al.* 2001). Although equipped to teach social skills, implementing social skills programming can be challenging for school personnel (teachers, therapists, psychologists, social workers), who often have limited time and resources. Recent meta-analysis research suggests that the effectiveness of social skills training can be enhanced by increasing the quantity (or intensity) of social skills interventions, providing instruction in the child's natural setting, matching the intervention strategy with the type of skill deficit, and ensuring treatment integrity (Bellini *et al.* 2007; Gresham, Sugai, and Horner 2001). Group-based social skills training is also considered a promising intervention approach for use with children with ASD because it provides the opportunity to practice newly learned skills in a relatively naturalistic format that may promote interaction with other children (Barry *et al.* 2003) The National Association of School Psychologists (2002) recommends the following when developing a social skills intervention strategy:

- Avoid a "one size fits all" approach and adapt the intervention to meet the needs of the individual or particular group.
- Focus on facilitating the desirable social behavior as well as eliminating the undesirable behavior.
- Emphasize the learning, performance, generalization, and maintenance of appropriate social behaviors through modeling, coaching, and role-playing.

- Employ primarily positive strategies and add corrective strategies only if the positive approach is unsuccessful and the behavior is of a serious and/or dangerous nature.
- Provide social skills training and practice opportunities in a number of settings with different individuals in order to encourage students to generalize new skills to multiple, real life situations.
- Use assessment strategies, including functional assessments of behavior, to identify children in need of more intensive interventions as well as target skills for instruction.
- Enhance social skills by increasing the frequency of an appropriate behavior in "normal" environments to address the naturally occurring causes and consequences.
- Include parents and caregivers as significant participants in developing and selecting interventions (they can help reinforce the skills taught at school to further promote generalization across settings).

The *type* of skill deficit (performance deficit versus skill deficit) should be considered when developing a social skills intervention plan. A *performance deficit* refers to a skill or behavior that is present but not demonstrated or performed, whereas a *skill acquisition deficit* refers to the absence of a particular skill or behavior. School professionals should make an intensive effort to systematically match the intervention strategy to the type of skill deficit exhibited by the child (Bellini *et al.* 2007). For instance, if the child lacks the skills necessary to join in an interaction with peers, an intervention strategy should be selected that promotes skill acquisition. In contrast, if the child has the skills to join in an activity but regularly fails to do so, a strategy should be selected that enhances the performance of the existing skill. The reader is invited to see Bellini (2008) for a comprehensive discussion of how to differentiate between a skill and a performance deficit, and for a list of social skills intervention strategies that promote skill acquisition and those that enhance the performance of existing skills.

BEST PRACTICE

Social skills instruction should be delivered throughout the day in various natural settings, using specific activities and interventions designed to meet age-appropriate, individualized social goals. Teachers should model, demonstrate, or role-play the appropriate social interaction skills.

Social skills in the classroom

Teachers should not assume that students with ASD understand the appropriate, socially accepted behavior for interacting with peers and adults. Effective prevention of challenging social behavior can be addressed through arranging the classroom environment and/or by adapting instruction and the curriculum. Changing the classroom environment or instruction may lessen the triggers or events that set off the challenging behavior. Teaching effective social interaction and communication as replacements for challenging behavior is also a preventive strategy for improving little used student social interaction and communication skills. Teachers can model, demonstrate, coach, or role-play the appropriate interaction skills. They can teach students to ask for help during difficult activities or negotiate alternative times to finish work. Encouraging positive social interactions such as conversational skills will help students with challenging behavior to effectively obtain positive peer attention. The following are examples of techniques for improving social skills and prosocial behaviors in the classroom (Vaughn *et al.* 2005).

Initiating interactions

Teachers might notice that when a student enters the classroom, group activity, or other social interaction, he or she may have difficulty greeting other students or starting a conversation. For example, they may joke, call each other names, laugh, or say something inappropriate. In this situation the student may have trouble initiating interactions or conversations. The teacher might talk to the student individually and offer suggestions for ways he or she can provide an appropriate greeting or introduce a topic of conversation.

> *Example:* "Why don't you ask students what they did last night, tell them about a TV show you watched, or ask if they finished their homework, rather than saying 'Hey, Stupid.' Students want to be your friend, but you make it difficult for them to talk with you."

Maintaining interactions

Many students with ASD struggle to maintain a conversation (e.g. turn taking). Some may dominate the conversation and make others feel that they have nothing to contribute, while other students may experience difficulty keeping up with the flow of conversation and asking questions. Students may also have limited topics of interest and discuss these topics repetitively.

> *Example:* "I've noticed that other students cannot share their thoughts and ideas with you when you start a conversation because you do all the talking. It may seem to them that you don't care what they have to say. Other students will be more willing to talk if you stop once you've

stated your idea or opinion and allow them a turn to talk. When you stop, they know you are listening. You can say to them, 'What do you think?' or 'Has this ever happened to you?'"

Terminating interactions

Some students with ASD may not know how to appropriately end a conversation. They may abruptly walk away, start talking with another student, or bluntly tell a student they don't know what they're talking about. Other students may interpret this as rude and impolite behavior. Teachers might point out to the student some acceptable ways of ending a conversation.

> *Example*: "You just walked away from that student when they were talking. Rather than walk away, you might say 'I have to go now,' 'It's time for my next class,' Or 'I'll see you later and we can finish our talk.'"

Recognizing body language

The recognition of body language or nonverbal cues is critical to successful social interactions. Students with ASD typically have difficulty interpreting these cues from teachers or other students. Body language tells students when they violate a person's personal space, a person needs to leave, or they need to change behavior. Teachers can incorporate these skills into their class time or school day.

> *Example*: Before leaving the classroom, demonstrate nonverbal cues by holding a finger to your lips and telling students that means "quiet," a hand held up with palm facing outward means "wait" or "stop," and both hands pushing downward means "slow down." You may need to demonstrate facial expressions you use to "deliver messages" and what they mean. Other students can demonstrate nonverbal cues they use. When students move through the halls, you may want to teach them the "arms length" rule for personal space.

Transitions

Many students with ASD have significant problems changing from one activity to the next or moving from one location to another. They may be easily upset by abrupt changes in routine and unable to estimate how much time is left to finish an activity and begin the next one. Poor executive function skills such as disorganization may also prevent them from putting materials away from the last activity or getting ready for the next activity. They may also need closure and preparation time for the transition. Problems arise if the teacher tries to push them to transition at the last minute. Some of these problems can be avoided if:

- the routine for making transitions is consistent
- the routine for making transitions is rehearsed ahead of time
- students are given 5–10 minute notices before the transition must be made
- a daily visual schedule is posted and reviewed throughout the day or class period
- students' individual schedules are posted or kept on or near their desks, if they differ from the class schedule. Individual schedules are reviewed with students after each activity or period
- changes are made on the posted classroom schedule and students' individual schedules to reflect any changes in the routine
- materials for activities are organized and easily accessible.

Example. About 10 minutes prior to the transition, refer to the classroom schedule and announce when the bell will ring or when the next activity will begin. Provide a 5-minute and then a 1-minute warning. This countdown helps students finish assignments or end favorite activities. For students that have difficulty getting started after a transition, place assignment folders on their desks so that they have their assignments and don't have to wait for instructions or materials. They can use the same folder to submit assignments (the folders can be left on their desks at the end of the period).

Some promising strategies for teaching social skills based on current research are shown in Table 6.1. You will also find several social skills programs appropriate for school-age children in the Appendix H listing of resources.

Behavior intervention plan (BIP)

Students with ASD who demonstrate serious and persistent behavioral challenges should be provided with an individual behavior support plan. The *IDEA* stipulates that a functional behavior assessment (FBA) be completed and a behavior intervention (or support) plan (BIP) implemented for students with disabilities when they are the subject of school discipline proceedings or being considered for an alternative placement. *IDEA* also requires that positive behavioral support programming be provided to eligible students who are in need; particularly when the behavior impedes learning or the learning of others.

As we have seen, functional behavior assessment (FBA) is an important component of providing positive behavioral support to students with ASD.

BEST PRACTICE

Functional assessment is a well-established tool for identifying and developing behavior intervention plans for students with ASD. Interventions developed from functional assessment information are more likely to result in significant behavior reduction.

Table 6.1 Promising strategies for teaching social skills

Goal	Strategies
Increase social motivation	Encourage self-awareness Intersperse new skills with previously mastered skills Begin with simple, easily learned skills
Increase social initiations	Make social rules clear and concrete Model age-appropriate initiation strategies Use natural reinforcers for social initiations Teach simple social "scripts" for common situations
Improve appropriate social responding	Teach social response scripts Reinforce response attempts Use modeling and role-play to teach skills
Reduce interfering behaviors	Make teaching structured and predictable Differentially reinforce positive behaviors Teach self-management skills Keep behavior charts for positive behavior Review socially appropriate and inappropriate behaviors via video or audiotape
Promote skill generalization	Coordinate peer involvement (e.g. prompting and initiating social interactions, physical proximity) Use several individuals with whom to practice skills Involve parents in training and practice Provide opportunities to apply learned skills in safe, natural settings (e.g. field trips) Use time between sessions to practice skills

Note: Adapted with kind permission from Springer Science and Business Media: *Journal of Autism and Developmental Disorders.* Social Skills Development in Children with Autism Disorders: A review of intervention research, 37, 2007, p. 1864, S. W. White, K. Koening, and L. Scahill, Copyright Springer Science and Business Media, LLC 2006.

FBA methods are considered best practice in identifying and designing behavioral interventions. A consistent finding has been that intervention plans developed from functional assessment information are more likely to result in a significant reduction of challenging behavior (Carr *et al.* 1999; Dunlap and Fox 1999; Horner *et al.* 2002).

An important goal of a functional assessment is to identify antecedents or environmental situations that will predict the occurrence and nonoccurrence of the student's challenging behavior. Another goal is to obtain and expand information that will improve the effectiveness and efficiency of intervention strategies. FBA identifies the function(s) that the behavior appears to serve for the student. For example, students might exhibit challenging behaviors with the goal of escape or the goal of seeking attention. When the curriculum is difficult or demanding, students may attempt to avoid or escape work through their behavior (e.g. refusal, passive aggression, disruption, etc.). They may also use challenging behavior to get attention from adults and peers. Because students with ASD have significant social and pragmatic skills deficits, they may experience difficulty effectively communicating their needs or influencing the environment. Thus, challenging classroom behavior may serve a purpose for communicating or a communicative function. When we understand the goal of student behavior then we can begin to teach alternative replacement behavior and new interactional skills.

The process of conducting an FBA is best described as 1. a strategy to discover the purposes, goals, or functions of a student's behavior; 2. an attempt to identify the conditions under which the behavior is most likely and least likely to occur; 3. a process for developing a useful understanding of how a student's behavior is influenced by or relates to the environment; and 4. an attempt to identify clear, predictive relationships between events in the student's environments and occurrences of challenging behavior and the contingent events that maintain the problem behavior. An FBA can be conducted in a variety of ways. There are two general assessment tools to assist in the collection of information about the variables and events that surround the occurrence (or nonoccurrence) of the student's challenging behavior. The first are interviews and rating scales that provide information from the individuals (parents, teachers) who know the student best, along with the student themselves. The second method is direct observation of the student in his or her natural daily environments. One observation strategy for collecting observational information is the **A-B-C** format. The observer records the **A**ntecedent to the behavior (what happened immediately before the behavior), describes the **B**ehavior, and the **C**onsequence of the behavior (what happened immediately after). Figure 6.1 shows a sample of an **A-B-C** recording form. The following steps are a general guide to developing a comprehensive student behavior intervention or support plan (*Autism Spectrum Disorders Handbook* 2006).

- Development of the plan should begin with a functional assessment of the problem behavior to understand the student and the nature of the challenging behavior in the context of the environment.
- Next, the professional team examines the results of the functional assessment and develops hypothesis statements as to why the student engages in the challenging behavior. The hypothesis statement is an informed, assessment-based explanation of the challenging behavior that indicates the possible function or functions served for the student.
- Once developed, the hypothesis provides the foundation for the development of intervention strategies. The focus of intervention plan is not only on behavior reduction, but for also teaching appropriate, functional (generally communicative) skills that serve as alternative/replacement behaviors for the undesirable behavior (Carr *et al.* 2002).
- Once the plan has been implemented, the team regularly reviews and evaluates its effectiveness and makes modifications as needed.

Readers interested in a more thorough discussion of issues related to functional assessment and the effective treatment of children with autism are referred to Alberto and Troutman 2006; Chandler and Dahlquist 2002; O'Neill *et al.* 1997; and Repp and Horner 1999.

ABC Recording form

Student Name _____   School:_____

D.O.B.: _____ Grade: _____ Teacher: _____

Date	Time	Antecedent Describe the activity and specific events that were present before the behavior occurred?	Behavior Describe exactly what the student did or said	Consequence Describe the events, reactions, and responses that followed the behavior

Comments:

Figure 6.1 Sample of A-B-C recording form

BEST PRACTICE

Supporting the family is a critically important aspect of the overall management of ASD.

Family support

Best practice requires that families who are experiencing stress in parenting their child with ASD be referred to the appropriate community resource in order to access mental health support services (National Research Council 2001). Parents and siblings of children with ASD experience more stress and depression than those of children who are typically developing or even those who have other disabilities (Estes *et al.* 2009). Supporting the family and ensuring the system's emotional and physical health is a very important aspect of overall management of ASD (Myers *et al.* 2007). When families receive a diagnosis of autism, a period of anxiety, insecurity, and confusion often follows. Some autism specialists have suggested that parents go through stages of grief and mourning similar to the stages experienced with a loss of a loved one (e.g. fear, denial, anger, bargaining/guilt, depression, and acceptance). Understanding this process can help school professionals provide support to families in the effort to cope with their child's diagnosis.

Professionals can also provide support to parents by educating them about ASD; provide guidance and training; assist them in obtaining access to resources; provide emotional support by listening and talking through problems; and help advocate for their child's or sibling's needs (National Research Council 2001).

A major strategy for helping families with children with ASD is providing information on the access to ongoing supports and services. Formal supports include publicly funded, state-administrated programs such as early intervention, special education, vocational and residential/living services, and respite services. Local parent advocacy groups, national autism and related disability organizations, early intervention and special education administrators, and SEN coordinators are often knowledgeable about various programs and their respective eligibility requirements. On a more personal level, school professionals should give parents a realistic interpretation of ASD and help them to understand their child's level of cognitive and adaptive functioning. It is also important to communicate the student's strengths and weaknesses and assure parents that they are not responsible for their child's social-communication deficits. Importantly, parents should be encouraged to play an active role in developing and implementing intervention plans and IEPs (Bloch, Weinstein, and Seitz 2005; Myers *et al.* 2007; Rogers and Vismara 2008).

BEST PRACTICE

Behavioral and educational interventions are currently the benchmark interventions for autism.

SUMMARY

Education is the most effective treatment for children with autism. To restate, the National Research Council recommends that all children identified with an ASD, regardless of subtype or severity, be considered eligible for special education services. Those school professionals most likely to be involved with assessments and the determination of autism eligibility (educational and school psychologists, speech/language pathologists) are advised to become thoroughly familiar with the criteria for autism specified in the *IDEA* and to keep in mind that the *DSM-IV* definition is not as a rule legally controlling (Fogt *et al.* 2003). The following are key components of a comprehensive educational program for a child with ASD (National Research Council 2001; Myles *et al.* 2005).

- An effective, comprehensive educational program should reflect an understanding and awareness of the challenges presented by autism.
- Parent—professional communication and collaboration are key components for making educational and treatment decisions.
- Ongoing training and education in autism is important for both parents and professionals. Professionals who are trained in specific methodology and techniques will be most effective in providing the appropriate services and in modifying curriculum based upon the unique needs of the individual child.
- Inclusion with typically developing peers is important for a child with ASD as peers provide the best models for language and social skills. However, inclusive education alone is insufficient, empirically based intervention and training is also necessary to address specific skill deficits.
- Assessment and progress monitoring of a student with ASD should be completed at specified intervals by an interdisciplinary team of professionals who have a knowledge base and experience in autism.
- A comprehensive IEP should be based on the child's unique pattern of strengths and weaknesses. Goals for a child with ASD commonly include the areas of communication, social behavior, adaptive skills, challenging behavior, and academic and functional skills. The IEP must address appropriate instructional and curricular modifications, together with related services such as counseling, occupational therapy, speech/language therapy, physical therapy and transportation needs. Transition goals must also be developed when the student reaches 16 years of age.
- Teaching social skills in the setting (classroom) in which they naturally occur is the most effective approach and helps the generalization of the skills to new environments.
- No single methodology is effective for all children with autism. Generally, it is best to integrate scientifically validated approaches according to a child's needs and responses.

The final chapter provides a discussion of the current status of the field, including intervention issues, programs, policy and training, and recommendations for future research.

Quick Reference

Comparison of DSM-IV and IDEA definitions of autism

	Social interaction	Communication	Behavior
DSM-IV:	Qualitative impairment in social interaction	Qualitative impairment in communication	Restricted repetitive and stereotyped patterns of behavior interests, and activities
IDEA:	A developmental disability that significantly affects social interaction	A developmental disability that significantly affects verbal and nonverbal communication	Engagement in repetitive activities and stereotyped movements, resistance to environmental change, change in daily routines, and unusual response to sensory experiences

Sources: American Psychiatric Association 2000. *Diagnostic and Statistical Manual of Mental Disorders* (4th edn text rev.) Washington, DC: APA. *Individuals with Disabilities Education Improvement Act of 2004*. Pub. L. No. 108–446, 108th Congress, 2nd Session. (2004).

Chapter 7

FUTURE DIRECTIONS AND CONCLUSION

Rapid developments in autism research require a periodic review of current best practices.

The multifaceted nature of autism, including coexisting disabilities, has significant implications for planning and intervention in the school, home, and community. Because the knowledge base in ASD is changing so rapidly, we are challenged to stay current with the latest methods of evaluation and treatment, acquire and become skilled with the most up-to-date screening and assessment tools, and maintain an awareness of community resources. Thus, one of the most critical needs is for both personnel preparation and ongoing education and training opportunities for all school professionals.

In addition to recognizing the red flags of autism, direct service providers such as teachers (regular and special education), speech/language pathologists, school and educational psychologists, and other support personnel must be familiar with current best practices for children with ASD. For example, some intervention and assessment procedures require a specific knowledge base and skills for successful implementation. It is important to ensure that service providers are skilled in effective best practice procedures across school, community, and home settings. Unfortunately, there continues to be a proliferation of unproven treatments and interventions in autism. School professionals are in of need accurate information in order to work with parents in identifying the most appropriate and effective intervention for the student. This requires a commitment on the part of all who work with children with ASD to periodically review current best practices and effectiveness research.

DIRECTIONS FOR FUTURE RESEARCH

Although there has been substantial progress in our understanding and treatment of children with autism over the past two decades, research is needed to improve early screening instruments, identify specific needs, and develop more effective intervention strategies (Klinger *et al.* 2003). There are several future research directions that are needed to help improve educational practice for children with autism. As we have seen, educational programs, behavioral techniques, cognitive approaches, social-learning approaches, and pharmacological interventions all have their place in the management of ASD. The challenge is to identify which interventions and programs have the best empirical support and value and for which children. It cannot be emphasized too often that there is no single best suited or universally effective intervention or treatment for all children and youth with ASD. The most effective programs are those that incorporate a variety of empirically supported practices and are designed to address and support the unique needs of individual students and families (National Research Council 2001).

Research is needed to examine the generalizability and transportability of interventions shown to be efficacious in research settings to the applied settings of home and school. This includes more research on the feasibility of using behavioral interventions in natural contexts by parents and teachers. Further research is also needed on how to ensure that functional assessments are conducted and used in the design of behavioral interventions and positive behavioral support. In addition to research on interventions that reduce or eliminate challenging behavior, attention should also be focused on the prevention of problem behaviors in the classroom and at home (Reeve and Carr 2000).

From the ages of 6 to 12, the child with ASD faces many challenges with transitions to new learning environments and contact with new peers and adults. As we saw in Sally's case, the social-communication domains of development become more divergent from typical expectations as the student with ASD progresses through school. Deficits in social interaction skills are the core, underlying feature of ASD and continue to be a major challenge for educators and parents (Weiss and Harris 2001). It is somewhat surprising that relatively few structured or manualized school-based social skills programs have been designed specifically for elementary school children with ASD. While there is preliminary support to suggest that social skills training may increase a student's awareness of social cues and his or her understanding of how to interact appropriately with peers, we have little information about how this knowledge is applied in the context of everyday situations. Thus, an important area for future research is to evaluate the generalization of social skills from training groups to the classroom. There is also a critical need for documenting the longer-term outcomes of social skills interventions for children with autism as well as publicized strategies such as the use of social stories and visual schedules.

A related area of investigation involves the accessibility of scientifically supported interventions. While many effective approaches are described in the literature, they are not often readily available to special educators. Teachers have difficulty developing effective intervention plans because empirical procedures used in research do not translate into real-world classroom application. Most are published in peer-reviewed scientific journals, which abbreviate the descriptions of the interventions and do not provide enough detail to permit replication in the classroom. We need to develop effective and efficient consumer friendly intervention strategies that are specifically designed and packaged for utilization in schools, community settings, and at home (Rogers 2000). Research should inform practice. Utilizing a research-to-practice framework will do much to enhance the development of effective interventions for children ASD in home and school settings.

Both clinical practice and research indicate a pressing need to examine the similarities and differences between boys and girls with ASD (Attwood 2006; Wilkinson 2008a). Although boys in our schools are being referred and identified in greater numbers, this is not the case for girls (Attwood 2006; Ehlers and Gillberg 1993; Wagner 2006). As noted earlier, referrals for evaluation of boys with higher-functioning ASD such as Asperger syndrome are ten times higher than for girls (Attwood 2006). Girls are also diagnosed with autism spectrum disorders at later ages relative to boys (Goin-Kochel et al. 2006). This gender gap should be empirically investigated as it raises serious questions regarding identification practices and delivery of services. If girls process language and social information differently than boys, then clinical and educational interventions based largely on research with boys may be inappropriate (Wilkinson 2008a). As a result, girls with ASD may receive less than optimal academic and behavioral interventions.

The success of intervention plans is largely dependent on the extent to which an intervention is implemented as intended or planned or what has been termed *treatment integrity* (Gresham 1989; Lane et al. 2004). As we saw earlier, literature reviews indicate that the measurement of treatment integrity is more the exception than the rule. Reporting treatment integrity is not only essential from a methodological point of view but from practical one as well. An absence of treatment integrity data makes it very difficult to determine whether a social skills intervention was unsuccessful because it is an ineffective strategy or because the intervention was poorly implemented. Without treatment fidelity, even empirically based interventions may fail. The social significance of the intervention outcomes or *social validity* is also of critical importance. Consumers (parents and teachers) must feel assured that the selected intervention strategies are effective and appropriate, and that the social objectives are important for the child to achieve. If the intervention lacks social validity, consumers are less likely to apply the effort necessary to implement the intervention, thus reducing intervention fidelity. Educators, parents and families expect (and hope) that research will produce interventions and treatments that will improve quality of life of children affected by autism. Thus, the measurement of treatment integrity and social validity should be a standard feature of intervention research.

CONCLUSION

The majority of children with autism are educated within the public school system, most often in general education classes, either full or part time. Teachers are now expected to instruct children with special educational needs who are included in their classroom. However, many do not have formal training in educating and intervening with children with ASD. Among the most pressing challenges is the need for more coordinated efforts among the various professionals for the training of teachers in evidence-based instruction and behavioral management practices, and for greater attention to the emotional and social well-being of children with ASD. While academic learning is important, this objective should not replace the need for developing social-communication skills. As our scientific knowledge and thinking about ASD continues to develop, professionals such as school and educational psychologists, behavior interventionists, social workers, and speech/language pathologists will play an increasingly important role in the educational programming of children with ASD by providing support, information, and recommendations to teachers, other school personnel and administrators, and families (Williams *et al.* 2005). Likewise, school professionals will be called on to provide consultation as to best practice in assessment and intervention. Therefore, it is critically important to remain current with the research and up to date on scientifically supported approaches that have direct application to the educational setting. While avoiding claims of cures or recovery, school professionals can help to ensure that the student with ASD receives an effective educational program. By being knowledgeable about assessment, intervention, and treatment approaches, including their strengths and limitations, we can help to form cohesive educational support networks for children with ASD (Bryson *et al.* 2003). It is hoped that this guide has made a contribution towards this goal.

FREQUENTLY ASKED QUESTIONS

1. What is the cause of autism spectrum disorders (ASD)?

Autism is a neurobiological disorder of unknown cause. There are no biological markers or laboratory tests that can reliably diagnose autism. Growing evidence suggest that genetic factors play a significant role in its etiology. Although autism may be associated with a variety of genetic mechanisms and no particular environmental factors have been scientifically validated, ongoing studies are examining a possible gene-environmental connection.

2. Do all children with ASD require special education?

It is rare for a child diagnosed with ASD not to need special educational services. All children and youth diagnosed or classified with ASD will benefit from individualized and specialized objectives and plans. According to the National Research Council (2001), a child who receives a diagnosis of any ASD should be eligible for special educational programming under the educational category of "autism," regardless of the specific diagnostic category within the autism spectrum (autistic disorder, Asperger's disorder, atypical autism, PDDNOS). Research supports the importance of initiating educational service as soon as a child is suspected of having an ASD.

3. What are the long-term outcomes for students with ASD?

There is no cure for autism. A diagnosis of ASD remains fairly stable throughout adolescence and adulthood. Although research has demonstrated substantial progress in response to scientifically based interventions over a relatively short period of time, few longitudinal studies have examined the long-term outcomes for children with ASD. Outcomes tend to be variable, with some children making significant improvement and gains and others showing little progress. However, recent research suggests that there is a trend toward improved outcomes for individuals with ASD in general. Increased opportunities for early intervention, improved educational programs and services, and parent and family support substantially increase the possibility of a more favorable outcome.

4. What is the difference between autism and Asperger syndrome?

Although autism and Asperger's disorder are classified as separate disorders by the *DSM-IV-TR*, there is continued debate whether there are clear, distinct boundaries between the two. Difficulties diagnosing Asperger's disorder using current *DSM-IV-TR* criteria center mainly on the differentiation from autistic disorder. Conceptually, it is difficult to identify individuals with significant impairment in social and behavioral domains that do not have some degree of accompanying communication deficits. Thus, it is possible that those who meet *DSM-IV-TR* criteria for Asperger's disorder may also meet the criteria for autistic disorder. Researchers continue to question the difference between Asperger's disorder and autism, and suggest that approaching the disorders as part of a continuum may be more appropriate. At the present time, empirical and clinical evidence suggest that there are no reliable methods of clearly distinguishing between autism without intellectual disability (high-functioning autism: HFA) and Asperger syndrome.

5. How early should intervention begin for children with ASD?

Researchers and practitioners suggest that children identified with autism should begin intensive behavioral treatment and receive educational services as early as possible in order to achieve the best possible outcomes. Specialized instruction should occur in a setting in which ongoing interventions occur with typically developing children. There is evidence that the early initiation of services is associated with a greater response to intervention and positive changes in language, social, or cognitive outcomes.

6. What's the difference between EIBI and early intervention?

Early Intensive Behavioral Intervention (EIBI) generally refers to interventions and programs that use a behavioral approach such as applied behavior analysis (ABA). These behavioral approaches may be varied and include any method that emphasizes changes in behavior in systematic and measurable ways. Early intervention models may include developmental approaches, or a combination of both developmental and behavioral components. Although there is no research to suggest that one model is superior to another, as a group these early intervention approaches can make a significant difference for many children on the autism spectrum.

7. Who should provide assessment services to children with ASD?

Both interdisciplinary and multidisciplinary processes stress the importance of gathering information from a variety of disciplines that provide unique knowledge of a particular aspect of the child and family. Professionals most often involved in the assessment and delivery of services to children with ASD include educational and school psychologists, clinical psychologists, psychiatrists, neurologists, pediatricians, speech/language pathologists, audiologists, occupational therapists, physical therapists, social workers, behavior interventionists, and special education teachers.

8. Can ASD occur with other childhood disorders?

Research suggests that anxiety and depression are more common in children with ASD than in the general population. Research estimates of coexisting (comorbid) anxiety and/or depression in individuals with ASD are as high as 65 percent. Although the *DSM-IV-TR* hierarchical rules prohibit the concurrent diagnosis of ASD/PDD and attention-deficit/hyperactivity disorder (ADHD), there is a relatively high frequency of impulsivity and inattention in children with higher-functioning ASD. ADHD is a relatively common initial diagnosis in young children with ASD. Some researchers have suggested that a subgroup of individuals on the autism spectrum also has ADHD.

9. Are interventions different for Asperger syndrome and HFA?

High-functioning autism (HFA) is not an official diagnostic category, but rather a description of a subset of individuals with autistic disorder who have relatively intact cognitive and language abilities. At present, research data are not available on the differential responsiveness of children with Asperger syndrome and HFA to empirically supported interventions and treatment. Interventions for pragmatic (social) language and social skills deficits are essentially the same for children with AS and HFA.

10. At what age do children develop ASD?

Autism is a lifelong disorder that begins in early childhood. Although normally present from birth, the age at which symptoms become apparent varies significantly. Research suggests that children with ASD may show signs of the disorder by 2 to 3 years of age. There is emerging evidence that both autistic disorder and Asperger's disorder can be diagnosed before 3 years of age. Advances have been made in identifying behavioral indicators as well as atypical development in children between the ages of 24 and 30 months who are later diagnosed with ASD. Parents and educators should be aware of the red flags that might indicate an ASD. Common signs of autistic disorder include:

- does not smile by the age of six months
- does not respond to his or her name
- does not cry
- does not babble or use gestures by 12 months
- does not point to objects by 12 months
- does not use words by 16 months
- does not use two-word phrases by 24 months
- regresses after mastering skills/loses previously mastered skills
- delays in milestones like crawling and walking.

11. Are sensory issues part of the diagnostic criteria for ASD?

Although unusual sensory reactions are apparent in some children with ASD, they are neither universal nor specific to the diagnosis of ASD. However, a lack of responsiveness, hypersensitivity to noise and the taste and texture of foods, and insensitivities to pain are more commonly observed in children with ASD than other developmental disabilities. Although sensory differences are not a specific indicator of ASD (nontriadic), their presence, together with impairments in social and communication skills, are helpful to identification and intervention planning.

12. To what extent do children with ASD have speech and language problems?

Impairment in communication is a core feature of ASD. It is important to stress the concept of "communication" in contrast to the more common focus of speech and language assessment and intervention. Although the range of language skills exhibited by children with ASD is varied, the primary difficulty is with communication or the use of pragmatic language. This is most evident in children described as having Asperger's disorder (who often have relatively intact structural language skills) and high-functioning autism (HFA).

13. What are the reasons for the dramatic increase in the number of children identified with ASD?

Contrary to popular reports of an autism "epidemic," the increase in prevalence over the last ten years is mostly due to better identification practices, broadening of the diagnostic criteria, diagnosis at an earlier age, and greater public awareness of the signs and symptoms of ASD. Although the number of children identified has clearly increased, it is unclear whether the actual number of children with ASD has increased dramatically.

14. What are controversial therapies and interventions for ASD?

Unfortunately, the field of autism has been especially vulnerable to the claims of a wide variety of unproven interventions and treatments. Because autism is a disorder with no known cure, controversial treatments provide hope to advocates, parents, and concerned professionals. "Controversial" is a reference to invalidated methods and strategies for which there is little scientific support for efficacy. Among so called controversial treatments are facilitated communication (FC) and auditory integration training (AIT). Many complementary and alternative therapies (CAM) are also controversial and lack scientific evidence supporting their effectiveness and safety in treating children with autism.

15. Why do more boys than girls receive a diagnosis of ASD?

Boys are at greater risk for nearly all developmental, behavioral, and learning disorders and are at least four times more likely than girls to receive a diagnosis of autism. The ratio increases to 10:1 with Asperger syndrome and HFA. Although there are no documented reasons for this gender difference, some researchers have suggested that a genetic mechanism or gender bias might play a role. It has been suggested that differences in brain organization might provide a protective factor for girls and lower the risk for developing the disorder. There is also some conjecture that expression of the behavioral phenotype might be different for girls than boys. Since females are socialized differently, ASD may not be manifest in the same way as typical male behavioral signs and patterns. There may also be a gender bias associated with a reliance on male criteria with respect to the diagnostic criteria for ASD.

16. Is there a possible link between ASD and childhood vaccines?

There continues to be a great deal of discussion and debate on the possibility of a link between childhood vaccines and ASD. The United States Centers for Disease Control and Prevention (CDC) reports that the most carefully designed research on the connection between autism and vaccines has not found a link. Epidemiological studies examining the preservative thimerosal and autism provided no evidence of an association despite utilization of different methods and examination of different populations (in Sweden, Demark, United States, and the United Kingdom). Despite rigorous follow-up studies and reports from the Institute of Medicine (IOM) and the CDC stating that there is no causal relationship between the MMR (measles, mumps, and rubella) vaccine and ASD, this issue continues to be discussed and debated.

17. What is meant by the broader autism phenotype?

The broader autism phenotype refers to children who demonstrate various behaviors and difficulties related to autistic disorder or autism, but who do not meet specific criteria for a clinical diagnosis. These behavioral and cognitive characteristics are milder but qualitatively similar to the defining features of autism. There is evidence to indicate that even mild deviance in development can have an adverse effect on school performance and adaptive behavior.

18. What intervention or treatment works best for children with ASD?

There is no single intervention or treatment that is right for every child with ASD and no specific program or model has been shown to be superior to another. According to the National Research Council (2001), research is not yet available to predict which intervention approaches work best with which children. As a result, no one approach or method is equally effective with all children, and not all children will make the same progress or gains. The most effective interventions and programs are those that are based on the individual child's unique needs, strengths and weaknesses.

19. What is ABA?

Applied Behavior Analysis (ABA) is perhaps the most popular approach to the treatment of autism and other pervasive developmental disorders. This method uses positive reinforcement, repetition and prompting to teach language, play and social skills. Discrete trial training (DTT) is the most common teaching technique incorporated into the ABA method. This approach involves breaking behaviors down into subcategories and teaching each subcategory through repetition, positive reinforcement and prompts that are gradually removed from the program as the child progresses. During this teaching, each subcategory is taught intensely and exclusively until the behavior is learned to help to ensure success for the child. Discrete trial training is a technique that can be an important element of a comprehensive educational program for the child with ASD.

20. What is Positive Behavior Support (PBS)?

Positive Behavior Support (PBS) is a systematic approach to preventing or reducing challenging behaviors, and, eventually, to enhancing the quality of life for individuals with autism and support providers. A central concept in PBS is the significance of the "function" of behavior. All behavior is considered to be meaningful, purposeful, and functional for the individual. The key objective of PBS is to determine the function of the problem behavior, and then to teach socially acceptable alternative/replacement skills and behaviors that are effective and efficient in accomplishing the function of the problem behavior.

21. What tests should be used by school professionals to identify students with ASD?

The Autism Diagnostic Interview-Revised (ADI-R) and Autism Diagnostic Observation Schedule (ADOS) are considered the "gold standard" instruments for assessing autism. Both require a substantial amount of experience, specialized training, and time to administer and interpret effectively. As a result, they may not be ideal instruments for use in school-based assessment. Although school professionals should be familiar with these instruments, there are other validated tools that yield important information about the autistic triad of impairments and may be included in an assessment battery to identify students with ASD. It is important to keep in mind that no single test will reliably identify ASD and that best practice requires multiple methods of assessment and sources of information.

22. Is there one set of forms or procedures that should be used when conducting a functional behavior assessment (FBA) for students with ASD?

An FBA provides a framework from which to plan and is not limited to a particular theory or model of assessment. There is no single set of procedures or one form that can be used with every student. Assessment forms and procedures vary, depending on the unique characteristics of the student, resources of the school, and the nature of challenging behaviors exhibited by the student. The more severe the behavior and/or complex the situation, the greater the degree of thoroughness required in the assessment process.

GLOSSARY OF TERMS

Adaptive behavior The age-appropriate or typical performance of daily activities based on social standards and expectations. It is an individual's ability to adjust to and apply new skills to other situations (e.g. different environments, tasks, objects, and people).

Algorithm A set of instructions or rules for performing a calculation or process to determine whether a score on a diagnostic test or set of observations meets specific criteria necessary to assign a diagnosis.

Anhedonia A symptom of depression characterized by diminished interest or pleasure in daily activities manifest as complaints of boredom, resistance to take part in any activity, reluctance to leave one's residence, and a lack of motivation.

Applied behavior analysis (ABA) The process of systematically applying interventions based upon the principles of learning theory to improve socially significant behaviors to a meaningful degree, and to demonstrate that the interventions employed are responsible for the improvement in behavior. A behavior therapist may use a variety of individual techniques (such as discrete trial training, modeling, shaping, and prompting).

Assessment for intervention planning Determination of the child's unique strengths and weaknesses across several domains of functioning with the objective of planning treatment and intervention based upon the child's individual profile. The intervention plan is designed to maximize child development and functional skills in both school and family contexts.

Autism spectrum disorder (ASD) An umbrella term for a group of neurobiological disorders that affect a child's ability to interact, communicate, relate, play, imagine, and learn. The terms pervasive developmental disorder (PDD) and ASD encompass a wide spectrum of autism-related disorders and are often used interchangeably.

Comorbid disorder A disorder that coexists with another diagnosis so that both share a primary focus of clinical and educational attention.

Comprehensive developmental approach An approach that emphasizes the assessment of multiple areas of functioning and the reciprocal impact of abilities and disabilities in order to understand the departure from normal developmental expectations that characterize ASD.

Developmental milestones Markers or guideposts to a child's learning, behavior, and development. Developmental milestones consist of skills or behaviors that most children perform by a certain age. While each child develops differently, some differences may indicate a slight delay and others may be a red flag or warning sign for greater concern.

Diagnostic and Statistical Manual of Mental Disorders (DSM-IV-TR) A handbook used widely by medical and mental health professionals in diagnosing and categorizing mental and developmental disorders. The *DSM-IV-TR* uses the term pervasive developmental disorders (PDD), also referred to as autism spectrum disorders (ASD) in other reference sources, as an overall term that includes five clinical disorders: autistic disorder, Rett's disorder, childhood disintegrative disorder, Asperger's disorder, and PDDNOS.

Diagnostic evaluation The process of gathering information via interview, observation, and specific testing in order to arrive at a diagnosis or categorical conclusion.

Discrete trial training A specific treatment approach or method of instruction based on the theory of ABA in which a task is isolated and taught by repeatedly presenting the same task to the person. It involves a three-part process: a presentation by a teacher (the antecedent); the child's response (the behavior); and a consequence (reinforcement). Each trial is a separate attempt to teach a new behavior or reinforce an existing behavior.

Early identification The identification of developmental delays through medical and developmental screening at the youngest age possible. Screening is provided to children school age or younger who are at risk of having a disability or other special need that may affect their development. Early identification increases the chances for improving developmental skills and positive outcome.

Echolalia The repetition of speech produced by others. The echoed words or phrases can include the same words and exact inflections as first heard, or they may be somewhat modified. Immediate echolalia refers to echoed words spoken immediately or a very brief time after they were heard. Delayed echolalia may occur several minutes, hours, days, or even weeks after the original speech was heard.

Ecological validity Skills or abilities evidenced under natural conditions such as the classroom or home setting that may not be demonstrated in structured assessment measures and tests.

Executive function A general term that refers to the mental processes that are required to maintain goal directed problem-solving behavior. Executive functions generally include response inhibition, working memory, cognitive flexibility, emotional control, self-regulation, and planning and organization.

Expressive language Refers to the language that the individual communicates to others. Generally, it indicates the ability to express thoughts, feelings, wants, and desires through oral speech.

Eye gaze An individual's eye contact with another person or with an object. Eye contact is a nonverbal form of communication and a way of regulating social interaction. Observing patterns of avoidance or initiation of eye gaze is important in identifying a child's capability for sharing of attention and affect.

Functional behavior assessment (FBA) A method of evaluating behaviors demonstrated by an individual by carefully observing what happens before (antecedent) and after (consequence) the behavior occurs. Specific behaviors are described in terms of the purposes of the behavior and the function the behaviors serve for the individual exhibiting the behavior.

High functioning autism (HFA) A non-clinical description of an individual with a diagnosis of autistic disorder who has average or near-average intellectual ability. Also referred to as autism without intellectual disability. High-functioning individuals with autism tend to demonstrate higher levels of functional adaptive and communication skills than those with classic autism.

Graduated approach A model of action and intervention in schools and early education settings to assist children with special educational needs. This approach recognizes that there is a continuum of special educational needs and that, where necessary, increasing specialist expertise and services are focused on the child's problems.

Hyperlexia An ability to learn to read at an early age and advanced level without instruction.

Hypersensitivity Heightened, often painful, reaction to sensory input.

Inclusion A situation in a school or community setting where children with special educational needs are included with children without disabilities.

Individualized education program (IEP) A special education program designed to meet each child's unique educational needs. The IEP is a planning, teaching, and progress monitoring tool and a working document for all children with special educational needs.

Individuals with Disabilities Education Act (IDEA) A United States federal law that governs how states and public agencies provide early intervention, special education, and related services to children with disabilities. It mandates free appropriate education for children in 13 specified categories of disability.

Interdisciplinary A coordinated effort among the various disciplines to complement (rather than duplicate) efforts and to develop a cohesive intervention plan and/or arrive at a diagnostic conclusion. Compare to multidisciplinary.

Joint attention The ability to share with another person the experience of an object of interest. Joint attention generally emerges between 8 and 12 months of age. A moving toy, for example, typically elicits a pointing behavior by the child, who looks alternately at the caregiver and the object.

Lovaas method Intensive behavioral therapy that often requires a minimum of 40 hours per week in one-on-one therapy. Discrete trial formats are one technique used in this method of therapy.

Multidisciplinary A process that involves separate evaluations by various professionals who often practice without benefit of collaboration with other evaluating professionals and who often reach separate conclusions based upon their particular experience. Compare to interdisciplinary.

Multidisciplinary team An assessment team with professional members from various disciplines (e.g. education, speech/language pathology, psychology, medicine) evaluate the total child.

Nonverbal communication Involves facial expressions, tone of voice, gestures, eye contact, and other types of expression involving no or minimal use of spoken language. Research suggests that nonverbal communication is critical to social development and communication.

Norm-referenced Refers to a standardized test or assessment that compares a child's performance to the performance of peers the same age or grade.

Percentile rank A derived score that indicates the percentage of individuals within the norm group who achieved this score or a lower one. For example, a student whose raw score converts to the 60th percentile can be said to perform at or above that of 60 percent of the norm group.

Perseveration The redundant repetition of a word, thought, or action without the ability to end or move forward. Includes repetitive movement or perseverative speech, or rigid adherence to one idea or task.

Pervasive developmental disorder (PDD) An umbrella term for a wide spectrum of disorders referred to as autism or autism spectrum disorders (ASD). The terms PDD and ASD are used interchangeably. They are a group of neurobiological disorders that affect a child's ability to interact, communicate, relate, play, imagine, and learn.

Phenotype The observable features produced by the interaction of the genotype and the environment. The "phenotypic" expression of a disorder refers to the behavioral expression of symptoms that may or may not share a similar etiology, course, or response to treatment.

Positive behavioral support (PBS) A systematic approach to preventing or reducing challenging behaviors, and, eventually, to enhancing quality of life for individuals and support providers. A key objective in PBS is to determine the function of the problem behavior, and then to teach socially acceptable alternative/replacement skills and behaviors.

Pragmatics Social rules for using functional spoken language in a meaningful context or conversation. It includes the rules about eye contact between speaker and listener, how close to stand, taking turns, selecting topics of conversation, and other requirements to ensure that satisfactory communication occurs. Challenges in pragmatics are a common feature of spoken language difficulties in children with ASD.

Prosody The rhythm and melody of spoken language expressed through rate, pitch, stress, inflection, or intonation to convey a meaning.

Receptive language The act of understanding that which is said, written, or signed.

Red flags for ASD Early indicators or warning signs for autism spectrum disorders (ASD). Common warning signs of autistic disorder include:

- does not smile by the age of six months
- does not respond to his or her name
- does not cry
- does not babble or use gestures by 12 months
- does not point to objects by 12 months
- does not use words by 16 months
- does not use two-word phrases by 24 months
- regresses after mastering skills/loses previously mastered skills
- delays in milestones like crawling and walking.

Restricted patterns of interest A preoccupation with a narrow range of interests and activities that is intense in focus. Also referred to as stereotyped or circumscribed patterns of interests because of the rigidity and narrowness of these interests.

Ritualistic behavior Rigid routines, such as insistence on eating particular foods or engaging in specific and seemingly meaningless behaviors repeatedly in certain situations or circumstances, such as turning the lights on and off several times when entering a room. Related terms are repetitive behaviors and restricted interests.

Screening The use of a specific test or instrument to identify those children in the population most likely to be at risk for a specified clinical disorder or disability. Screening for a particular disorder such as ASD may occur at a specific age or when concerns of parents and/or educators or results of routine developmental surveillance indicate that a child is at risk for developmental difficulties. Screening is not intended to provide definitive diagnoses but rather to suggest a need for further evaluation and assessment for intervention planning.

SEN Code of Practice A guide for early education settings, state schools and local education authorities (LEAs) in the United Kingdom on providing help to children with special educational needs. Schools and LEAs must take account of the Code when they deal with a child with special educational needs.

Sensory integration The organization of sensory input for use by the individual. Parts of the nervous system work together through sensory integration so that an individual can effectively interact with the environment.

Sensory integration therapy Treatment involving sensory stimulation and adaptive responses according to the child's neurologic needs. SI is implemented by an occupational therapist and usually involves full body movements that provide vestibular, proprioceptive and tactile stimulation. The goal of therapy is to improve the way the brain processes and organizes sensations.

Social reciprocity The back-and-forth flow of social interaction or how the behavior of one person influences and is influenced by the behavior of another person and vice versa. Also, mutual responsiveness in the context of interpersonal contact, such as awareness of and ability to respond appropriately to other people.

Special educational needs *IDEA* defines a "child with a disability" as "a child with mental retardation, hearing impairments (including deafness), speech or language impairments, visual impairments (including blindness), serious emotional disturbance, orthopedic impairments, autism, traumatic brain injury, other health impairments, or specific learning disabilities, and who because of the condition needs special education and related services." According to the *SEN Code of Practice*, children have special educational needs (SEN) if they have learning difficulties that require a provision for special education and related services. Children with special educational needs require extra or different help from that given to other children of the same age.

SPELL An educational framework for understanding and responding to the needs of children and adults on the autism spectrum by creating an atmosphere which has Structure, Positive approaches and expectations, is Empathetic, Low arousal and maintains vital Links. SPELL promotes development in social communication, social skills and social imagination and emphasizes consistency of approach and the importance of mainstream opportunities and settings.

Splinter skills An isolated ability that often does not generalize across learning environments. These abilities are often widely discrepant from other areas of functioning.

Statement of special educational needs A document that specifies a child's special educational needs and the services required to meet those needs.

Stereotyped behaviors An abnormal or excessive repetition of an action carried out in the same way over time. This may include repetitive movement of objects or repetitive and complex motor mannerisms including hand or whole body movement such as clapping, finger flapping, body rocking, swaying, finger flicking, etc.).

Structured interview An interview that follows a fixed protocol for gathering information in which the interviewer asks standard questions and codes the answers in accordance with predefined criteria.

T-score Raw scores on a norm-referenced test that have been transformed so that they have a predetermined mean and standard deviation. Although they can vary from measure to measure, many tests set the mean at 100 and the standard deviation at 15. If a student's raw score converts to a standard score of 100, the student performed at the mean or in the average range.

Tangential Responding to a question in an indirect or irrelevant way.

TEACCH A structured teaching intervention developed by Division TEACCH of the University of North Carolina at Chapel Hill. The components of the program include physical structure, schedules, individual work systems, visual structure, and routines.

Visual support Written schedules, lists, charts, picture sequences, and other visuals that convey meaningful information in a permanent format for later reference. Visual supports allow the person with autism to function more independently without constant verbal directions.

GLOSSARY OF ACRONYMS

AAC	Alternative and augmentative communication
ABA	Applied behavior analysis
ADI-R	Autism Diagnostic Interview—Revised
ADOS	Autism Diagnostic Observation Schedule
AIT	Auditory integration training
AS	Asperger syndrome
ASA	Autism Society of America
ASD	Autistic spectrum disorder
CAM	Complementary and alternative medicine
CARS	Childhood Autism Rating Scale
CBT	Cognitive behavioral therapy
CDD	Childhood disintegrative disorder (Heller's syndrome)
CELF-4	Clinical Evaluation of Language Fundamentals-4th Edition
DD	Developmental Disability
DSM-IV-TR	*Diagnostic and Statistical Manual of Mental Disorders, Fourth Edition, Text Revision*
DTT	Discrete trial training
EIBI	Early intensive behavioral intervention
FBA	Functional behavior assessment
FAPE	Free appropriate public education
FC	Facilitated Communication
GF-CF	Gluten-free and casein-free diet
HFA	High-functioning autism
ICD-10	International classification of Diseases, 10th Edition
IDEA	Individuals with Disabilities Education Act
IEP	Individual educational program or plan
InD	Intellectual disability

IQ	Intelligence quotient
LRE	Least restrictive environment
MR	Mental retardation
NAS	National Autistic Society
OSEP	Office of Special Education Programs
PBS	Positive behavioral support
PDD	Pervasive developmental disorder
PDDNOS	Pervasive developmental disorder not otherwise specified
PECS	Picture Exchange Communication System
PRT	Pivotal response treatment
SEN	Special educational needs
SI	Sensory integration
SPELL	An educational approach which has **S**tructure, **P**ositive approaches and expectations, is **E**mpathetic, **L**ow arousal, and maintains vital **L**inks
SSRI	Selective serotonin reuptake inhibitor
TEACCH	**T**reatment and **E**ducation of **A**utistic and related **C**ommunication handicapped **Ch**ildren

APPENDIX A

The Autism Spectrum Quotient-Children's Version (AQ-Child)

	Definitely Agree	Slightly Agree	Slightly Disagree	Definitely Disagree
1. S/he prefers to do things with others rather than on her/his own.				
2. S/he prefers to do things the same way over and over again.				
3. If s/he tries to imagine something, s/he finds it very easy to create a picture in her/his mind.				
4. S/he frequently gets so strongly absorbed in one thing that s/he loses sight of other things.				
5. S/he often notices small sounds when others do not.				
6. S/he usually notices house numbers or similar strings of information.				
7. S/he has difficulty understanding rules for polite behaviour.				
8. When s/he is reading a story, s/he can easily imagine what the characters might look like.				
9. S/he is fascinated by dates.				
10. In a social group, s/he can easily keep track of several different people's conversations.				
11. S/he finds social situations easy.				

The Autism Spectrum Quotient-Children's Version (AQ-Child)

	Definitely Agree	Slightly Agree	Slightly Disagree	Definitely Disagree
12. S/he tends to notice details that others do not.				
13. S/he would rather go to a library than a birthday party.				
14. S/he finds making up stories easy.				
15. S/he is drawn more strongly to people than to things.				
16. S/he tends to have very strong interests, which s/he gets upset about if s/he can't pursue.				
17. S/he enjoys social chit-chat.				
18. When s/he talks, it isn't always easy for others to get a word in edgeways.				
19. S/he is fascinated by numbers.				
20. When s/he is read a story, s/he finds it difficult to work out the characters' intentions or feelings.				
21. S/he doesn't particularly enjoy fictional stories.				
22. S/he finds it hard to make new friends.				
23. S/he notices patterns in things all the time.				
24. S/he would rather go to the cinema than a museum.				
25. It does not upset him/her if his/her daily routine is disturbed.				
26. S/he doesn't know how to keep a conversation going with her/his peers.				

The Autism Spectrum Quotient-Children's Version (AQ-Child)

	Definitely Agree	Slightly Agree	Slightly Disagree	Definitely Disagree
27. S/he finds it easy to "read between the lines" when someone is talking to her/him.				
28. S/he usually concentrates more on the whole picture, rather than the small details.				
29. S/he is not very good at remembering phone numbers.				
30. S/he doesn't usually notice small changes in a situation, or a person's appearance.				
31. S/he knows how to tell if someone listening to him/her is getting bored.				
32. S/he finds it easy to go back and forth between different activities.				
33. When s/he talks on the phone, s/he is not sure when it's her/his turn to speak.				
34. S/he enjoys doing things spontaneously.				
35. S/he is often the last to understand the point of a joke.				
36. S/he finds it easy to work out what someone is thinking or feeling just by looking at their face.				
37. If there is an interruption, s/he can switch back to what s/he was doing very quickly.				
38. S/he is good at social chit-chat.				
39. People often tell her/him that s/he keeps going on and on about the same thing.				

The Autism Spectrum Quotient-Children's Version (AQ-Child)

	Definitely Agree	Slightly Agree	Slightly Disagree	Definitely Disagree
40. When s/he was in preschool, s/he used to enjoy playing games involving pretending with other children.				
41. S/he likes to collect information about categories of things (e.g. types of car, types of bird, types of train, types of plant, etc.).				
42. S/he finds it difficult to imagine what it would be like to be someone else.				
43. S/he likes to plan any activities s/he participates in carefully.				
44. S/he enjoys social occasions.				
45. S/he finds it difficult to work out people's intentions.				
46. New situations make him/her anxious.				
47. S/he enjoys meeting new people.				
48. S/he is good at taking care not to hurt other people's feelings.				
49. S/he is not very good at remembering people's date of birth.				
50. S/he finds it very to easy to play games with children that involve pretending.				

Source: Reprinted with kind permission from Springer and Business Media: *Journal of Autism and Developmental Disorders*, The Autism Spectrum Quotient: Children's Version (AQ-Child), 38, 2008, pp. 1230–1240, Auyeung, B., Baron-Cohen, S., Wheelwright, S., and Allison, C. Copyright Springer Science+Business Media, LLC 2008.

APPENDIX B

The Childhood Autism Spectrum Test (CAST)

1. Does s/he join in playing games with other children easily?	Yes No
2. Does s/he come up to you spontaneously for a chat?	Yes No
3. Was s/he speaking by 2 years old?	Yes No
4. Does s/he enjoy sports?	Yes No
5. Is it important to him/her to fit in with the peer group?	Yes No
6. Does s/he appear to notice unusual details that others miss?	Yes No
7. Does s/he tend to take things literally?	Yes No
8. When s/he was 3 years old, did s/he spend a lot of time pretending (e.g. play-acting being a superhero, or holding teddy's tea parties)?	Yes No
9. Does s/he like to do things over and over again, in the same way all the time?	Yes No
10. Does s/he find it easy to interact with other children?	Yes No
11. Can s/he keep a two-way conversation going?	Yes No
12. Can s/he read appropriately for his/her age?	Yes No
13. Does s/he mostly have the same interests as his/her peers?	Yes No
14. Does s/he have an interest which takes up so much time that s/he does little else?	Yes No
15. Does s/he have friends, rather than just acquaintances?	Yes No
16. Does s/he often bring you things s/he is interested in to show you?	Yes No
17. Does s/he enjoy joking around?	Yes No
18. Does s/he have difficulty understanding the rules for polite behavior?	Yes No
19. Does s/he appear to have an unusual memory for details?	Yes No
20. Is his/her voice unusual (e.g. overly adult, flat, or very monotonous)?	Yes No
21. Are people important to him/her?	Yes No
22. Can s/he dress him/herself?	Yes No
23. Is s/he good at turn-taking in conversation?	Yes No
24. Does s/he play imaginatively with other children, and engage in role-play?	Yes No

The Childhood Autism Spectrum Test (CAST)

25. Does s/he often do or say things that are tactless or socially inappropriate?	Yes	No
26. Can s/he count to 50 without leaving out any numbers?	Yes	No
27. Does s/he make normal eye-contact?	Yes	No
28. Does s/he have any unusual and repetitive movements?	Yes	No
29. Is his/her social behavior very one-sided and always on his/her own terms?	Yes	No
30. Does s/he sometimes say "you" or "s/he" when s/he means "I"?	Yes	No
31. Does s/he prefer imaginative activities such as play-acting or story-telling, rather than numbers or lists of facts?	Yes	No
32. Does s/he sometimes lose the listener because of not explaining what s/he is talking about?	Yes	No
33. Can s/he ride a bicycle (even if with stabilizers)?	Yes	No
34. Does s/he try to impose routines on him/her, or on others, in such a way that it causes problems?	Yes	No
35. Does s/he care how s/he is perceived by the rest of the group?	Yes	No
36. Does s/he often turn conversations to his/her favourite subject rather than following what the other person wants to talk about?	Yes	No
37. Does s/he have odd or unusual phrases?	Yes	No
SPECIAL NEEDS SECTION Please complete as appropriate	Yes	No
38. Have teachers/health visitors ever expressed any concerns about his/her development?	Yes	No
If Yes, please specify…		
39. Has s/he ever been diagnosed with any of the following?		
Language delay	Yes	No
Hyperactivity/Attention Deficit Disorder (ADHD)	Yes	No
Hearing or visual difficulties	Yes	No
Autism Spectrum Condition, incl. Asperger syndrome	Yes	No
A physical disability	Yes	No
Other (please specify)	Yes	No

APPENDIX C

ASD Assessment Worksheet

Date:_____ Student Name:_____
Birth Date:_____ Age:_____ Grade:_____
Pre-Eval. Meeting Date:_____ Eval. Meeting Date:_____ Eval. Due Date:_____

Sensory Status:
☐ Record/File Review
☐ Vision Screening
☐ Pure Tone and Tymp Screening

Academic and Functional Performance:
☐ Record/File Review
☐ Wechsler Individual Achievement Test-2nd Edition (WIAT-2)
☐ Woodcock-Johnson NU Achievement Tests-3rd Edition (WJ NU III)
☐ Kaufman Test of Educational Achievement-2nd Edition (KTEA-II)
☐ Classroom observation
☐ Informational Assessments
☐ Other_____

Autism Spectrum Disorders Assessment:
☐ Record/File Review
☐ Parent/Teacher Interviews
☐ Behavioral Observation
☐ Childhood Autism Rating Scale (CARS)
☐ Social Responsiveness Scale (SRS)
☐ Autism Diagnostic Interview (ADI)
☐ Autism Diagnostic Observation Schedule (ADOS)
☐ Social Communication Questionnaire (SCQ)

Communication (Language):
☐ Record/File Review
☐ Clinical Evaluation of Language Fundamentals-4th Edition (CELF-4)
☐ Expressive One Word Picture Vocabulary Test (EOWPVT)
☐ Peabody Picture Vocabulary Test-4th Edition (PPVT-4)
☐ Test of Pragmatic Language-2nd Edition (TOPL-2)
☐ Children's Communication Checklist (CCC-2)
☐ Pragmatic Language Skills Inventory (PLSI)
☐ Test of Auditory Comprehension of Language (TACL)
☐ Comprehensive Assessment of Spoken Language (CASL)
☐ Language Sample
☐ Observation

Motor Skills:
☐ Record/File Review

☐ Bruininks-Oseretsky Test of Motor Proficiency-2nd Edition (BOT-2)
☐ Developmental Test of Visual Motor Integration-5th Edition (VMI-5)

Intellectual/Cognitive Functioning:
☐ Record/File Review
☐ Informal Interviews: Parent, Teacher, and Student
☐ Wechsler Intelligence Scale for Children-4th Edition (WISC-IV)
☐ Wechsler Preschool and Primary Scale of Intelligence-III (WPPSI-III)
☐ Differential Ability Scales-Second Edition (DAS-II)
☐ Stanford-Binet Intelligence Scale-5th Edition (SB-5)

Executive Function and Attention:
☐ Record/File Review
☐ Conners' Rating Scales (Conners 3)
☐ Wide Range Assessment of Memory and Learning (WRAML2)
☐ Behavior Rating Inventory of Executive Function (BRIEF)

Emotional/Social and Behavior Functioning:
☐ Record/File Review
☐ Informal Interviews: Parent, Teacher, and Student
☐ Achenbach System of Empirically Based Assessment (ASEBA)
☐ Behavior Assessment System for Children-2nd Edition (BASC-II)
☐ Children's Depression Inventory (CDI)
☐ Revised Children's Manifest Anxiety Scale-2nd Edition (RCMAS-2)
☐ Other_____

Adaptive and Functional Skills:
☐ Record/File Review
☐ Behavioral Observation
☐ Informal Interviews: Parent, Teacher, and Student
☐ Vineland Adaptive Behavior Scales—2nd Edition (VABS-II): Parent, Teacher
☐ Adaptive Behavior Assessment System—2nd Edition (ABAS-II): Parent; Teacher
☐ Developmental Profile-3rd Edition (DP-3)

Sensory Processing:
☐ Sensory Profile (SP)
☐ Sensory Profile School Companion

Family System:
☐ Interview
☐ Parenting Stress Index (PSI)

Comments:

APPENDIX D

ASD Observation Checklist

Qualitative Impairments in Social Interaction:
___wanting and needing to be left alone at times
___trouble with back and forth social interactions
___inability to respond to social cues (verbal and nonverbal)
___inability to understand how someone else might feel (perspective taking)
___inappropriate giggling or laughing
___impaired imitation—not engaging in simple games
___lack of socially directed smiles when young
___little sense of other people's boundaries
___engaging in stereotypic question asking as interaction pattern
___inappropriately intrusive in social situations
___mimicking actions from TV, but not in reciprocal manner
___inappropriate use of eye contact, avoidance or extended staring
___poor use of nonverbal gestures

Qualitative Impairments in Communication:
___problems with pronouns
___problems getting the order of words in sentences correct
___problems answering questions
___problems responding to directions
___problems understanding multiple meaning of words
___problems understanding jokes, sarcasm, idioms, and figurative speech
___echoing what is said directly, later, or in a slightly changed way (echolalia)
___limited spontaneous communication
___difficulty understanding abstract concepts
___difficulty with concepts that are time bound or lack concreteness
___difficulty with long sentences
___difficulty keeping up with the flow of conversation
___problems with reciprocal conversations
___problems using speed, tone, volume appropriately (prosody)

Restricted Repetitive and Stereotyped Patterns of Behavior, Interests, or Activities:
___lining up and/or ordering objects
___strong attachment to inanimate objects (strings, bottles)
___fascination with movement (spinning wheels, fans, door and drawers)
___pacing or running back and forth, rocking
___exploring environment through licking, smelling, touching
___overly sensitive to sounds or lights
___insistence on routines, resists change
___negative reaction to change in environment

___perfectionist, problems with correction or "mistake"
___difficulty with unstructured time
___difficulty waiting
___impaired response to temperature or pain
___staring at patterns, lights, or shiny surfaces
___lack of fear of real danger
___excessive fearfulness of some harmless objects or situations
___defensive to touch that isn't self initiated

Learning Characteristics:
___uneven profile of skills
___well developed long term memory
___ability to manipulate items better than paper-pencil abilities
___over and under generalization of learning
___good visual skills
___overactive
___short attention span for some activities and not for others
___impulsivity
___delayed response time
___problems organizing and planning
___sequential learner
___needs help to problem solve

Observable Problem Behaviors:
___aggression (verbal and physical)
___self-injurious behaviors
___temper tantrums
___argumentative
___non-compliance and oppositional behavior

Source: Adapted with permission from the *Technical Assistance Manual on Autism for Kentucky Schools.* Copyright 1997, Kentucky Department of Education.

Note: This checklist should be used as part of the assessment process when observing, interviewing parent/teacher, and/or directly interacting with the student. It should not be used as the sole measure for making a decision regarding eligibility classification or educational programming.

APPENDIX E

IDEA Disability Categories

Individuals with Disabilities Education Improvement Act of 2004 (IDEA)

1. **Autism** means a developmental disability significantly affecting verbal and nonverbal communication and social interaction, generally evident before age three, that adversely affects a child's educational performance. Other characteristics often associated with autism are engagement in repetitive activities and stereotyped movements, resistance to environmental change or change in daily routines, and unusual responses to sensory experiences.
   a. Autism does not apply if a child's educational performance is adversely affected primarily because the child has an emotional disturbance, as defined in paragraph (c)(4) of this section.
   b. A child who manifests the characteristics of autism after age three could be identified as having autism if the criteria in paragraph (c)(1)(i) of this section are satisfied.
2. **Deaf-blindness** means concomitant hearing and visual impairments, the combination of which causes such severe communication and other developmental and educational needs that they cannot be accommodated in special education programs solely for children with deafness or children with blindness.
3. **Deafness** means a hearing impairment that is so severe that the child is impaired in processing linguistic information through hearing, with or without amplification that adversely affects a child's educational performance.
4. **Emotional disturbance** means a condition exhibiting one or more of the following characteristics over a long period of time and to a marked degree that adversely affects a child's educational performance:
   a. An inability to learn that cannot be explained by intellectual, sensory, or health factors.
   b. An inability to build or maintain satisfactory interpersonal relationships with peers and teachers.
   c. Inappropriate types of behavior or feelings under normal circumstances.
   d. A general pervasive mood of unhappiness or depression.
   e. A tendency to develop physical symptoms or fears associated with personal or school problems.
   Emotional disturbance includes schizophrenia. The term does not apply to children who are socially maladjusted, unless it is determined that they have an emotional disturbance under paragraph (c)(4)(i) of this section.
5. **Hearing impairment** means an impairment in hearing, whether permanent or fluctuating, that adversely affects a child's educational performance but that is not included under the definition of deafness in this section.
6. **Mental retardation** means significantly subaverage general intellectual functioning, existing concurrently with deficits in adaptive behavior and manifested during the developmental period, that adversely affects a child's educational performance.

7. **Multiple disabilities** means concomitant impairments (such as mental retardation-blindness or mental retardation-orthopedic impairment), the combination of which causes such severe educational needs that they cannot be accommodated in special education programs solely for one of the impairments. Multiple disabilities does not include deaf-blindness.

8. **Orthopedic impairment** means a severe orthopedic impairment that adversely affects a child's educational performance. The term includes impairments caused by a congenital anomaly, impairments caused by disease (e.g. poliomyelitis, bone tuberculosis), and impairments from other causes (e.g. cerebral palsy, amputations, and fractures or burns that cause contractures).

9. **Other health impairment** means having limited strength, vitality, or alertness, including a heightened alertness to environmental stimuli, that results in limited alertness with respect to the educational environment, that—
   a. Is due to chronic or acute health problems such as asthma, attention deficit disorder or attention deficit hyperactivity disorder, diabetes, epilepsy, a heart condition, hemophilia, lead poisoning, leukemia, nephritis, rheumatic fever, sickle cell anemia, and Tourette syndrome; and
   b. Adversely affects a child's educational performance.

10. **Specific learning disability** means a disorder in one or more of the basic psychological processes involved in understanding or in using language, spoken or written, that may manifest itself in the imperfect ability to listen, think, speak, read, write, spell, or to do mathematical calculations, including conditions such as perceptual disabilities, brain injury, minimal brain dysfunction, dyslexia, and developmental aphasia.
    a. Disorders not included. Specific learning disability does not include learning problems that are primarily the result of visual, hearing, or motor disabilities, of mental retardation, of emotional disturbance, or of environmental, cultural, or economic disadvantage.

11. **Speech or language impairment** means a communication disorder, such as stuttering, impaired articulation, a language impairment, or a voice impairment, that adversely affects a child's educational performance.

12. **Traumatic brain injury** means an acquired injury to the brain caused by an external physical force, resulting in total or partial functional disability or psychosocial impairment, or both, that adversely affects a child's educational performance. Traumatic brain injury applies to open or closed head injuries resulting in impairments in one or more areas, such as cognition; language; memory; attention; reasoning; abstract thinking; judgment; problem-solving; sensory, perceptual, and motor abilities; psychosocial behavior; physical functions; information processing; and speech. Traumatic brain injury does not apply to brain injuries that are congenital or degenerative, or to brain injuries induced by birth trauma.

13. **Visual impairment** including blindness means an impairment in vision that, even with correction, adversely affects a child's educational performance. The term includes both partial sight and blindness.

Source: Individuals with Disabilities Education Improvement Act of 2004. Pub. L. No. 108–446, 108th Congress, 2nd Session (2004).

APPENDIX F

A Summary of DSM IV-TR Criteria for the Pervasive Developmental Disorders

Autistic Disorder

Qualitative impairment in social interaction, as shown by at least two of the following:
- impairment in the regulation of social interaction through the use of non-verbal behavior, such as eye-contact, facial expression, body posture, and gestures
- failure to develop peer relationships that are appropriate to developmental level
- absence of spontaneous seeking to share achievements, interests, or pleasure with others
- poor social or emotional reciprocity

Qualitative impairment in communication, as shown by a least one of the following:
- delayed or absence of spoken language which is not accompanied by attempts to communicate with gestures
- impairment in ability to initiate or sustain a conversation with others when adequate speech is present
- language that is repetitive, stereotyped, or idiosyncratic
- lack of developmentally appropriate social imitative play or make-believe play

Repetitive, restricted, and stereotyped interests, activities, and behavior, as shown by a least one of the following:
- significant preoccupation with one or more stereotyped and restricted interests that are abnormal in focus and intensity
- inflexible adherence to specific routines or rituals that are nonfunctional
- repetitive and stereotyped motor movements such as hand flapping or complex whole body movements
- persistent preoccupation with parts of objects

Delayed or abnormal functioning in at least one of the following prior to age three:
- social interaction
- language used in social communication
- imaginative or symbolic play

The impairment is not better accounted for by Rett's disorder or childhood disintegrative disorder.

Asperger's Disorder

Qualitative impairment in social interaction, as shown by at least two of the following:
- marked impairment in the use of multiple non-verbal behaviors such as eye-contact, facial expression, body posture, and gestures
- lack of peer relationships that are appropriate to developmental level

- lack of significant spontaneous seeking to share achievements, interests, and pleasure with others
- lack of emotional or social reciprocity

Repetitive, restricted, and stereotyped interests, activities, and behavior, as shown by a least one of the following:

- significant preoccupation with one or more stereotyped or restricted interests that are abnormal in focus and intensity
- inflexible adherence to specific routines or rituals that are nonfunctional
- repetitive and stereotyped motor movements such as hand flapping and complex whole body movements
- persistent preoccupation with parts of objects

The symptoms cause clinically significant impairment in social, occupational or other areas of personal functioning

Absence of a clinically significant general language delay (e.g. single words by age two and communicative phrases by age three)

Absence of a clinically significant delay in cognitive development, age appropriate self-help skills, adaptive behavior (except social interaction), and curiosity about the environment

Criteria are not met for another specific pervasive developmental disorder or schizophrenia

---

Pervasive Developmental Disorder Not Otherwise Specified (Including Atypical Autism)

This diagnostic classification is used for children who demonstrate severe developmental impairment in reciprocal social interaction associated with impairment in either verbal or nonverbal communication skills or with the presence of stereotyped behavior, interests, and activities and who do not meet the criteria for a specific pervasive developmental disorder or for schizophrenia, schizotypal personality disorder, or avoidant personality disorder.

Source: Summarized criteria from the Diagnostic and Statistical Manual of Mental Disorders, Fourth Edition, Text Revision, Copyright 2000. American Psychiatric Association.

APPENDIX G

Sample IEP Goals and Objectives for Students with Autism Spectrum Disorders

1. ___will develop social understanding skills as measured by the benchmarks listed below.
   a. Will raise his/her hand and wait to be called on before talking aloud in group settings 4 out of 5 opportunities.
   b. Will work cooperatively with peers in small group settings (i.e. share materials, permit peers to share different thoughts) 4 out of 5 opportunities.
   c. Will develop an understanding of the relationship between his/her verbalizations and actions/effect on others 4 out of 5 opportunities.
   d. Will engage in appropriate cooperative social play interactions initiated by others 4 out of 5 opportunities.
   e. Will engage in cooperative social play interactions by allowing others to make changes or alter the play routine 4 out of 5 opportunities.
   f. Will engage in appropriate turn-taking skills by attending to peer's turn and waiting for own turn 4 out of 5 opportunities.
   g. Will appropriately acknowledge an interaction initiated by others by giving an appropriate response, either verbal or nonverbal.
   h. Will develop an understanding of the rationale for various social skills by stating the reason when asked (e.g. Why do we say excuse me?)
   i. Will increase social awareness of environment by stating what is taking place in environment or imitating actions of others 4 out of 5 opportunities.
   j. Will identify appropriate social rules and codes of conduct for various social situations 4 out of 5 opportunities.
   k. Will stop interrupting others by exhibiting appropriate social interaction skills 4 out of 5 opportunities.
2. ___will increase perspective taking skills as measured by the benchmarks listed below.
   a. Will identify various emotional states in others 4 out of 5 opportunities.
   b. Will state why a person might be feeling a particular emotion 4 out of 5 opportunities.
   c. Will identify various simple emotional states in self 4 out of 5 opportunities.
   d. Will state why he/she might be feeling a particular emotion 4 out of 5 opportunities.
   e. Will state what would be an appropriate emotional/behavioral response to specific social situations 4 out of 5 opportunities.
3. ___ will increase social communication skills as measured by the benchmarks listed below.

    a. Will initiate communicative interactions with others 4 out of 5 opportunities.

    b. Will initiate varied appropriate topics with others 4 out of 5 opportunities.

    c. Will initiate communicative interactions with others by asking questions 4 out of 5 opportunities.

    d. Will engage in conversational turn-taking with others across 3–4 conversational turns, 4 out of 5 opportunities (topics initiated by self/others).

    e. Will ask questions of others regarding topics initiated by self or others to sustain conversation for conversational turn-taking 4 out of 5 opportunities.

    f. Will identify and understand various nonverbal social communication behaviors (i.e. tone of voice, personal space, vocal volume, body orientation, facial expressions) by stating their implied meaning 4 out of 5 opportunities.

    g. Will spontaneously seek assistance/ ask for help/seek additional information given visual prompts 4 out of 5 opportunities.

    h. Will spontaneously use a verbal or nonverbal message to indicate to the speaker that he needs additional "wait" time to process information editorially 4 out of 5 opportunities.

    i. Will identify breakdowns in communication and make appropriate adjustments 4 out of 5 opportunities.

4. ___ will increase his/her ability to function appropriately within the school environment as measured by the benchmarks listed below.

    a. Given visual and verbal prompts participate in tasks/activities to completion by exhibiting appropriate behaviors, __ percent of the time.

    b. Will transition appropriately from tasks and activities and school environments __ percent of the time given visual and verbal prompts.

    c. Will accept changes in routine/schedule by exhibiting appropriate behaviors given visual and verbal cues __ percent of the time.

    d. Will follow classroom rules and directives given visual and verbal prompts __ percent of the time.

    e. Will independently ask to take a break given visual and verbal prompts __ percent of the time.

Empirically supported strategies to focus on above goals:

- social stories
- individual visual schedule
- self-management strategies
- peer-mediated strategies
- incidental teaching
- social skills group
- pivotal response treatment
- video-tapes.

Source: Adapted with permission from the *Technical Assistance Manual on Autism for Kentucky Schools.* Copyright 1997, Kentucky Department of Education.

APPENDIX H

Resources for Further Information

ORGANIZATIONS, AGENCIES, AND SUPPORT GROUPS

American Academy of Pediatrics www.pediatrics.org
Association for Science in Autism Treatment www.asatonline.org
Australian Advisory Board on Autism Spectrum Disorders www.autismaus.com.au
Autism Europe www.autismeurope.org/portal/
Autism Society of America www.autism-society.org/
Autism Society Canada http://autismsocietycanada.ca
Autism Speaks www.autismspeaks.org/
Center for Autism and Related Disabilities (CARD) http://card-usf.fmhi.usf.edu/
Center for Disease Control and Prevention www.cdc.gov/ncbddd/autism/index.html
National Autistic Society www.nas.org.uk
National Information Center for Children and Youth with Disabilities (NICHCY) www.nichcy.org
National Institute of Child Health and Human Development Autism Site www.nichd.nih.gov/autism
National Institutes of Health Autism Research Network www.autismresearchnetwork.org/
National Research Council www.nap.edu
Organization for Autism Research www.researchautism.org/
Research Autism www.researchautism.net/

UNIVERSITIES AND CENTERS

Cambridge University, Autism Research Centre www.autismresearchcentre.com/
Geneva Center for Autism www.autism.net
Indiana University, Indiana Resource Center for Autism www.iidc.indiana.edu/irca
Kennedy Krieger Institute www.kennedykrieger.org/index.jsp
La Trobe University, Olga Tennison Autism Research Centre www.latrobe.edu.au/otarc/centre.html
Nova Southeastern University, Mailman Segal Institute www.nova.edu/msi/autism/
University of Bristol, Bristol Autism Research Group http://barg.psy.bris.ac.uk/
University of California, M.I.N.D. Institute www.ucdmc.ucdavis.edu/mindinstitute/
University of Kansas, Kansas Institute for Positive Behavior Support www.kipbs.org/new_kipbs/index.html
University of Michigan, Autism and Communication Disorders Center www.umaccweb.com/
University of North Carolina, Treatment and Education of Autistic and Related Communication Handicapped Children www.teacch.com/
University of Sunderland, The Autism Research Unit http://centres.sunderland.ac.uk/autism/
Yale Child Study Center Developmental Disabilities Clinic www.autism.fm

EDUCATOR, PARENT, AND SERVICE PROVIDER INFORMATION

American Academy of Pediatrics (2005) *Understanding Autism Spectrum Disorders* [pamphlet]. Elk Grove Village, IL: American Academy of Pediatrics.

Autistic Spectrum Disorders: Good Practice Guidance (2002) Department for Education and Skills. Available at www.teachernet.gov.uk/wholeschool/sen/asds/asdgoodpractice (accessed October 2009).

Chandler, L. K. and Dahlquist, C. M. (2002) *Functional Assessment: Strategies to Prevent and Remediate Challenging Behavior in School Settings.* New Jersey: Merrill Prentice Hall.

Department for Education and Employment (2001) *The Code of Practice on the Identification and Assessment of Special Educational Needs.* London: HMSO.

DfES (Department for Education and Skills) (2002) *Autistic Spectrum Disorders: Good Practice Guidance.* London: DfES.

First Signs www.Firstsigns.org

Fouse, B. (1999) *Creating a Win-Win IEP for Students with Autism: A How-to Manual for Parents and Educators.* Arlington, TX: Future Horizons.

Individuals with Disabilities Education Improvement Act of 2004. Pub. L. No. 108–446, 108th Congress, 2nd Session. Available at idea.ed.gov/ (accessed October 2009).

Life Journey through Autism: An Educator's Guide to Asperger Syndrome. Arlington, VA: Organization for Autism Research. Available at www.researchautism.org/resources/reading/index.asp (accessed October 2009).

Life Journey through Autism: A Parent's Guide to Research. Arlington, VA: Organization for Autism Research.

Life Journey through Autism: A Parent's Guide to Assessment. Arlington, VA: Organization for Autism Research.

National Autistic Society (2003) *Approaches to Autism: An Easy to Use Guide to Many and Varied Approaches to Autism* (5th edn.) London: National Autistic Society.

National Autistic Society (2006) "What is the SPELL framework?" Available at www.nas.org.uk/nas/jsp/polopoly.jsp?d=297&a=3362 (accessed October 2009).

Office of Special Education Programs (2000) *A Guide to the Individualized Education Program.* Available at www.ed.gov/offices/OSERS/OSEP/Products/IE_Guide (accessed October 2009).

Persons with Autism Spectrum Disorders: Identification, Understanding, and Intervention. Available at www.autismeurope.org/portal (accessed October 2009).

Positive Behavior Support: A Classroom-Wide Approach to Successful Student Achievement and Interactions (2005) Tampa, FL: Louis de la Parte Florida Mental Health Institute. Available at http://cfs.fmhi.usf.edu/Policy/RMRT/PDF/4Pasco-PBS.pdf (accessed October 2009).

Special Educational Needs (SEN) Tool Kit. Available at www.teachernet.gov.uk/wholeschool/sen/sentoolkit/

Sen Code of Practice (2001) Department for Education and Skills. Available at www.teachernet.gov.uk/wholeschool/sen/sencodeintro/ (accessed October 2009).

Twachtman-Cullen, D. and and Twachtman-Reilly, J. (2003) *How Well Does Your Child's IEP Measure Up? Quality Indicators for Effective Service Delivery.* London: Jessica Kingsley Publishers.

Winner, M. (2005) *Think Social: A Social Thinking Curriculum for School Age Students.* San Jose, CA: Think Social Publishing.

SOCIAL SKILLS TRAINING AND OTHER INTERVENTIONS

Alberto, P. and Troutman, A. (2006) *Applied Behavior Analysis for Teachers,* 7th edn. New York: Prentice-Hall.

Attwood, T. (2004) *Exploring Feelings: Cognitive Behaviour Therapy to Manage Anxiety.* Arlington, TX: Future Horizons.

Attwood, T. (2004) *Exploring Feelings: Cognitive Behaviour Therapy to Manage Anger.* Arlington, TX: Future Horizons.

Baker, J. E. (2003) *Social Skills Training for Children and Adolescents with Asperger Syndrome and Social-Communication Problems.* Shawnee Mission, KS: Autism Asperger Publishing Company.

Baron-Cohen, S. (2007) *Mind Reading: The Interactive Guide to Emotions.* London: Jessica Kingsley Publishers.

Bellini, S. (2008) *Building Social Relationships: A Systematic Approach to Teaching Social Interaction Skills to Children and Adolescents with Autism Spectrum Disorders and Other Social Difficulties.* Shawnee Mission, KS: Autism Asperger Publishing Company.

Bondy, A. S. and Frost, L. A. (2002) *A Picture's Worth: PECS and Other Visual Communication Strategies in Autism.* Bethesda, MD: Woodbine House.

Dunn, M. A. (2006) *S.O.S. Social Skills in our Schools: A Social Skills Program for Children with Pervasive Developmental Disorders, Including High-Functioning Autism and Asperger Syndrome, and their Typical Peers.* Shawnee Mission, KS: Autism Asperger Publishing Company.

Elliott, S. N. and Gresham, F. M. (1991) *Social Skills Intervention Guide.* Circle Pines, MN: American Guidance Service.

Faherty, C. (2000) *Asperger's...What Does it Mean to Me?: A Workbook Explaining Self Awareness and Life Lessons to the Child or Youth with High-Functioning Autism or Asperger's.* Arlington, TX: Future Horizons.

Gray, C. (2000) *The New Social Story Book, Illustrated Edition.* Arlington, TX: Future Horizons.

Gray, C. (2000) *Writing Social Stories with Carol Gray.* Arlington, TX: Future Horizons.

Howlin, P., Baron-Cohen, S. and Hadwin, J. (1999) *Teaching Children with Autism to Mindread: A Practical Guide.* London: Wiley.

Koegel, R. L. and Koegel, L. K. (2006) *Pivotal Response Treatments for Autism: Communication, Social, and Academic Development.* Baltimore, MD: Paul H. Brookes Publishing.

McGinnis, E. and Goldstein, A. P. (1997) *Skillstreaming the Elementary School Child: New Strategies and Perspectives for Teaching Prosocial Skills.* Champaign, IL: Research Press.

Myles, B. S., Trautman, M. L., and Schelvan, R. L. (2004) *The Hidden Curriculum: Practical Solutions for Understanding Unstated Rules in Social Situations*. Shawnee Mission, KS: Autism Asperger Publishing Company.

Prizant, B. M., Wetherby, A., Rubin, E., Laurent A., and Rydell, P. (2005) *The SCERTS Model: A Comprehensive Educational Approach for Children with Autism*. Baltimore, MD: Paul Brooks Publishing.

Rathvon, N. (2008) *Effective School Interventions: Evidence-based Strategies for Improving Student Outcomes*, 2nd edn. New York: Guilford.

Shapiro, E. S. and Kratochwill, T. R. (eds.) (2000) *Behavioral Assessment in Schools*. New York: Guilford.

Sprick, R. and Garrison, M. (2008) *Interventions: Evidence-based Behavioral Strategies for Individual Students*, 2nd edn. Eugene, OR: Pacific Northwest Publishing. University Press.

Winner, M. G. (2002) *Thinking about You. Thinking about Me*. San Jose, CA: Think Social Publishing.

Witt, J. C. and Beck, R. (2000) *One-minute Academic Functional Assessment and Interventions: "Can't" Do It...or "Won't" Do It?* Longmont, CO: Sopris West.

JOURNALS

Autism: The International Journal of Research and Practice

Focus on Autism and Other Developmental Disabilities

Intervention in School and Clinic

Journal of Autism and Developmental Disorders

Journal of Clinical Child and Adolescent Psychology

Journal of Positive Behavior Interventions

Remedial and Special Education

GENERAL INFORMATION ON AUTISM SPECTRUM DISORDERS

Attwood, T. (2006) *The Complete Guide to Asperger's Syndrome*. London: Jessica Kingsley Publishers.

Baron-Cohen, S. (2008) *Autism and Asperger Syndrome: The Facts*. New York: Oxford.

Goldstein, S., Naglieri, J. A., and Ozonoff, S. (eds.) (2009) *Assessment of Autism Spectrum Disorders*. New York: Guilford.

Klin, A., Volkmar, F. R. and Sparrow, S. S. (eds.) (2000) *Asperger's Syndrome*. New York: Guilford.

House, A. E. (2002) *DSM-IV Diagnosis in the Schools*. New York: Guilford.

Mesibov, G. B., Shea, V., and Schopler, E. (with Adams, L., Burgess, S., Chapman, S.M., Merkler, E., Mosconi, M., Tanner, C. and Van Bourgondien, M. E.). (2005) *The TEACCH Approach to Autism Spectrum Disorders*. New York: Kluwer Academic/Plenum.

Ozonoff, S., Dawson, G., and McPartland, J. (2002) *A Parent's Guide to Asperger Syndrome and High-functioning Autism: How to Meet the Challenges and Help Your Child Thrive*. New York: Guilford.

National Research Council (2001) *Educating Children with Autism*. Washington, DC: National Academy Press.

Volkmar, F. R., Paul, R., Klin, A., and Cohen, D. (eds.) (2005) *Handbook of Autism and Pervasive Developmental Disorders*, 3rd edn. (vols. 1 and 2). Hoboken, NJ: John Wiley & Sons.

PERIODICALS

Autism Spectrum Quarterly www.asquarterly.com/

Autism-Asperger's Digest www.autismdigest.com/

INDEX TO BEST PRACTICE RECOMMENDATIONS

SCREENING

ASSESSMENT

The identification of parenting stress and parent—child relationship problems can alert the assessment team to the need for additional family support or counseling.   70

A screening of potential coexisting (comorbid) behavioral/emotional issues, such as anxiety and depression, should be conducted to determine the need for a more detailed evaluation (possibly including referral to specialists).   71

INTERVENTION AND TREATMENT

Although no professional can be an expert on every method and make a detailed study of the literature, we should be cautious about accepting at face value widely reported interventions and treatments that are often presented as self-evident facts and infrequently challenged.   100

Different approaches to intervention have been found to be effective for children with autism, and no comparative research has been conducted that demonstrates one approach is superior to another. The selection of a specific intervention should be based on goals developed from a comprehensive assessment.   101

Positive behavioral support has been shown to be an effective proactive approach to eliminate, minimize, and prevent challenging behavior.   102

PECS can increase a student's ability to function and communicate in the classroom.   103

Interventions and programs should capitalize on children's natural tendency to respond to visual structure, routines, schedules, and predictability.   106

Social skills interventions have the potential to produce noticeable effects in the social interactions and social relationships of children with autism, if appropriately designed and delivered.   108

Relying on ineffective and potentially harmful treatments puts the child at risk and uses valuable time that could be utilized in more productive educational or remedial activities.   109

No one methodology is effective for all children with autism. Generally, it is best to integrate approaches according to a student's individual needs and responses. 111

School professionals should strongly encourage parents to investigate thoroughly any CAM treatment approach or nontraditional therapy prior to implementing them with their children.   111

Medication has the potential to improve symptom functioning and the ability to benefit from other types of interventions.   113

Regardless of the method, school professionals and interventionists should make a concentrated effort to collect data related to intervention integrity (fidelity).   114

Empirically supported strategies such as self-management have shown considerable promise as a method for teaching students with ASD to be more independent, self-reliant, and less dependent on external control and continuous supervision.   115

SPECIAL NEEDS EDUCATION

ABOUT THE AUTHOR

Lee A. Wilkinson, PhD, **NCSP** is an applied researcher and practitioner with a special interest in development psychopathology. He is a nationally certified school psychologist, chartered educational psychologist, chartered scientist, and certified cognitive-behavioral therapist. Dr. Wilkinson is currently a school psychologist in the Florida public school system where he provides diagnostic and consultation services for children with autism spectrum disorders and their families. He is also a university educator and teaches graduate courses in psychological assessment, clinical intervention, and child and adolescent psychopathology. His research and professional writing has focused primarily on behavioral consultation and therapy, and children and adults with Asperger syndrome and high-functioning autism spectrum disorders. He has published numerous journal articles on these topics both in the United States and the United Kingdom.

REFERENCES

Abidin, R. R. (1995) *Parenting Stress Index*, 3rd edn. Odessa, FL: Psychological Assessment Resources.

Achenbach, T. M. and Rescorla, L. A. (2001) *Manual for the ASEBA School-age Forms and Profiles*. Burlington: University of Vermont, Research Center for Children, Youth, and Families.

Adreon, D. and Stella, J. (2001) "Transition to middle and high school: Increasing the success of students with Asperger syndrome." *Intervention in School and Clinic 36*, 266–271.

Alberto, P. and Troutman, A. (2006) *Applied Behavior Analysis for Teachers*, 7th edn. New York: Prentice-Hall.

Allison, C., Williams, J., Scott, F., Stott, C., *et al.* (2007) "The Childhood Asperger Syndrome test (CAST): Test retest reliability in a high scoring sample." *Autism 11*, 173–185.

Alpern, G., Boll, T., and Shearer, M. (2007) *Developmental Profile*, 3rd edn. Austin, TX: Pro-Ed.

American Psychiatric Association (1994) *Diagnostic and Statistical Manual of Mental Disorders*. Washington, DC: APA.

American Psychiatric Association (2000) *Diagnostic and Statistical Manual of Mental Disorders*, 4th edn, text rev. Washington, DC: APA.

Attwood, T. (2005) "Cognitive behaviour therapy for children and adults with Asperger's syndrome." *Behaviour Change 21*, 147–161.

Attwood, T. (2006) *The Complete Guide to Asperger's Syndrome*. London: Jessica Kingsley Publishers.

Autism Education Trust (2008) *Education Provision for Children and Young People on the Autism Spectrum Living in England: A Review of Current Practice, Issues and Challenges*. London: National Autism Society.

Autism Europe (2008) *Persons with Autism Spectrum Disorders: Identification, Understanding, Intervention*. Brussels: Autism Europe. Available at www.autismeurope.org/portal (accessed October 2009).

Autism Spectrum Disorders Handbook (2006) Sioux Falls, SD: Sanford School of Medicine, University of South Dakota, Center for Disabilities.

Auyeung, B., Baron-Cohen, S., Wheelwright, S., and Allison, C. (2008) "The Autism Spectrum Quotient: Children's Version (AQ-Child)." *Journal of Autism and Developmental Disorders 38*, 1230–1240.

Bailey, A., Phillips, W., and Rutter, M. (1996) "Autism: towards an integration of clinical, genetic, neuropsychological, and neurobiological perspectives." *Journal of Child Psychology and Psychiatry 37*, 89–126.

Baird, G., Simonoff, E., Pickles, A., Loucas, T., Meldrum, D., and Charman, T. (2006) "Prevalence of disorders of the autism spectrum in a population cohort of children in South Thames: The special needs project (SNAP)." *Lancet 368*, 179–181.

Baranek, G. T. (2002) "Efficacy of sensory and motor interventions for children with autism." *Journal of Autism and Developmental Disorders 32*, 397–422.

Barnhill, G. P., Cook, K. T., Tebbenhamp, K., and Myles, B. S. (2002) "The effectiveness of social skills intervention targeting nonverbal communication for adolescents with Asperger syndrome and related pervasive developmental delays." *Focus on Autism and Other Developmental Disabilities 17*, 112–118.

Baron-Cohen, S. (2008a) "Autism—in 100 words." *British Journal of Psychiatry 193*, 321.

Baron-Cohen, S. (2008b) *Autism and Asperger Syndrome: The Facts*. New York: Oxford University Press.

Barry, T. D., Klinger, L. G., Lee, J. M., Palardy, N., Gilmore, T., and Bodin, S. D. (2003) "Examining the effectiveness of an outpatient clinic-based social skills group for high-functioning children with autism." *Journal of Autism and Developmental Disorders 33*, 685–701.

Bebko, J. M., Konstantareas, M. M., and Springer J. (1987) "Parent and professional evaluations of family stress associated with characteristics of autism." *Journal of Autism and Developmental Disorders 17*, 565–576.

Beery, K., Buktenica, N. A., and Beery, N. A. (2004) *Beery-Buktenica Developmental Test of Visual-Motor Integration*, 5th edn. San Antonio, TX: Psychological Corporation.

Bellini, S. (2006) "The development of social anxiety in high functioning adolescents with autism spectrum disorders." *Focus on Autism and Other Developmental Disabilities 21*, 138–145.

Bellini, S. (2008) *Building Social Relationships: A Systematic Approach to Teaching Social Interaction Skills to Children and Adolescents with Autism Spectrum Disorders and Other Social Difficulties*. Shawnee Mission, KS: Autism Asperger Publishing Company.

Bellini, S., Peters, J. K., Benner, L., and Hopf, A. (2007) "A meta-analysis of school-based interventions for children with autism spectrum disorders." *Remedial and Special Education 28*, 153–162.

Bishop, D. V. M. (2003) *Children's Communication Checklist*, 2nd edn. London: Psychological Corporation.

Bishop, D. V. M. (2006) *Children's Communication Checklist*, 2nd edn, U.S. San Antonio, TX: Psychological Corporation.

Bishop, D. V. M. and Norbury, C. F. (2002) "Exploring the borderlands of autistic disorder and specific language impairment: A study using standardized instruments." *Journal of Child Psychology and Psychiatry 43*, 917–930.

Bloch, J., Weinstein, J., and Seitz, M. (2005) "School and Parent Partnerships in the Preschool Years." In D. Zager (ed.) *Autism Spectrum Disorders: Identification, Education, and Treatment*, 3rd edn. Mahwah, NJ: Lawrence Erlbaum Associates.

Bolte, S., Dickhut, H., and Poustka, F. (1999) "Patterns of parent-reported problems indicative in autism." *Psychopathology 32*, 93–97.

Bolte, S. and Poustka, F. (2002) "The relation between general cognitive level and adaptive behavior domains in individuals with autism with and without co-morbid mental retardation." *Child Psychiatry and Human Development 33*, 165–172.

Bondy, A. and Frost, L. A. (1994) "The picture exchange communication system." *Focus on Autistic Behavior 9*, 1–19.

Bondy, A. S. and Frost, L. A. (2001) "The picture exchange communication system." *Behavior Modification 25*, 725–744.

Brock, S. E., Jimerson, S. R., and Hansen, R. L. (2006) *Identifying, Assessing, and Treating Autism at School*. New York: Springer.

Brownell, R. (2000) *Expressive One-Word Picture Vocabulary Test*. Novato, CA: Academic Therapy.

Bruininks, R. H. and Bruininks, B. D. (2006) *Bruininks-Oseretsky Test of Motor Proficiency*, 2nd edn. San Antonio, TX: Psychological Corporation.

Bryan L. C. and Gast D. L. (2000) "Teaching on-task and on-schedule behaviors to high-functioning children with autism via picture activity schedules." *Journal of Autism and Developmental Disorders 30*, 553–567.

Bryson, S. E., Rogers, S. J., and Fombonne, E. (2003) "Autism spectrum disorders: Early detection, intervention, education, and psychopharmacological management." *Canadian Journal of Psychiatry 48*, 506–516.

Bryson, S. E., Koegel, L. K., Koegel, R. L., Openden, D., Smith, I. M., and Nefdt, N. (2007) "Large scale dissemination and community implementation of pivotal response treatment: Program description and preliminary data." *Research and Practice for Persons with Severe Disabilities 32*, 142–153.

California Department of Developmental Services (2002) *Autistic Spectrum Disorders: Best Practice Guidelines for Screening, Diagnosis and Assessment*. Sacramento, CA: California Department of Developmental Services.

Callahan, K. and Rademacher, J. A. (1999) "Using self-management strategies to increase the on-task behavior of a student with autism." *Journal of Positive Behavior Interventions 1*, 117–122.

Campbell, J. M. (2005) "Diagnostic assessment of Asperger's disorder: A review of five third-party rating scales." *Journal of Autism and Developmental Disorders 35*, 25–35.

Carpenter, L. A., Soorya, L., and Halpern, D. (2009) "Asperger's syndrome and high-functioning autism." *Pediatric Annals 38*, 30–35.

Carr, E. G., Horner, R. H., Turnbull, A. P., Marquis, J. G., *et al.* (1999) "Positive behavior support for people with developmental disabilities: A research synthesis." *American Association on Mental Retardation Monograph Series*, Washington, DC.

Carr, E. G., Dunlap, G., Horner, R. H., Koegel, R. L., *et al.* (2002) "Positive behavior support: Evolution of an applied science." *Journal of Positive Behavior Interventions 4*, 4–16.

Carrow-Woolfolk, E. (1999) *Comprehensive Assessment of Spoken Language*. Circle Pines, MN: American Guidance Service.

Carter, A. S., Davis, N. O., Klin, A., and Volkmar, F. R. (2005) "Social Development in Autism." In F. R. Volkmar, R. Paul, A. Klin, and D. Cohen (eds.) *Handbook of Autism and Pervasive Developmental Disorders: Vol. 1. Diagnosis, Development, Neurobiology, and Behavior*. Hoboken, NJ: John Wiley and Sons.

Centers for Disease Control and Prevention (CDC) (2002) "Prevalence of autism spectrum disorders." *Autism and Developmental Disabilities Monitoring Network, 14 Sites*, United States, 2002. MMWR SS 2007; 56(SS-1) (2).US Government report

Chakrabarti, S. and Fombonne, E. (2001) "Pervasive developmental disorders in preschool children." *Journal of the American Medical Association 285*, 3093–3099.

Chandler, S., Charman, T., Baird, G., Simonoff, E., *et al.* (2007) "Validation of the Social Communication Questionnaire in a population cohort of children with autism spectrum disorders." *Journal of the American Academy of Child and Adolescent Psychiatry 46*, 1324–1332.

Chandler, L. K. and Dahlquist, C. M. (2002) *Functional Assessment: Strategies to Prevent and Remediate Challenging Behavior in School Settings*. New Jersey: Merrill Prentice Hall.

Charlop-Christy M.H., and Carpenter M. H. (2000) "Modified incidental teaching sessions: A procedure for parents to increase spontaneous speech in their children with autism." *Journal of Positive Behavior Interventions 2*, 98–112.

Charlop-Christy, M. H., and Kelso, S. E. (1999) "Autism." In V. L. Schwean and D. H. Saklofske (eds.) *Handbook of Psychosocial Characteristics of Exceptional Children.* New York: Kluwer Academic/Plenum Publishers.

Charlop-Christy, M. H., Carpenter, M., H., LeBlanc, L. A., and Kellet, K. (2002) "Using the Picture Exchange Communication System (PECS) with children with autism: Assessment of PECS acquisition, speech, social-communicative behavior, and problem behavior." *Journal of Applied Behavior Analysis 35,* 213–231.

Charman, T., Baird, G., Simonoff, E., Loucas, T., *et al.* (2007) "Efficacy of three screening instruments in the identification of autistic-spectrum disorders." *British Journal of Psychiatry 191,* 554–559.

Cimera, R. E. and Cowan, R. J. (2009) "The costs of services and employment outcomes achieved by adults with autism in the US." *Autism 13,* 285–302

Clark, C., Prior, M., and Kinsella, G. (2002) "The relationship between executive function abilities, adaptive behavior, and academic achievement in children with externalizing behavior problems." *Journal of Child Psychology and Psychiatry 43,* 785–796.

Cole, C. L. and Bambara, L. M. (2000) "Self-monitoring: Theory and Practice." In E. S. Shapiro and T. R. Kratochwill (eds.) *Behavioral Assessment in Schools: Theory, Research, and Clinical Foundations,* 2nd edn. New York: Guilford Press.

Cole, C. L., Marder, T., and McCann, L. (2000) "Self-monitoring." In E. S. Shapiro and T. R. Kratochwill (eds.) *Conducting School-based Assessments of Child and Adolescent Behavior.* New York: Guilford Press.

Conners, C. K. (2008) *Conners 3rd Edition.* North Tonawanda, NY: Multi-Health Systems.

Constantino, J. N., Davis, S. A., Todd, R. D., Schindler, M. K., *et al.* (2003) "Validation of a brief quantitative measure of autistic traits: Comparison of the Social Responsiveness Scale with the Autism Diagnostic Interview-Revised." *Journal of Autism and Developmental Disorders 33,* 427–433.

Constantino, J. N. and Todd, R.D. (2003) "Autistic traits in the general population: A twin study." *Archives of General Psychiatry 60,* 524–530.

Constantino, J. N. and Gruber, C. P. (2005) *Social Responsiveness Scale.* Los Angeles: Western Psychological Services.

Cook, D. G. and Dunn, W. (1998) "Sensory Integration for Students with Autism." In R. L. Simpson and B. S. Myles (eds.) *Educating Children and Youth with Autism: Strategies for Effective Practice.* Austin, TX: Pro-Ed.

Coonrod, E. E. and Stone, W. L. (2005) "Screening for Autism in Young Children." In F. R. Volkmar, R. Paul, A. Klin, and D. Cohen (eds.) *Handbook of Autism and Pervasive Developmental Disorders: Vol. 2. Assessment, Interventions, and Policy,* 3rd edn. New York: John Wiley.

Cooper, M. J., Griffith, K. G., and Filer, J. (1999) "School intervention for inclusion of students with and without disabilities." *Focus on Autism and Other Developmental Disabilities 14,* 110–115.

Corsello, C., Hus, V., Pickles, A., Risi, S., *et al.* (2007) "Between a ROC and a hard place: Decision making and making decisions about using the SCQ." *Journal of Child Psychology and Psychiatry 48,* 932–940.

Crane, L., Goddard, L., and Pring, L. (2009) "Sensory processing in adults with autism spectrum disorders." *Autism 13,* 215–228.

Dawson, G. and Osterling, J. (1997) "Early Intervention in Autism." In M. Guralnick (ed.) *The Effectiveness of Early Intervention.* Baltimore, MD: Paul H. Brookes Publishing.

Dawson, G. and Watling, R. (2000) "Interventions to facilitate auditory, visual, and motor integration in autism: A review of the evidence." *Journal of Autism and Developmental Disorders 30,* 415–421.

Department for Education and Employment (2001) *The Code of Practice on the Identification and Assessment of Special Educational Needs.* London: HMSO.

Department for Education and Skills (2002) *Autistic Spectrum Disorders: Good Practice Guidance.* London: DfES.

Deprey, L. and Ozonoff, S. (2009) "Assessment of Comorbid Psychiatric Conditions in Autism Spectrum Disorders." In S. Goldstein, J. A. Naglieri, and S. Ozonoff (eds.) *Assessment of Autism Spectrum Disorders.* New York: Guilford Press.

DiSalvo, D. A. and Oswald, D. P. (2002) "Peer-mediated interventions to increase the social interaction of children with autism: Consideration of peer expectancies." *Focus on Autism and Other Developmental Disabilities 17,* 198–208.

Duarte, C. S., Bordin, I. A. S., deOliveira, A., and Bird, H. (2003) "The CBCL and the identification of children with autism and related conditions in Brazil: Pilot findings." *Journal of Autism and Developmental Disorders 33,* 703–707.

Dunlap, G. and Fox, L. (1999) "A demonstration of behavioral support for young children with autism." *Journal of Positive Behavior Interventions 1,* 77–87.

Dunlap, G., Carr, E. G., Horner, R. H., Zarcone, J. R., and Schwartz, I. (2008) "Positive behavior support and applied behavior analysis: A familial alliance." *Behavior Modification 32,* 682–698.

Dunn, W. (1999) *Sensory Profile.* San Antonio, TX: Psychological Corporation.

Dunn, W. (2001) "The sensations of everyday life: Empirical, theoretical, and pragmatic considerations." *American Journal of Occupational Therapy 55,* 608–620.

Dunn, L. and Dunn, L. (2007) *Peabody Picture Vocabulary Test*, 4th edn. Circle Pines, MN: American Guidance Service.

Eaves, R.C., Campbell, H., and Chambers, D. (2000) "The criterion-related and construct validity of the Pervasive Developmental Disorders Rating Scale and the Autism Behavior Checklist." *Psychology in the Schools 37*, 311–321.

Ehlers, S. and Gillberg, C. (1993) "The epidemiology of Asperger syndrome: A total population study." *Journal of Child Psychology and Psychiatry 34*, 1327–1350.

Ehlers, S., Gillberg, C., and Wing, L. (1999) "A screening questionnaire for Asperger syndrome and other high-functioning autism spectrum disorders in school-age children." *Journal of Autism and Developmental Disorders 29*, 129–141.

Eikeseth, S., Smith, T., Jahr, E., and Eldevik, S. (2002) "Intensive behavioral intervention at school for 4- to 7-year old children with autism." *Behavior Modification 26*, 49–68.

Eldevik, S., Hastings, R. P., Hughes, C. J., Jahr, E., Eikeseth, S., and Cross, S. (2009) "Meta-analysis of early intensive behavioral intervention for children with autism." *Journal of Clinical Child and Adolescent Psychology 38*, 439–450.

Elliott, C. (2007) *Differential Abilities Scale*, 2nd edn. San Antonio, TX: Psychological Corporation.

Elliott, S. N. and Busse, R. T. (1993) "Effective Treatments with Behavioral Consultation." In J. E. Zins, T. R. Kratochwill, and S. N. Elliott (eds.) *Handbook of Consultation Services for Children: Applications in Educational and Clinical Settings*. San Francisco, CA: Jossey-Bass.

Estes, A., Munson, J., Dawson, G., Koehler, E., Zhou, X., and Abbott, R. (2009) "Parenting stress and psychological functioning among mothers of preschool children with autism and developmental delay." *Autism 13*, 375–387.

Filipek, P. A., Accardo, P. J., Baranek, G. T., Cook, E. H. Jr., *et al.* (1999) "The screening and diagnosis of autistic spectrum disorders." *Journal of Autism and Developmental Disorders 29*, 439–494.

Filipek, P. A., Accardo, P. J., Ashwal, S., Baranek, G. T., *et al.* (2000) "Practice parameter: Screening and diagnosis of autism: Report of the Quality Standards Subcommittee of the American Academy of Neurology and the Child Neurology Society." *Neurology 55*, 468–479.

Filipek, P. A., Steinberg-Epstein, R., and Book, T. M. (2006) "Intervention for autistic spectrum disorders." *Neurotherapeutics 3*, 207–216.

Fogt, J. B., Miller, D. N., and Zirkel, P. A. (2003) "Defining autism: Professional best practices and published case law." *Journal of School Psychology 41*, 201–216.

Fombonne, E. (2003) "The prevalence of autism." *Journal of the American Medical Association 289*, 87–89.

Fombonne, E. (2005) "The changing epidemiology of autism." *Journal of Applied Research in Intellectual Disabilities 18*, 281–294.

Fombonne, E., Simmons, H., Ford, T., Meltzer, H., and Goodman, R. (2001) "Prevalence of pervasive developmental disorders in the British Nationwide Survey of Child Mental Health." *Journal of the American Academy of Child and Adolescent Psychiatry 40*, 820–827.

Fombonne, E., Zakarian, R., Bennett, A., Meng, L., and McLean-Heywood, D. (2006) "Pervasive developmental disorders in Montreal, Quebec, Canada: Prevalence and links with immunizations." *Pediatrics 118*, 139–150.

Forness, S. and Kavale, K. (1999) "Teaching social skills in children with learning disabilities: A meta-analysis of the research." *Learning Disability Quarterly 19*, 2–13.

Fouse, B. (1999) *Creating a Win-Win IEP for Students with Autism: A How-to Manual for Parents and Educators*. Arlington, TX: Future Horizons.

Freeman, B. J., Del'Homme, M., Guthrie, D., and Zhang, F. (1999) "Vineland Adaptive Behavior Scale scores as a function of age and initial IQ in 210 autistic children." *Journal of Autism and Developmental Disorders 29*, 379–384.

Ganz, J. B. (2008) "Self-monitoring across age and ability levels: Teaching students to implement their own positive behavioral interventions." *Preventing School Failure 53*, 39–48.

Ghaziuddin, M. (2002) "Asperger syndrome: Associated psychiatric and medical conditions." *Focus on Autism and Other Developmental Disabilities 17*, 138–143.

Ghaziuddin, M. (2005) *Mental Health Aspects of Autism and Asperger Syndrome*. London: Jessica Kingsley Publishers.

Ghaziuddin, M., Weidmer-Mikhail, E., and Ghaziuddin, N. (1998) "Comorbidity of Asperger syndrome: A preliminary report." *Journal of Intellectual Disability Research 42*, 279–283.

Gilliam, J. E. (1995) *Gilliam Autism Rating Scale*. Austin, TX: Pro-Ed.

Gilliam, J. E. (2001) *Gilliam Asperger's Disorder Scale*. Austin, TX: Pro-Ed.

Gilliam, J. E. and Miller, L. (2006) *Pragmatic Language Skills Inventory*. Austin, TX: Pro-Ed.

Gioia, G. A., Isquith, P. K., Guy, S. C, and Kenworthy, L. (2000) *Behavior Rating Inventory of Executive Function*. Lutz, FL: Psychological Assessment Resources.

Gioia, G. A., Isquith, P. K., Kenworthy, L., and Barton, R. M. (2002) "Profiles of everyday executive function in acquired and developmental disorders." *Child Neuropsychology 8*, 121–137.

Goddard, J. A., Lehr, R., and Lapadat, J. C. (2000) "Parents of children with disabilities: Telling a different story." *Canadian Journal of Counselling 34*, 273–289.

Goin-Kochel, R. P., Mackintosh, V. H., and Myers, B. J. (2006) "How many doctors does it take to make an autism spectrum diagnosis?" *Autism 10*, 439–451.

Goldstein, G., Johnson, C. R., and Minshew, N. J. (2001) "Attentional processes in autism." *Journal of Autism and Developmental Disorders 31*, 433–440.

Goldstein, H. (2002) "Communication intervention for children with autism: A review of treatment efficacy." *Journal of Autism and Developmental Disorders 32*, 375–395.

Goldstein, S. (2002) "Review of the Asperger Syndrome Diagnostic Scale." *Journal of Autism and Developmental Disorders 32*, 611–614.

Goldstein, S. and Naglieri, J.A. (2009) *Autism Spectrum Scales.* North Tonawanda, New York, NY: Health Systems, Inc.

Gray, C. A. (1998) "Social Stories and Comic Strip Conversations with Students with Asperger Syndrome and High-Functioning Autism." In E. Schopler, G. B. Mesibov, and L. J. Kunce (eds.) *Asperger Syndrome or High-functioning Autism?* New York: Plenum Press.

Gresham, F. M. (1989) "Assessment of treatment Integrity in school consultation and prereferral intervention." *School Psychology Review 18*, 37–50.

Gresham, F. M., Gansle, K. A., and Noell, G. H. (1993) "Treatment integrity in applied behavior analysis with children." *Journal of Applied Behavior Analysis 26*, 257–263.

Gresham, F. M. and MacMillan, D. L. (1998) "Early intervention project: Can its claims be substantiated and its effect replicated?" *Journal of Autism and Developmental Disorders 28*, 5–13.

Gresham, F. M., Beebe-Frankenberger, M. E., and MacMillan, D. L. (1999) "A selective review of treatments for children with autism: Description and methodological considerations." *School Psychology Review 28*, 559–575.

Gresham, F. M., Sugai, G., and Horner, R. H. (2001) "Interpreting outcomes of social skills training for students with high-incidence disabilities." *Teaching Exceptional Children 67*, 331–344.

Gutkin, T. B. (1993) "Conducting Consultation Research." In J. E. Zins, T. R. Kratochwill, and S. N. Elliott (eds.) *Handbook of Consultation Services for Children: Applications in Educational and Clinical Settings.* San Francisco, CA: Jossey-Bass.

Hall, L. J. (1997) "Effective behavioural strategies for the defining characteristics of autism." *Behaviour Change 14*, 139–154.

Hanley, G. P., Iwata, B. A., and Thompson, R. H. (2001) "Reinforcement schedule thinning following treatment with functional communication training." *Journal of Applied Behavior Analysis 34*, 17–38.

Hare, D. J. (1997) "The use of cognitive-behavioural therapy with people with Asperger's syndrome." *Autism 1*, 215–225.

Hare D. J. (2004) "Developing cognitive behavioural work with people with ASD." *Good Autism Practice 5*, 18–22.

Harris, S. (1994) "Treatment of Family Problems in Autism." In E. Schopler and G. Mesibov (eds.) *Behavioral Issues in Autism.* New York, NY: Plenum Press.

Harris, S. L. and Handleman, J. S. (2000) "Age and IQ at intake as predictors of placement for young children with autism: A four- to six-year follow-up." *Journal of Autism and Developmental Disorders 30*, 137–142.

Harris, S. L. and Delmolino, L. (2002) "Applied behavior analysis: Its application in the treatment of autism and related disorders in young children." *Infants and Young Children 14*, 11–17.

Harrison, J. and Hare, D. J. (2004) "Brief report: Assessment of sensory abnormalities in people with autism spectrum disorders." *Journal of Autism and Developmental Disorders 34*, 727–730.

Harrison, P. and Oakland, T. (2003) *Adaptive Behavior Assessment System*, 2nd edn. San Antonio, TX: Psychological Corporation.

Harrower, J. K. and Dunlap, G. (2001) "Including children with autism in general education classrooms: A review of effective strategies." *Behavior Modification 25*, 762–785.

Hart, S. L. and Banda, D. R. (2009) "Picture Exchange Communication System with individuals with developmental disabilities: A meta-analysis of single subject studies." *Remedial and Special Education*, August 26, 2009. DOI: 10.1177/0741932509338354.

Hill, E. L. (2004) "Evaluating the theory of executive dysfunction in autism." *Developmental Review 24*, 189–233.

Hoffman, C. D., Sweeney, D. P., Hodge, D., Lopez-Wagner, M. C., and Looney, L. (2009) "Parenting stress and closeness: Mothers of typically developing children and mothers of children with autism." *Focus on Autism and Other Developmental Disabilities 24*, 178–187.

Horner, R. H., Carr, E. G., Strain, P. S., Todd, A. W., and Reed, H. K. (2002) "Problem behavior interventions for young children with autism: A research synthesis." *Journal of Autism and Developmental Disorders 32*, 5, 423–446.

Howlin, P. (1998) *Children with Autism and Asperger's Syndrome: A Guide for Practitioners and Carers.* New York: John Wiley and Sons.

Howlin, P. (2005) "Outcomes in Autism Spectrum Disorders." In F. R. Volkmar, R. Paul, A. Klin, and D. Cohen (eds.) *Handbook of Autism and Pervasive Developmental Disorders: Vol. 1. Diagnosis, Development, Neurobiology, and Behavior,* 3rd edn. New York: John Wiley and Sons.

Howlin, P. and Rutter, M. (1987) *Treatment of Autistic Children.* New York: John Wiley and Sons.

Howlin, P. and Moore, A. (1997) "Diagnosis in autism: A survey of over 1200 patients in the UK." *Autism 1*, 135–162.

Howlin, P. and Asgharian, A. (1999) "The diagnosis of autism and Asperger syndrome: Findings from a survey of 770 families." *Developmental Medicine and Child Neurology* 41, 834—9.

Hume, K., Bellini, S., and Pratt, C. (2005) "The usage and perceived outcomes of early intervention and early childhood programs for young children with autism spectrum disorder." *Topics in Early Childhood Special Education 25*, 195–207.

Hwang, B., and Hughes, C. (2000) "The effects of social interactive training on early social communicative skills of children with autism." *Journal of Autism and Developmental Disorders 30*, 331–343.

Individuals with Disabilities Education Improvement Act of 2004. Pub. L. No. 108–446, 108th Congress, 2nd Session (2004).

Iovannone, R., Dunlap, G., Huber, H., and Kincaid, D. (2003) "Effective educational practices for students with autism spectrum disorders." *Focus on Autism and Other Developmental Disabilities 18*,150–165.

Johnson, C. P., Myers, S. M., and Council on Children with Disabilities (2007) "Identification and evaluation of children with autism spectrum disorders." *Pediatrics 120*, 1183–1215.

Johnston, J. M., Foxx, R. M., Jacobson, J. W., Green, G., and Mulick J. A. (2006) "Positive behavior support and applied behavior analysis." *Behavior Analyst 29*, 51–74.

Jordan, R. (2003) School-based intervention for children with specific learning difficulties. In M. Prior (ed.) *Learning and Behavior Problems in Asperger Syndrome.* New York: Guilford Press.

Kamps D., Kravits T., Gonzalez-Lopez A., Kemeret, K., Potucek J., and Garrison-Harrell L. (1998) "What do the peers think? Social validity of peer-mediated programs." *Education and Treatment of Children 21*, 107–134.

Kamps, D., Royer, J., Dugan, E., Kravits, T., *et al.* (2002) "Peer training to facilitate social interaction for elementary students with autism and their peers." *Exceptional Children 68*, 173–187.

Kamphaus, R. W., Reynolds, C. R., and Imperato-McCammon, C. (1999) "Roles of Diagnosis and Classification in School Psychology." In C. R. Reynolds and T. B. Gutkin (eds.) *The Handbook of School Psychology,* 3rd edn. New York: John Wiley and Sons.

Kaufman, A. S. and Kaufman, N. L. (2004) *Kaufman Test of Educational Achievement,* 2nd edn. San Antonio, TX: Psychological Corporation.

Kern, J. K., Trevidi, M. H., Grannemann, B. D., Garver, C. R., *et al.* (2007) "Sensory correlations in autism." *Autism 11*, 123–134.

Kim, A., Szatmari, P., Bryson, S., Streiner, D., and Wilson, F. (2000) "The prevalence of anxiety and mood problems among children with autism and Asperger syndrome." *Autism 4*, 117–132.

Klin, A., Sparrow, S. S., Marans, W. D., Carter, A. and Volkmar, F. R. (2000) "Assessment Issues in Children and Adolescents with Asperger's Syndrome." In A. Klin, F. R. Volkmar, and S. S. Sparrow (eds.) *Asperger's Syndrome.* New York: Guilford Press.

Klin, A. and Volkmar, F. R. (2000) "Treatment and Intervention Guidelines for Individuals with Asperger Syndrome." In A. Klin, F.R. Volkmar, and S. S. Sparrow (eds.) *Asperger's Syndrome.* New York: Guilford Press.

Klin, A., Saulnier, C., Tsantsanis, K., and Volkmar, F. R. (2005) "Clinical Evaluation in Autism Spectrum Disorders: Psychological Assessment within a Transdisciplinary Framework." In F. R. Volkmar, R. Paul, A. Klin, and D. Cohen (eds.) *Handbook of Autism and Pervasive Developmental Disorders: Vol. 2. Assessment, Interventions, and Policy,* 3rd edn. New York: John Wiley.

Klinger, L. G., Dawson, G., and Renner, P. (2003) "Autistic Disorder." In E. Mash and R. Barkley (eds.) *Child Psychopathology,* 2nd edn. New York: Guilford Press.

Klinger, L. G., O'Kelley, S. E., and Mussey, J. L. (2009) "Assessment of Intellectual Functioning in Autism Spectrum Disorders." In S. Goldstein, J. A. Naglieri, and S. Ozonoff (eds.) *Assessment of Autism Spectrum Disorders.* New York: Guilford Press.

Koegel, L. K., Koegel, R. L., Hurley, C., and Frea, W. D. (1992) "Improving social skills and disruptive behavior in children with autism through self-management." *Journal of Applied Behavior Analysis 25*, 341–353.

Koegel, L. K., Robinson, S., and Koegel, R. L. (2009) "Empirically supported intervention practices for autism spectrum disorders in school and community settings: Issues and practices." In Sailor, W., Dunlap, G., Sugai, G., and Horner, R. (eds.) *Handbook of Positive Behavior Support*. New York: Springer.

Koegel, R. L., Schreibman, L., Loos, L. M., and Dirlich-Wilhelm, H. (1992) "Consistent stress profiles in mothers of children with autism." *Journal of Autism and Developmental Disorders* 22, 205–216.

Koegel, R. L. and Koegel, L. K. (eds.) (1995) *Teaching Children with Autism: Strategies for Initiating Positive Interactions and Improving Learning Opportunities*. Baltimore, MD: Paul H. Brookes Publishing.

Koegel, R. L., Koegel, L. K., and Parks, D. R. (1995) "'Teach the Individual' Model of Generalization: Autonomy through Self-management." In R. L. Koegel and L. K. Koegel (eds.) *Teaching Children with Autism: Strategies for Initiating Positive Interactions and Improving Learning Opportunities*. Baltimore, MD: Paul H. Brookes Publishing.

Koegel, R. L., Koegel, L. K., and Carter, C. M. (1999) "Pivotal teaching interactions for children with autism." *School Psychology Review 28*, 576–594.

Koegel, R. L. and Koegel, L. K. (2006) *Pivotal Response Treatments for Autism: Communication, Social, and Academic Development*. Baltimore, MD: Paul H. Brookes Publishing.

Koegel, R. L., Openden, D., Fredeen, R. M., and Koegel, L. K. (2006) "The Basics of Pivotal Response Treatment." In R. L. Koegel and L. K. Koegel (eds.) *Pivotal Response Treatments for Autism: Communication, Social, and Academic Development*. Baltimore, MD: Paul H. Brookes Publishing.

Kovacs, M. (1992) *Children's Depression Inventory*. North Tonawanda, NY: Multi-Health Systems.

Krug, D. A., Arick, J. R., and Almond, P. J. (1988) *Autism Behavior Checklist*. Austin, TX: Pro-Ed.

Kunce, L. (2003) "The Ideal Classroom." In M. Prior (ed.) *Learning and Behavior Problems in Asperger Syndrome*. New York: Guilford Press.

La Greca, A. M. and Lopez, N. (1998) "Social anxiety among adolescents: Linkages with peer relations and friendships." *Journal of Clinical Child Psychology 26*, 83–94.

Lainhart, J. E. (1999) "Psychiatric problems in individuals with autism, their parents and siblings." *International Review of Psychiatry 11*, 278–298.

Lainhart, J. E. and Folstein, S. E. (1994) "Affective disorders in people with autism: A review of published cases." *Journal of Autism and Developmental Disorders 24*, 587–601.

Landa R. (2000) "Social Language Use in Asperger Syndrome and High-Functioning Autism." In A. Klin, F. Volkmar, and S. Sparrow (eds.) *Asperger Syndrome*. New York: Guilford Press.

Lane, K. L., Bocian, K. M., MacMillan, D. L., and Gresham, F. M. (2004) "Treatment integrity: An essential—but often forgotten—component of school-based interventions." *Preventing School Failure 48*, 36–43.

Ledford, J. R., Gast, D. L., Luscre, D., and Ayres, K. M. (2008) "Observational and incidental learning by children with autism during small group instruction." *Journal of Autism and Developmental Disorders 38*, 86–103.

Lee, L., David, A. B., Rusyniak, J., Landa, R., and Newschaffer, C. J. (2007) "Performance of the Social Communication Questionnaire in children receiving preschool special education services." *Research in Autism Spectrum Disorders 1*, 126–128.

Lee, S., Simpson, R. L., and Shogren, K. A. (2007) "Effects and implications of self-management for students with autism: A meta-analysis." *Focus on Autism and Other Developmental Disabilities 22*, 2–13.

Lincoln, A. J., Allen, M. H., and Kilman, A. (1995) "The Assessment and Interpretation of Intellectual Abilities in People with Autism." In E. Schopler and G. B. Mesibov (eds.) *Learning and Cognition in Autism*. New York: Plenum.

Liss, M., Bullard, S., Robins, D. and Fein, D. (2000) "Brief report: Cognitive estimation in individuals with pervasive developmental disorders." *Journal of Autism and Developmental Disorders 30*, 613–618.

Lopata, C., Thomeer, M. L., Volker, M. A., and Nida, R. E. (2006) "Effectiveness of a cognitive-behavioral treatment on the social behaviors of children with Asperger disorder." *Focus on Autism and Other Developmental Disabilities 21*, 237–244.

Lord, C. (2000) "Diagnosis of Autism Spectrum Disorders in Young Children." In A. Wetherby and B. Prizant (eds.) *Autism, a Transactional, Developmental Perspective*. Baltimore: Paul H. Brookes Publishing.

Lord, C., Rutter, M., and LeCouteur, A. (1994) "Autism diagnostic interview-revised: A revised version of a diagnostic interview for caregivers of individuals with possible pervasive developmental disorder." *Journal of Autism and Developmental Disorders 24*, 659–685.

Lord, C., Pickles, A., McLennan, J., Rutter, M., *et al.* (1997) "Diagnosing autism: Analyses of data from the Autism Diagnostic Interview." *Journal of Autism and Developmental Disorders 27*, 501–517.

Lord, C., Risi, S., Lambrecht, L., Cook, E. H., *et al.* (2000) "The Autism Diagnostic Observation Schedule-Generic: A standard measure of social and communication deficits associated with the spectrum of autism." *Journal of Autism and Developmental Disorders 30*, 205–223.

Lord, C., Rutter, M., DiLavore, P. C., and Risi, S. (2001) *Autism Diagnostic Observation Schedule*. Los Angeles: Western Psychological Services

Lord, C. and Corsello, C. (2005) "Diagnostic Instruments in Autistic Spectrum Disorders." In F. R. Volkmar, R. Paul, A. Klin, and D. Cohen (eds.) *Handbook of Autism and Pervasive Developmental Disorders: Vol. 2. Assessment, Interventions, and Policy,* 3rd edn. New York: John Wiley.

Lovaas, O. I. (1987) "Behavioral treatment and normal educational and intellectual functioning in young autistic children." *Journal of Autism and Developmental Disorders 9,* 315–323.

Loveland K. A. and Tunali-Kotoski, B. (1997) "The School Age Child with Autism." In D. J. Cohen and F. R. Volkmar (eds.) *Handbook of Autism and Pervasive Developmental Disorders,* 2nd edn. New York: Wiley and Sons.

Macintosh, K. and Dissanayake, C. (2004) "Annotation. The similarities and differences between autistic disorder and Asperger's disorder: A review of the empirical evidence." *Journal of Child Psychology and Psychiatry 45,* 421–434.

Macintosh, K. and Dissanayake, C. (2006) "Social skills and problem behaviors in school aged children with high-functioning autism and Asperger's disorder." *Journal of Autism and Developmental Disorders 36,* 1065–1076

Mandlawitz, M. R. (2002) "The impact of the legal system on educational programming for young children with autism spectrum disorder." *Journal of Autism and Developmental Disorders 32,* 495–508.

Marans, W. D. (1997) "Communication Assessment." In D. Cohen and F. R. Volkmar (eds.) *Handbook of Autism and Pervasive Developmental Disorders,* 2nd edn. New York: John Wiley and Sons.

Mayes, S. and Calhoun, S. (2003) "Relationship between Asperger Syndrome and High-functioning Autism." In M. Prior (ed.) *Learning and Behavior Problems in Asperger Syndrome.* New York: Guilford Press.

Mayes, S. D., Calhoun, S. L., and Crites, D. L. (2001) "Does *DSM-IV* Asperger's disorder exist?" *Journal of Abnormal Child Psychology 29,* 263–271.

McClannahan, L. E. and Krantz, P. J. (1999) *Activity Schedules for Children with Autism: Teaching Independent Behavior.* Bethesda, MD: Woodbine House.

McConnell, S. R. (2002) "Interventions to facilitate social interaction for young children with autism: Review of available research and recommendations for educational intervention and future research." *Journal of Autism and Developmental Disorders 32,* 351–370.

McGee, G. G. and Daly, T. (2007) "Incidental teaching of age-appropriate social phrases to children with autism." *Research and Practice for Persons with Severe Disabilities 32,* 112–123.

Medical Research Council (2001) *MRC Review of Autism Research: Epidemiology and Causes.* London: MRC.

Mesibov, G., Schopler, E., and Hearsey, K. A. (1994) "Structured Teaching." In E. Schopler and G. Mesibov (eds.) *Behavioral Issues in Autism.* New York: Plenum.

Mildenberger, K., Sitter, S., Noterdaeme, M., and Amorosa, H. (2001) "The use of the ADI-R as a diagnostic tool in the differential diagnosis of children with infantile autism and children with receptive language disorder." *European Child and Adolescent Psychiatry 10,* 248–255.

Minshew, N., Goldstein, G., and Siegel, D. J. (1995) "Speech and language in high functioning autistic individuals." *Neuropsychology 9,* 255–261.

Minshew, N. J., Sweeney, J. A., and Bauman, M. L. (1997) "Neurological Aspects of Autism." In D. D. Cohen and F. R. Volkmar (eds.) *Handbook of Autism and Pervasive Developmental Disorders,* 2nd edn. New York: Wiley.

Morrison, R. S., Sainato, D. M., BenChaaban, D., and Endo, S. (2002) "Increasing play skills of children with autism using activity schedules and correspondence training." *Journal of Early Intervention 25,* 58–72.

Myers, S. M., Johnson, C. P., and Council on Children with Disabilities (2007) "Management of children with autism spectrum disorders." *Pediatrics 120,* 1162–1182.

Myles, B. S., Bock, S. J., and Simpson, R. L. (2001) *Asperger Syndrome Diagnostic Scale.* Los Angeles: Western Psychological Services.

Myles, B. S. and Simpson, R. L. (2002) "Asperger syndrome: An overview of characteristics." *Focus on Autism and Other Developmental Disabilities 17,* 132–137.

Myles, B. S. and Simpson, R. L. (2003) *Asperger Syndrome: A Guide for Educators and Parents,* 2nd edn. Austin, TX: Pro-Ed.

Myles, B. S., Adreon, D. A., Hagen, K., Holverstott, J., *et al.* (2005) *Life Journey through Autism: An Educator's Guide to Asperger Syndrome.* Arlington, VA: Organization for Autism Research.

Naglieri, J. A. and Chambers, K. M. (2009) "Psychometric Issues and Current Scales for Assessing Autism Spectrum Disorders." In S. Goldstein, J. A. Naglieri, and S. Ozonoff (eds.) *Assessment of Autism Spectrum Disorders.* New York: Guilford Press.

National Association of School Psychologists (2002) *Promoting Positive Behavior, Academic Success, and School Safety.* Bethesda, MD: NASP.

National Autistic Society (2003) *Approaches to Autism: An Easy to Use Guide to Many and Varied Approaches to Autism,* 5th edn. London: National Autistic Society.

National Autistic Society (2006) "What is the spell framework?" Available at www.nas.org.uk/nas/jsp/polopoly.jsp?d=297&a=3362 (accessed October 2009).

National Institute of Mental Health (2004) *Autism Spectrum Disorders: Pervasive Developmental Disorders.* Bethesda, MD: NIMH. Available at www.nimh.nih.gov (accessed October 2009).

National Research Council (2001) *Educating Children with Autism*, ed. C. Lord and J. P. McGee. Committee on Educational Interventions for Children with Autism. Division of Behavioral and Social Sciences and Education. Washington, DC: National Academy Press.

Norris, C. and Datillo, J. (1999) "Evaluating effects of a social story intervention on a young girl with autism." *Focus on Autism and Other Developmental Disabilities 14*, 180–186.

Odom, S. L., Brown, W. H., Frey, T., Karasu, N., Smith-Canter, L. L., and Strain, P. S. (2003) "Evidence-based practices for young children with autism: Contributions for single-subject design research." *Focus on Autism and Other Developmental Disabilities 18*, 166–175.

Office of National Statistics (2005) *Mental Health of Children and Young People in Great Britain.* London: Palgrave Macmillan.

O'Neil, M. and Jones, R. S. (1997) "Sensory-perceptual abnormalities in autism: A case for more research?" *Journal of Autism and Developmental Disorders 3*, 283–93.

O'Neill, R. E., Horner, R. H., Albin, R. W., Sprague, J. R., Storey, K. and Newton, J. S. (1997) *Functional Assessment and Program Development for Problem Behavior.* Pacific Grove, CA: Brooks Cole.

Osborne, L. A., McHugh, L., Saunders, J., and Reed, P. (2008) "The effect of parenting behaviors on subsequent child behavior problems in autistic spectrum conditions." *Research in Autism Spectrum Disorders 2*, 249–263.

Owen-DeSchryver, J. S., Carr, E. G., Cale, S. I., and Blakeley-Smith, A. (2008) "Promoting social interactions between students with autism spectrum disorders and their peers in inclusive school settings." *Focus on Autism and Other Developmental Disabilities 23*, 15–28.

Ozdemir S. (2008) "The effectiveness of social stories on decreasing disruptive behaviors of children with autism: Three case studies." *Journal of Autism and Developmental Disorders 38*, 1689–1696.

Ozonoff, S. (1997) "Components of Executive Function in Autism and Other Disorders." In J. Russell (ed.) *Autism as an Executive Disorder.* New York: Oxford University Press.

Ozonoff, S., Pennington, B. F., and Rogers, S. J. (1991) "Executive function deficits in high functioning autistic individuals: Relationship to theory of mind." *Journal of Child Psychology and Psychiatry 3*, 1081–1105.

Ozonoff, S. and Cathcart, K. (1998) "Effectiveness of a home-program intervention for young children with autism." *Journal of Autism and Developmental Disorders 28*, 25–32.

Ozonoff, S., Dawson, G., and McPartland, J. (2002a) *A Parent's Guide to Asperger Syndrome and High-functioning Autism: How to Meet the Challenges and Help Your Child to Thrive.* New York: Guilford Press.

Ozonoff, S., Provencal, S., and Solomon, M. (2002b) "The effectiveness of social skills training programs for autism spectrum disorders." Paper presented at the annual meeting of the American Academy of Child and Adolescent Psychiatry, San Francisco.

Ozonoff, S., Goodlin-Jones, B. L., and Solomon, M. (2005a) "Evidence-based assessment of autism spectrum disorders in children and adolescents." *Journal of Clinical Child and Adolescent Psychology 34*, 523–540.

Ozonoff, S., South, M., and Provencal, S. (2005b) "Executive Functions." In F. R. Volkmar, A. Klin, and R. Paul (eds.) *Handbook of Autism and Pervasive Developmental Disorders*, 3rd edn. New York: Wiley.

Paul, R. and Wilson, K. P. (2009) "Assessing Speech, Language, and Communication in Autism Spectrum Disorders." In S. Goldstein, J. A. Naglieri, and S. Ozonoff (eds.) *Assessment of Autism Spectrum Disorders.* New York: Guilford Press.

Pennington, B.-F. and Ozonoff, S. (1996) "Executive functions and developmental psychopathologies." *Journal of Child Psychology and Psychiatry 37*, 51–87.

Phelps-Terasaki, D. and Phelps-Gunn, T. (2007) *Test of Pragmatic Language*, 2nd edn. Austin, TX: Pro-Ed.

Pierce, K. L. and Schreibman, L. (1994) "Teaching daily living skills to children with autism in unsupervised settings through pictorial self-management." *Journal of Applied Behavior Analysis 27*, 471–481.

Pierce, K. and Schreibman, L. (1995) "Increasing complex social behaviors in children with autism: Effects of peer-implemented pivotal response training." *Journal of Applied Behavior Analysis 28*, 285–295.

Pierce, K. and Schreibman, L. (1997) "Multiple peer use of pivotal response training to increase social behaviors of classmates with autism: Results from trained and untrained peers." *Journal of Applied Behavior Analysis 30*, 157–160.

Posserud, M., Lundervold, A. J., and Gillberg, C. (2006) "Autistic features in a total population of 7–9 year old children assessed by the ASSQ (Autism Spectrum Screening Questionnaire)." *Journal of Child Psychology and Psychiatry 47*, 167–175.

Posserud, M., Lundervold, A. J., and Gillberg, C. (in press) "Validation of the Autism Spectrum Screening Questionnaire in a total population sample." *Journal of Autism and Developmental Disorders.*

Posserud, M., Lundervold, A. J., Steijen, M. C., Verhoven, S., Stormark, K. M., and Gillberg, C. (2008) "Factor analysis of the Autism Spectrum Screening Questionnaire." *Autism 12*, 99–112.

Prizant, B. M. and Wetherby, A. M. (1993) "Communication assessment of young children." *Infants and Young Children 5*, 20–34.

Quill, K. A. (ed.) (1995) *Teaching Children with Autism: Strategies to Enhance Communication and Socialization.* New York: Delmar Publishers.

Rao, P. A., Beidel, D. C., and Murray, M. J. (2008) "Social skills interventions for children with Asperger's syndrome or high-functioning autism: A review and recommendations." *Journal of Autism and Developmental Disorders 38*, 353–361.

Rathvon, N. (2008) *Effective School Interventions: Evidence-based Strategies for Improving Student Outcomes*, 2nd edn. New York: Guilford.

Reaven, J. A., Blakeley-Smith, A., Nichols, S., Dasari, M., Flanigan, E., and Hepburn, S. (2009) "Cognitive-behavioral group treatment for anxiety symptoms in children with high-functioning autism spectrum disorders: A pilot study." *Focus on Autism and Other Developmental Disabilities 24*, 27–37.

Reeve, C. E. and Carr, E. G. (2000) "Prevention of severe behavior problems in children with developmental disorders." *Journal of Positive Behavior Interventions 2*, 144–160.

Repp, A. and Horner, R. H. (eds.) (1999) *Functional Analysis of Problem Behavior: From Effective Assessment to Effective Support.* Belmont, CA: Wadsworth Publishing.

Reynolds, C. R. and Kamphaus, R. W. (2003) *Reynolds Intellectual Assessment Scales.* Lutz, FL: Psychological Assessment Resources.

Reynolds, C. R. and Kamphaus, R. W. (2004) *Behavior Assessment System for Children*, 2nd edn. Circle Pines, MN: American Guidance Publishing.

Reynolds, C. R. and Richmond, B. O. (2008) *Revised Children's Manifest Anxiety Scale*, 2nd edn. Los Angeles, CA: Western Psychological Services.

Rogers, S. (2000) "Interventions that facilitate socialization in children with autism." *Journal of Autism and Developmental Disorders 30*, 399–409.

Rogers, S. J. (1998) "Empirically supported comprehensive treatments for young children with autism." *Journal of Clinical Child Psychology 27*, 167–178.

Rogers, S. J. and Vismara, L. A. (2008) "Evidence-based comprehensive treatments for early autism." *Journal of Clinical Child and Adolescent Psychology 37*, 8–38.

Roid, G. H. (2003) *Stanford-Binet Intelligence Scale*, 5th edn. Itasca, IL: Riverside.

Roid, G. and Miller, L. (1997) *Leiter International Test of Intelligence-Revised.* Chicago: Stoelting.

Rutter, M., Bailey, A., and Lord, C. (2003) *Social Communication Questionnaire.* Los Angeles: Western Psychological Services.

Rutter, M., Le Couteur, A., and Lord, C. (2003) *Autism Diagnostic Interview-Revised.* Los Angeles: Western Psychological Services.

Sandall, S., Hemmeter, M. L., Smith, B.J., and McLean, M.E. (2005) *DEC Recommended Practices, A Comprehensive Guide for Practical Application in Early Intervention/Early Childhood Special Education.* Longmont, CO: Sopris West Ed. Services.

Sansosti, F. J., Powell-Smith, K. A., and Kincaid, D. (2004) "A research synthesis of social story interventions for children with autism spectrum disorders." *Focus on Autism and Other Developmental Disabilities 19*, 194–204.

Sattler, J. M. and Hoge, R. D. (2006) *Assessment of Children: Behavioral, Social, and Clinical Foundations*, 5th edn. San Diego, CA: Sattler.

Schopler, E. (2005) "Comments on 'Challenges in evaluating psycho-social interventions for autistic spectrum disorders' by Lord *et al.*" *Journal of Autism and Developmental Disorders 35*, 709–711.

Schopler, E., Reichler, R., and Renner, B. (1988) *The Childhood Autism Rating Scale* (CARS). Los Angeles: Western Psychological Services.

Schopler, E., Mesibov, G. B., and Hearsey, K. (1995) *Structured Teaching in the TEACCH System: Learning and Cognition in Autism.* New York: Plenum.

Schopler, E. Van Bourgondien, M.E., Wellman, G.J., and Love, S. (2010) *Childhood Autism Rating Scale*, 2nd ed. San Antonio, TX: Psychological Corporation.

Scott, F. J., Baron-Cohen, S., Bolton, P., and Brayne, C. (2002) "The CAST (Childhood Asperger Syndrome Test): Preliminary development of a UK screen for mainstream primary-school-age children." *Autism 6*, 9–31.

Shapiro, E. S. and Cole, C. L. (1994) *Behavior Change in the Classroom: Self-management Interventions.* New York: Guilford Press.

Shattuck, P. T., Durkin, M., Maenner, M. Newschaffer, C., *et al.* (2009) "Timing of identification among children with an autism spectrum disorder: Findings from a population-based surveillance study." *Journal of the American Academy of Child and Adolescent Psychiatry 48*, 474–483.

Shea, V. (2004) "A perspective on the research literature related to early intensive behavioral intervention (Lovaas) for young children with autism." *Autism 8*, 349–367.

Sheinkopf, S. and Siegel, B. (1998) "Home-based treatment of young children with autism." *Journal of Autism and Developmental Disorders 28*, 15–23.

Sheslow, D. and Adams, W. (2003) *Wide Range Assessment of Memory and Learning*, 2nd edn. Wilmington, DE: Wide Range Incorporated.

Shriver, M. D., Allen, K. D., and Mathews, J. R. (1999) "Effective assessment of the shared and unique characteristics of children with autism." *School Psychology Review 28*, 538–558.

Shulman, B. (1985) *Test of Pragmatic Skills*. Tucson, AZ: Communication Skill Builders.

Siegel, D., Minshew, N., and Goldstein, G. (1996) "Wechsler IQ profiles in diagnosis of high-functioning autism." *Journal of Autism and Developmental Disorders 26*, 389–406.

Simpson, R. L. (2005) "Evidence-based practices and students with autism spectrum disorders." *Focus on Autism and Other Developmental Disabilities 20*, 3, 140–149.

Simpson, R. L. and Myles, B. S. (1998) "Aggression among children and youth who have Asperger's syndrome: A different population requiring different strategies." *Preventing School Failure 42*, 149–153.

Simpson, R. L. and Zionts, P. (2000) *Autism: Information and Resources for Professionals and Parents*. Austin, TX: Pro-Ed.

Skuse, D. H., Mandy, W., and Scourfield, J. (2005) "Measuring autistic traits: Heritability, reliability and validity of the social and communication disorders checklist." *British Journal of Psychiatry 187*, 568–572.

Skuse, D. H., Mandy, W., Steer, C., Miller, L. L., *et al.* (2009) "Social communication competence and functional adaptation in a general population of children: Preliminary evidence for sex-by-verbal IQ differential risk." *Journal of the American Academy of Child and Adolescent Psychiatry 48*, 2, 128–137.

Smith, T. (1999) "Outcome of early intervention for children with autism." *Clinical Psychology: Science and Practice 6*, 33–49.

Solomon, M., Goodlin-Jones, B. L., and Anders, T. F. (2004) "A social adjustment enhancement intervention for high functioning autism, Asperger's syndrome, and pervasive developmental disorder NOS." *Journal of Autism and Developmental Disorders 34*, 649–668.

South, M., William, B. J., McMahon, W. M., Owley, T., *et al.* (2002) "Utility of the Gilliam Autism Rating Scale in research and clinical populations." *Journal of Autism and Developmental Disorders 32*, 593–599.

Sparrow, S. S., Balla, D., and Cicchetti, D. V. (2005) *Vineland Adaptive Behavior Scales*, 2nd edn. Circle Pines, MN: American Guidance Service.

Spence, S. H., Donovan, C., and Brechman-Toussaint, M. (2000) "The treatment of childhood social phobia: The effectiveness of a social skills training-based, cognitive-behavioural intervention, with and without parental involvement." *Journal of Child Psychology and Psychiatry 41*, 713–726.

Spencer, V. G., Simpson, C. G., and Lynch, S. A. (2008) "Using social stories to increase positive behaviors for children with autism spectrum disorders." *Intervention in School and Clinic 44*, 58–61.

Sprick, R. and Garrison, M. (2008) *Interventions: Evidence-based Behavioral Strategies for Individual Students*, 2nd edn. Eugene, OR: Pacific Northwest Publishing.

Stevens, M. C, Fein, D. A., Dunn, M., Allen, *et al.* (2000) "Subgroups of children with autism by cluster analysis: A longitudinal examination." *Journal of the American Academy of Child and Adolescent Psychiatry 39*, 346–352.

Stone, W. L. (2006) *Does My Child Have Autism? A Parent's Guide to Early Detection and Intervention in Autism Spectrum Disorders*. San Francisco, CA: Jossey Bass.

Stone, W. L. and Caro-Martinez, L. M. (1990) "Naturalistic observations of spontaneous communication in autistic children." *Journal of Autism and Developmental Disorders 20*, 437–453.

Stone, W. L. and Yoder, P. J. (2001) "Predicting spoken language level in children with autism spectrum disorders." *Autism 5*, 341–361.

Sugai, G., Horner, R. H., Dunlap, G., Hieneman, M., *et al.* (2000) "Applying positive behavioral support and functional behavioral assessment in schools." *Journal of Positive Behavioral Interventions 2*, 131–143.

Sulzer-Azaroff, B., Hoffman, A. O., Horton, C. B., Bondy, A., and Frost, L. (2009) "The Picture Exchange Communication System (PECS): What do the data say?" *Focus on Autism and Other Developmental Disabilities 24*, 89–103.

Szatmari, P., Bryson, S. E., Boyle, M. H., Streiner, D. L., and Duku, E. (2003) "Predictors of outcome among high functioning children with autism and Asperger syndrome." *Journal of Child Psychology and Psychiatry 44*, 520–528.

Tager-Flusberg, H., Paul, R., and Lord, C. (2005) "Language and Communication in Autism." In F. R. Volkmar, R. Paul, A. Klin, and D. Cohen (eds.) *Handbook of Autism and Pervasive Developmental Disorders: Vol. 2. Assessment, Interventions, and Policy*, 3rd edn. New York: John Wiley.

Tantam, D. (2000) "Psychological disorder in adolescents and adults with Asperger syndrome." *Autism 4*, 47–62.

Tantam, D. (2003) "Assessment and Treatment of Comorbid Emotional and Behavior Problems." In M. Prior (ed.) *Learning and Behavior Problems in Asperger Syndrome*. New York: Guilford Press.

Towbin, K. E. (2005) "Pervasive Developmental Disorder Not Otherwise Specified." In F. R. Volkmar, R. Paul, A. Klin, and D. Cohen (eds.) *Handbook of Autism and Pervasive Developmental Disorders Vol. 1: Diagnosis, Development, Neurobiology, and Behavior*, 3rd edn. Hoboken, NJ: Wiley.

Tse, J., Strulovitch, J., Tagalakis, V., Meng, L., and Fombonne, E. (2007) "Social skills training for adolescents with Asperger syndrome and high-functioning autism." *Journal of Autism and Developmental Disorders 37,* 1960–1968.

Tutt, R., Powell, S., and Thorton, M. (2006) "Educational approaches in autism: What we know about what we do." *Educational Psychology in Practice 22,* 69–81.

Twachtman-Cullen, D. (1998) "Language and Communication in HFA and AS." In E. Schopler, G. B. Mesibov, and L. J. Kunce (eds.) *Asperger Syndrome or High-functioning Autism?* New York: Plenum Press.

Twachtman-Cullen, D. and Twachtman-Reilly, J. (2003) *How Well Does Your Child's IEP Measure Up? Quality Indicators for Effective Service Delivery.* London: Jessica Kingsley Publishers.

U. S. Department of Education, Office of Special Education and Rehabilitative Services (2006) *Twenty-sixth Annual Report to Congress on the Implementation of the Individuals with Disabilities Education Act.* Washington, DC: U. S. Department of Education, Office of Special Education and Rehabilitative Services.

U. S. Department of Education, Office of Special Education Programs, Data Analysis System (DANS), OMB #1820—0043: *Children with disabilities receiving special education under Part B of the Individuals with Disabilities Education Act 2006.* Data updated as of July 15, 2007.

Van Bourgondien, M., Marcus, L., and Schopler, E. (1992) "Comparison of DSM-III-R and Childhood Autism Rating Scale diagnoses of autism." *Journal of Autism and Developmental Disorders 22,* 493–506.

Vaughn, B., Duchnowski, A., Sheffield, S., and Kutash, K. (2005) *Positive Behavior Support: A Classroom-wide Approach to Successful Student Achievement and Interactions.* Tampa, FL: University of South Florida, Department of Child and Family Studies, Louis de la Parte Florida Mental Health Institute.

Velting, O. N., Setzer, N. J., and Albano, A. M. (2004) "Update on and advances in assessment and cognitive-behavioral treatment of anxiety disorders in children and adolescents." *Professional Psychology: Research and Practice 35,* 42–54.

Venter, A., Lord, C, and Schopler, E. (1992) "A follow-up study of high-functioning autistic children." *Journal of Child Psychology and Psychiatry 33,* 489–507.

Verte, S., Geurts, H. M., Roeyers, H., Rosseel, Y., Oosterlaan, J., and Sergeant, J. A. (2006) "Can the Children's Communication Checklist differentiate autism spectrum subtypes?" *Autism 10,* 266–287.

Volkmar, F. R. (2005) "International Perspectives." In F. R. Volkmar, R. Paul, A. Klin, and D. Cohen (eds.) *Handbook of Autism and Pervasive Developmental Disorders: Vol. 2. Assessment, Interventions, and Policy,* 3rd edn. New York: John Wiley.

Volkmar, F., Cook, E. H. Jr., Pomeroy, J., Realmuto, G. and Tanguay, P. (1999) "Practice parameters for the assessment and treatment of children, adolescents, and adults with autism and other pervasive developmental disorders." *Journal of the American Academy of Child and Adolescent Psychiatry 38* (Suppl.), 32S–54S.

Volkmar, F. R., Lord, C., Bailey, A., Schultz, R. T., and Klin, A. (2004) "Autism and pervasive developmental disorders." *Journal of Child Psychology and Psychiatry 45,* 135–170.

Volkmar, F. R., and Klin, A. (2005) "Issues in the Classification of Autism, Related Conditions." In F. R. Volkmar, R. Paul, A. Klin, and D. Cohen (eds.) *Handbook of Autism and Pervasive Developmental Disorders, Vol. 1: Diagnosis, Development, Neurobiology, and Behavior,* 3rd edn. Hoboken, NJ: Wiley.

Wagner, S. (2006) "Educating the female student with Asperger's." In *Asperger's and Girls.* Arlington, TX: Future Horizons.

Wechsler, D. (1991) *Wechsler Intelligence Scale for Children,* 3rd edn. San Antonio, TX: Psychological Corporation.

Wechsler, D. (1999) *Wechsler Abbreviated Scale of Intelligence.* San Antonio, TX: The Psychological Corporation.

Wechsler, D. (2002a) *Wechsler Preschool and Primary Scale of Intelligence,* 3rd edn. San Antonio, TX: Psychological Corporation.

Wechsler, D. (2002b) *Wechsler Individual Achievement Test,* 2nd edn. San Antonio, TX: Psychological Corporation.

Wechsler, D. (2003) *Wechsler Intelligence Scale for Children,* 4th edn. San Antonio, TX: Psychological Corporation.

Weiss, M. J. and Harris, S. L. (2001) "Teaching social skills to people with autism." *Behavior Modification 25,* 785–802.

Welsh, M., Park, R. D., Widaman, K., and O'Neil, R. (2001) "Linkages between children's social and academic competence: A longitudinal analysis." *Journal of School Psychology 39,* 463–481.

Wetherby, A. M., Schuler, A. L., and Prizant, B. M. (1997) "Enhancing Language and Communication Development: Theoretical Foundations." In D. J. Cohen and F. R. Volkmar (eds.) *Handbook of Autism and Pervasive Developmental Disorders,* 2nd edn. New York: Wiley.

Wheeler, J. J., Baggett, B. A., Fox, J., and Blevins, L. (2006) "Treatment integrity: A review of intervention studies conducted with children with autism." *Focus on Autism and Other Developmental Disabilities 21,* 45–54.

White, S. W., Koening, K., and Scahill, L. (2007) "Social skills development in children with autism spectrum disorders: A review of the intervention research." *Journal of Autism and Developmental Disorders 37*, 1858–1868.

Wickstrom, K. F., Jones, K. M., LaFleur, L. H., and Witt, J. C. (1998) "An analysis of treatment integrity in school—based behavioural consultation." *School Psychology Quarterly 13*, 141–54.

Wiggins, L. D., Bakeman, R., Adamson, L. B., and Robins, D. L. (2007) "The utility of the Social Communication Questionnaire in screening for autism in children referred for early intervention." *Focus on Autism and Other Disabilities 22*, 33–38.

Wiig, E. and Secord, W. (1989) *Test of Language Competence.* San Antonio, TX: Psychological Corporation.

Wiig, E., Secord, W., and Semel, E. (2003) *Clinical Evaluation of Language Fundamentals*, 4th edn. San Antonio, TX: Psychological Corporation.

Wilkinson, L. A. (2005) "Supporting the inclusion of a student with Asperger syndrome: A case study using conjoint behavioral consultation and self-management." *Educational Psychology in Practice 21*, 307–326.

Wilkinson, L. A. (2006) "Monitoring treatment integrity: An alternative to the 'consult and hope' strategy in school-based behavioural consultation." *School Psychology International 27*, 426–438.

Wilkinson, L. A. (2008a) "The gender gap in Asperger syndrome: Where are the girls?" *Teaching Exceptional Children Plus 4*, 1–10. Available at http://escholarship.bc.edu/education/tecplus/vol4/iss4/art3 (accessed October 2009).

Wilkinson, L. A. (2008b) "Self-management for high-functioning children with autism spectrum disorders." *Intervention in School and Clinic 43*, 150–157.

Wilkinson, L. A. (2009) "Facilitating the identification of autism Spectrum Disorders in school-age children." *Remedial and Special Education*, July 1, 2009, DOI: 10.1177/0741932509338372.

Williams, J., Allison, C., Scott, F., Stott, C., Baron-Cohen, S., and Brayne, C. (2006) "The Childhood Asperger Syndrome Test (CAST): Test-retest reliability." *Autism 10*, 415–427

Williams, S. K., Johnson, C., and Sukhodolsky, D. G. (2005) "The role of the school psychologist in the inclusive education of school-age children with autism spectrum disorders." *Journal of School Psychology 43*, 117–136.

Wing, L. (1981) "Asperger's syndrome: A clinical account." *Psychological Medicine 11*, 115–129.

Wing, L. (1988) "The Continuum of Autistic Characteristics." In E. Schopler and G. Mesibov (eds.) *Diagnosis and Assessment in Autism.* New York: Plenum Press.

Wing, L. (1993) "The definition and prevalence of autism: A review." *European Child and Adolescent Psychiatry 2*, 61–74.

Wing, L. (2005) "Problems of Categorical Classification Systems." In F. R. Volkmar, R. Paul, A. Klin, and D. Cohen (eds.) *Handbook of Autism and Pervasive Developmental Disorders: Vol. 1. Diagnosis, Development, Neurobiology, and Behavior*, 3rd edn. New York: John Wiley.

Wing, L. and Gould, J. (1979) "Severe impairments of social interaction and associated abnormalities in children: epidemiology and classification." *Journal of Autism and Developmental Disorders 9*, 11–29.

Wing, L. and Potter, D. (2002) "The epidemiology of autism spectrum disorders: Is the prevalence rising?" *Mental Retardation and Developmental Disabilities Research Reviews 8*, 51–161.

Witt, J. C. and Beck, R. (2000) *One-minute Academic Functional Assessment and Interventions: "Can't" Do It…Or "Won't" Do It?* Longmont, CO: Sopris West.

Witwer, A. N. and Lecavalier, L. (2008) "Examining the validity of autism spectrum disorder subtypes." *Journal of Autism and Developmental Disorders 38*, 1611–1624.

Woodcock, R. W., McGrew, K. S., and Mather, N. (2007) *Woodcock-Johnson III NU.* Rolling Meadows, IL: Riverside Publishing.

World Health Organization (1993) *The ICD-10 Classification of Mental and Behavioral Disorders: Diagnostic Criteria for Research.* Geneva, Switzerland: WHO.

Yang, N. K., Schaller, J. L., Huang, T., Wang, M. H., and Tsai, S. (2003) "Enhancing appropriate social behaviors for children with autism in general education classrooms: An analysis of six cases." *Education and Training in Developmental Disabilities 38*, 405–416.

Yeargin-Allsopp, M., Rice, C., Karapurkar, T., Doernberg, N., Boyle, C., and Murphy, C. (2003) "Prevalence of autism in a US metropolitan area." *Journal of the American Medical Association 289*, 49–58.

Young, E. C., Diehl, J. J., Morris, D., Hyman, S. L., and Bennetto, L. (2005) "The use of two language tests to identify pragmatic language problems in children with autism spectrum disorders." *Language, Speech, and Hearing Services in Schools 36*, 62–72.

SUBJECT INDEX

AUTHOR INDEX